THE
RIVER
YOU
TOUCH

ALSO BY CHRIS DOMBROWSKI

NONFICTION
Body of Water

POETRY
Ragged Anthem
Earth Again
By Cold Water

THE
RIVER
YOU
TOUCH

MAKING A LIFE
ON MOVING WATER

CHRIS
DOMBROWSKI

MILKWEED EDITIONS

(800) 520-6455
milkweed.org

First paperback edition, published 2023 by Milkweed Editions
Printed in the United States
Cover design by Mary Austin Speaker
Cover art by Karim Iliya
Author photo by Erick Petersen
23 24 25 26 27 5 4 3 2 1

978-1-63955-085-2

Library of Congress Cataloging-in-Publication Data

Names: Dombrowski, Chris, 1976- author.
Title: The river you touch : making a life on moving water / Chris Dombrowski.
Description: Minneapolis : Milkweed Editions, 2022. | Summary: "We are matter and long to be received by an Earth that conceived us, which accepts and reconstitutes us, its children, each of us, without exception, every one. The journey is long, and then we start homeward, fathomless as to what home might make of us."-- Provided by publisher.
Identifiers: LCCN 2022014627 (print) | LCCN 2022014628 (ebook) | ISBN 9781639550630 (Hardcover) | ISBN 9781571319531 (ePub)
Subjects: LCSH: Rivers. | Home.
Classification: LCC GB1203.2 .D66 2022 (print) | LCC GB1203.2 (ebook) | DDC 910/.01--dc23/eng20220613
LC record available at https://lccn.loc.gov/2022014627
LC ebook record available at https://lccn.loc.gov/2022014628

Milkweed Editions is committed to ecological stewardship. We strive to align our book production practices with this principle, and to reduce the impact of our operations in the environment. We are a member of the Green Press Initiative, a nonprofit coalition of publishers, manufacturers, and authors working to protect the world's endangered forests and conserve natural resources. *The River You Touch* was printed on acid-free 100% postconsumer-waste paper by Sheridan Saline.

for my mother, Dianne Dombrowski
and for Mary, Luca, Molly, and Lily—
five luminous guides

CONTENTS

"In rivers, the water that you touch is the last of what has passed and the first of that which comes; so with present time."

LEONARDO DA VINCI

PREFACE

At its uppermost source, this book began as a love song to the rivers on which I've guided for twenty-five years and the land through which they pulse like veins. "Land" here means everything from the cloud-hung peaks down to our toenails, antlers, and beaks made of reconstituted earth; means the ever-evolving relationships between these things; means us. As the songwriter Jeffrey Foucault once told me, "a true love song succeeds on the element of doubt." Per Foucault's prerequisite, this oarsman's ode is rife with apprehension: a young father's fear of ushering children into a periled world, his awareness of his own complicity in the destruction of that which he claims to adore, as well as that pervading sense of dread that seems a preexisting condition in our over-informed epoch.

But as a wise elder once remarked, our doubts are our traitors. It is of course easier to nestle beneath the goose down comforter of irony in our age of complicity than to entertain the hard questions. "What does a mindful, sustainable inhabitance on this small planet look like in the Anthropocene?" is no longer an academic question but rather a necessary qualifier to each step we take. For answers, we who have proven ourselves such untrustworthy stewards of our home might look to what Barry Lopez called "myriad enduring relationships of the landscape," to our predecessors, in other words, whose voices are the bells that must sound before any gritty ceremony of community can truly begin. Whether we accept it or not, the land itself is our earliest predecessor, the main character of all our stories, and listening to it, after all, is not a onetime undertaking but a practice.

Lest I imply some shoddy metaphysics here: "listening," refers to direct contact, engagement, what the forager Jenna Rozelle calls the "primacy of immediate experience." Callouses on palms formed by friction between human skin and oar handle. Shoulder muscles straining to pull oar blade through current, the oar stroke negotiating with the wave train's brute liquid force. After thousands of days in such physical dialogue—as much of my adult life spent on moving water as on solid ground—I have come to know a single Montana watershed better than I know most of my human acquaintances, which is to say I am intimate with the rivers' daily and seasonal rhythms, and altered by the way the watershed has moved around and through me.

Despite the nontraditional lifestyle that my occupation affords, however, I have lately fallen prey to the plague of screens and a generic brand of informed cynicism, to an existence that appears rife with concentration but that in truth is fragmented and increasingly short on profound impression. I live among the homogenized throngs chained to the assumption that our moment-to-moment ability to "virtually connect" literally connects us, but as our collective actions exhibit, we have failed to truly comprehend our infinite ties. What are we if not inextricably linked, and yet blind to this blunt fact? Day by day, at nearly mythic speed, our failure to face this truth brings forth bold consequences.

Pre-fatherhood, I might have blamed my succumbing to such trends on domesticity, but there is nothing as wild and vital in my life as our children: three free beings in whom flourishes an essential kind of knowing—what David Abram called "a sensorial empathy with the living land"—and whose capacity for wonder may be the beacon by which we see ourselves through this dark epoch. The faculty of wonder—which, in this context, is simply the unsentimental ability to identify with astonishment the earth and its inhabitants as relational—is diminishing as quickly as any endangered species. If it vanishes as an inevitable byproduct of decreased direct encounters with the physical world, so, too, may go the instinct to protect the very places that sustain us.

By purest chance, our family has come to live a few hundred yards from just such a place, a creek called Rattlesnake that descends from peaks and snow-fed lakes in an undeveloped wilderness and flows, by way of the Clark Fork of the Columbia River, to the Pacific. On summer days, especially these recent blowtorch-hot ones, we swim in the creek nearly every afternoon. I call it "our creek," a phrase that I realize is rife with postcolonial complications, because it is *our* creek: mine and yours and whomever swam in it before, human beings of all ages and genders, trout and whitefish, deer and elk and bear, mayflies and stoneflies, leeches and dragonflies, ouzels and migratory ducks, gloriously interpenetrated from time immemorial by native species and invasive ones alike.

Most evenings after guiding, I walk leisurely down to the swimming hole, taking a steep, tight trail on the west bank over the bulbous roots of cottonwoods, a cumbersome and shady way the kids call the "elf path." But other days, as when I've been watching the news on my phone, I have to bike down, so desperate am I for a brief immersion, the icy kick of an elemental martini, what my grandmother would have called "a good belt." This drought-racked August has been particularly choked with haze from forest fires, embers blown all the way from California or Washington: "not our smoke," I'm tempted to say, except that it's all our smoke, and I refuse to indulge another foolish round of us-versus-them.

One recent morning, we took a chilly family dip in the creek, all feral five of us, then jumped into the car and followed the floodplain down Interstate 90, aimed west when the big river bent north, and wound through the beetle-blighted forests and over two steep passes, across the Palouse and the parched agricultural plains, up and over another mountain pass, then finally down through sprawl, city, and more sprawl, until we eventually reached the Pacific. Good friends were there to greet us on the gravelly shore of a bay with a meal of fresh-caught Dungeness crab and spot prawns. Starved as we were after nearly five hundred miles in the car, though, we found the gently breaking waves too inviting to resist, and one by one we changed into our suits and dove in. Treading breathless in the chilly waters of the sound, cooled to the core after nine hours at the wheel, I pondered a deliciously unsolvable equation: How long would it take for, say, a gallon of the creek we swam in this morning to reach the same body of water we were floating in now?

Like a child, moving water is a treatise on impermanence, a constant reminder of the ungraspable. I was in my late twenties when our firstborn, Luca, arrived. Suddenly (or what seemed like it), facing the far side of my forties, I found myself wondering how to properly celebrate our son's sixteenth birthday. The answer was a midnight paddle in a borrowed sea kayak on a bay come wildly alive with bioluminescence. Above us, perched somewhere in the moss-draped cedars, a heron rasped out its frightful call, and far above bird and boat, the stars convened. Somehow on this new-moon August night we had timed our paddle with the peak light emission from trillions of marine invertebrates, and as we entered the darkest recess of a cove, our paddles stirred emerald whirlpools above scintillating creatures: fracturing schools of salmon smolt, undulating moon jelly-fish, and frantic backstroking crabs.

"Liquid phosphorus," Darwin had called the spectacle while aboard the HMS *Beagle* in the *Rio de la Plata*, but I read on my smartphone's blinding screen that the unicellular organisms' emission of light was actually a seven-chemical reaction that produced oxidized luciferin, and that organisms from dinoflagellates to giant squids use the process for attraction, defense, warning, even mimicry. I was of a mind to share some of my research with Luca when there was a *thunk* on the bottom of the boat.

Raw fright struck the body first. Then the adrenaline-quickened brain calculated known dangers (very rare orcas, even rarer blue whales, and scantly aggressive seals) in rela-tion to my makeshift weapon (a small paddle to be wielded against ocean-borne tooth and muscle) versus possibility of flight. We had life vests and the distance from shore was a swimmable seventy yards, though the fifty-eight-degree water would make muscles seize. Then rational thought nudged in. As a tingling wash of nerves receded, I guessed *harbor seal*: we'd seen several basking at sunset on a nearby island. Apparently curious, the mysterious creature cir-cled us with a fish's fluidity, disappeared again, and, after a moment in hiding, popped its head up to regard us, its bris-tled whiskers gleaming like a lathered moustache.

Otter!

I doubted my cell phone's camera could capture an image of the creature at such a low aperture, but I was determined to commemorate the encounter, a birthday visitation of sorts. Holding the paddle in one hand, I defiled the night with the phone's flash and snapped the shot.

To reconstitute an old haiku: *Cold ocean, phone falls in: the sound of water.*

The kayak tipped precariously starboard as I reached for the phone.

"Dad," Luca gasped, as he steadied the rocking craft with his hands. Together we watched a spiraling line of light afford a momentary visual connection to the plummeting device.

"Well, that's that," I said, surprised at my instantaneous detachment, considering how tightly I usually clung to the device. The pang of material loss and self-chiding would arrive in the morning when, at dead-low tide, we'd find the phone comically lodged in a purple urchin's spines, the salt-water having already corroded volume buttons and rendered the system unusable despite the device's protective case. But for the moment, watching our craft push a pale wake, I felt pleasantly unmoored.

How might it have felt, I wondered, to encounter this phenomenon millennia ago, before science explained it, and epochs before I'd access some scant understanding of it from a billion-dollar satellite? Could a man steering a small cedar dugout across a coastal bay have paused from his paddling, reached down, turned the rippling water to a ghostly flame, and not felt himself a holy part of the living world, the animate universe?

I scanned our ambit for further sign of the otter, weighing the value of what I'd beamed in on 4G versus the salt drying on the hand Luca had dragged through the water. I sensed the latter would form a more lasting kind of knowing.

And sudden as the otter's tail-thwack against our boat, I stopped paddling, gobsmacked. What hubris! Sixteen years a parent, and I had just now arrived at the notion that our three children have served as *my* guides, and not the other way around? Momentarily, as the bow of the kayak slowed and stalled against the shoreline, I saw with clarity how they have—progressing meander by meander, discovery by discovery—sustained me, often sparing me from my own mind.

Once ashore, Luca knelt, ran his fingers through the wave-worn pebbles, the stones sparking and crackling, and dug out a skipper stone. As a yearling his first word was "light," and long before he could speak, before he was a bright form tumbling weightlessly through the galaxy of Mary's womb, our frantic bodies making him made light.

Slung out, the stone hopped several times across the water and, glowing as it fell, left a pale, unspooling thread in its wake.

In pursuit of that thread, I launched this boat made of words: a chronicle of wonder at the place we humbly call home and an attempt to preserve the quality of attention that our children, those messengers of a hopeful reality, so often emit, without which we will find ourselves mortally far out at sea.

I.

YOUNG MOUNTAINS

"It's a landscape that has to be seen to be believed. And as I say on occasion, it may have to be believed in order to be seen."

—N. SCOTT MOMADAY

HEADWATERS
2004

Mary wakes me in the dark, bounding onto the mattress to tell me what she carries. I strain up, flanks aching, then sink back into the pillows and a latent dream of the river we skied alongside last night: the current like a spill of ink against cleaving tiers of ice, the floes buoyant, clunking against the cobble bed with a strangely hollow sound. Down the hill on the rails, a train snaking its way through the canyon whistles once, twice, three times. I hike myself out from the warmth of the covers, perch my weight on my elbows.

"You're what?" I ask.

Another exultant, whispered declaration.

"You are?"

Whatever fears jotted in the margins of the mind, whatever worries held in the heart's palm like a sliver—these evaporate, fail to manifest. We somersault out of bed somehow holding on to each other and are soon dancing across the living room hardwood, fleet with the news of Mary's pregnancy, as the gentle slope of the mountain under which we live begins to distinguish itself from the predawn sky.

If I make my way upstream in memory toward this story's source, I find myself parked alongside the Big Hole River near its headwaters, where I have stopped to gather some wildflowers for Mary's birthday. From my knees I pluck several scarlet Indian paintbrush and one pollen-laden balsamroot to accent the group, then fill a jam jar from the tea-colored river. Galloping past its lush banks, this ocean-bound water—what doesn't evaporate to form clouds or isn't siphoned off for irrigation—will travel farther than any fluvial body on the continent before reaching its eventual, albeit temporary, destination and merging with the Gulf of Mexico. *Godspeed*, I say, placing the glass in the cup holder, gauging the bouquet's red against that of the sunstruck rimrock. I aim the truck for Boise, hoping to arrive before the flowers wilt.

I choose the two-lanes over the interstate, a straighter, crow-flown line, but at midnight remain hours from Mary's door. Third of July and there's snow on the switchbacks! Spent from rowing fishing clients all day under a punishing sun, I doze off, the wheel following my tilting head toward the shoulder of the road. The rumble strip snaps me to attention and simultaneously startles a bull elk that feints from the high beams and clomps into the forest. In Stanley, I dig change from between the seats and make an apologetic call from a payphone: I'd worked late and thought coming down the Salmon River corridor would be faster. Mirthful voices in the background, a song I can almost recognize on the stereo. Just a little party, she says in a beer-softened voice that makes my stomach leap. Everyone's leaving soon. I'll wait up.

True to her word, at 2:00 a.m. she leans against the frame of an open window in her third-story apartment, one slim leg slung over the sill.

"Hey," I call from the quiet street, my truck parked, flowers in tow.

Rising slowly, she shudders awake and for a nanosecond is yanked gravitationally toward the sidewalk—she steadies her leaning body, though, gripping the brick facing with her thigh and free hand.

"What are you doing up there?" I ask, fully adrenalized again.

"Watching for you. Must've nodded off." She hoists a beer from the sill as if to toast me. "Lucky I put this down."

Two country-drunk midwestern transplants guzzling the bottom out of the dusty bottle that is the West, we talk until dawn on the futon she's dragged into the living room to afford us privacy from her roommate. At sunrise, a slight breeze lofts through an open window, parting the accumulated air like drapery. Gooseflesh. We pull the sheet over our bodies.

I was nineteen—the Yellowstone River flowing around my hips swept quicksilver-streaked beneath the vast moonlit snowfields of the Crazy Mountains—when the continent turned briefly on its axis and the West became my true north.

In my truck's smudged rearview lay the distant scablands of the auto industry and my forbearers' General Motors jobs, the once fertile riparian corridors stripped bare by corporate greed, and the massacre-haunted Great Plains. Following a map of sorts—one sketched in part by beloved books—I had come in search of wild trout, vast systems of unfettered freestone water, and, as one revered author had it, "eternity compressed into a moment." High-minded? Of course: I was jobless, barely out of high school, and hopped up on the transcendentalists, just a kid with a fly rod in search of rare ore.

Scratching free of the Midwest's fertilized comforts, Mary also jettisoned neighborhoods and subdivisions named for animals that no longer resided there—Wolf Court, Elk Meadows—for the promise of a life less bound by convention, less dictated by the status quo and occupational demands than by one's passions. One Friday evening after clocking off from her second job, she caught the California Zephyr out of Chicago Union Station, fell asleep in the cocktail car, and woke to the sun breaking over the foothills of the Rockies. A few hours later, in the passenger seat of a friend's van, she watched the Denver skyline shrink behind her, and by dusk, wearing stiff hiking boots, was pitching a tent at twelve thousand feet. Sometime after midnight she was startled awake by something—the quiet—and stepped outside the tent to marvel at her own shadow cast by the long-traveled light of uncountable stars. She crouched and touched the tender, blistered skin at her heels. What day was it, anyway? Checked her watch. Sunday, of course, and this would clearly pass for church.

For a while the wind blew her around the region like pine duff—Oregon, Colorado, Idaho—until she landed a teaching job just outside a charming foothills town that was hell-bent on becoming a city. On her first day of school, walking into the old farmstead converted in the 1960s by some freethinkers into several primary classrooms, she recognized the name of a student's parent, a writer and whitewater guide whose book I toted around in my backpack. "You'll never believe whose daughter is in my class," she wrote to me soon after in a letter. We had been sending dispatches from our respective valleys every couple of weeks, courting old-fashioned-like, noncommittal in that

I-really-dig-you-but-I'm-having-my-own-adventure sort of way. "You should come meet my students," she offered, finally, after some weeks.

Whenever I envisioned her teaching—overall clad, guitar in hands, seated on the floor with her bright-eyed students—my heart chakra hummed. But when I finally saw her navigating her natural element, I nearly lost my footing.

To watch her in the classroom was to witness a born-to-do-just-this genius. She was creek water, limpid, nimble, present and attentive to the disposition and abilities of every child, determined to connect on multiple pedagogical and emotional levels. Her undeniable engagement with the invisible, with what lay core-deep inside her students, floored me.

Later that evening over beers at Bar Gernika, I tried to put words to what I'd seen, but my mouth turned to mush. I picked at the Basque food we'd ordered and blamed my inarticulateness on road fatigue. She must have read my eyes, though, their smitten intention. Before long there were two sleeping pads in the bed of the red pickup.

Fair to say, then, that if the landscape teased us from our respective suburban confines, took us by the lip, the people inhabiting that landscape subsequently tethered us here. River-hewn folks like Randall and Tee, sixty-something raft guides in Glacier National Park who taught school during the academic year and, when they weren't behind the oars, farmed organic garlic near the shores of Flathead Lake. We met at a boat launch campground, and after a couple of early morning conversations beside the tailgate camp stove, they offered Mary and me a place to crash. One night I sat up fireside in the backyard paging through a book I had found on their shelf, Carlo Rovelli's *The Order of Time*, which explained by way of theoretical physics how people who live in the mountains age more rapidly than those who live at, say, sea level, closer to the center of the planet, because time passes more quickly the farther one is from gravitational mass. The physics was beyond my remit but, watching Randall and Tee pack coolers and dry bags by headlamp in preparation for a five-day float through the Bob Marshall Wilderness, I was inclined to buy in. Were these folks who lived with wise urgency, who cobbled together lives in lieu of careers, somehow intellectually more liberated, as anthropologists suggested, for all the open space the West afforded? They appeared to be.

Another couple, Kate and Thomas, who worked for the Park Service as grizzly bear biologists, put us up for a few days while we backpacked through Yellowstone. Late evenings after a few glasses of wine, they would play Guy Clark cassettes in the living room of their one-bedroom employee-housing cabin, spinning yarns about so-called problem bears, a phrase Kate scoffed at. One particular grizzly they recounted, a stubborn sow that frequented a campground, had to be tranquilized and caged for transport to a more remote wilderness than even Yellowstone could offer. After giving the captured bear a couple of hours to regain its consciousness, Thomas, standing several feet back, slipped a watering hose between the bars, intending to fill a bowl—at which point the sow grabbed hold of the nozzle and yanked so hard that Thomas was jerked off his feet and slammed into the cage. He knelt there a moment, nose to nose with the bear, her wet breath on his fear-locked face, before rolling away.

Listening to Thomas, I noticed that my hand, or Mary's, which I held, had begun to shake. And with a jolt, the charge came clear again: the aim, then, was not only to scratch out a life in this most demanding of paradises, but to somehow, one day, come to speak of it from a place of authenticity, to render it in such a way that the land, for the listener, might come alive with the story.

The sun crests the mountain we live beneath and sends spindles of light downhill through the pines.

From the kitchen with my back to the stove, I watch Mary, just returned from her ritual run along the river, load her bike's panniers with the schoolbooks she will read aloud to her kindergartners in a voice that is as beckoning as a lit hearth. All the while, her body will tend its tiny seed, her calm demeanor belying the cacophony of cellular activity beneath her skin: veins and arteries channeling about five hundred gallons of blood per day to the placenta, and so unfathomably on. Waiting for the water to boil, I marvel at the confluence of teachers in my life—the free-flowing natures of rivers and Mary, and surely now the tiny force of nature that she bears, an extension of the land itself, small as a droplet but powered by its first-formed organ, the heart a cluster of conjoined cells the size of a comma that already beats with the fingerprint-singular rhythm it will carry with it for the duration. But before I can voice my gratitude, Mary is peddling off to work, denim skirt flaring, guitar case banging against her hip.

THUNDERBIRD MOTEL

For someone who has spent most of his adult life around rivers, logging thousands of days astream as a fishing guide, I'm strangely averse to the notion of change, and pending fatherhood is no exception. Moving water may indeed be a potent reminder of the present tense, but that's a condition I'm adept at avoiding.

After a couple of weeks of initial elation over the news of Mary's pregnancy and a skewed sense of accomplishment, I return to my old mental heel dragging, insisting that I'm not ready for parenthood because my "career" isn't yet on track; because we struggle to make rent each month; because we haven't been married long enough, even after nearly four years, to know whether we'll make compatible co-parents. . . ad infinitum. At age sixteen, I declared Tom Waits's "I Don't Wanna Grow Up" the national anthem of my ungovernable country, and to this day, when faced with the slightest bit of responsibility, I flee from it, hearkening instead toward Waits's desperate, growling chorus. On my way into the grocery store one afternoon to pick up some liverwurst and a three-piece of fried chicken for the ever-hungry Mary, I'm humming Waits's ragged anthem under my breath when my friend Esteban, on his way out, catches me.

"Singing is one thing," he says, squaring his stance and adjusting the large black art portfolio under his left arm. "But if I catch you talking to yourself, I'm calling a professional."

"Won't be long," I joke. Embarrassed, I point at the fresh baguette protruding from his backpack. "Dinner?"

"The insatiable appetite of a nursing mother," he says. Esteban's partner, our friend Amelia, recently gave birth to a son, Taro, who was forced to undergo emergency connective sinus surgery before leaving the hospital, and though the baby's health has fully stabilized, the early weeks were tenuous. I avoid mentioning the grave trials his family endured, and instead inquire about his new series of paintings.

"So, when are you guys going to take the plunge?" Esteban responds, dodging my small talk. "I've seen Mary holding Taro. Don't tell me she's not ready."

An angler long practiced at bluffing and obscuring locations, I counter with some vague clichés. We're not quite ready, too many variables, not enough money saved, you know how things go.

He smiles deeply, as if reading me from a great distance.

"What's it like, though?" I ask. "With a newborn in the house?"

The early days are the perfect balance of boredom and panic, he assures me. Then he places a gloved hand on my shoulder, leans in with some weight.

"Just so you know. There's no *prepping* for it." He smiles again, quote-fingers popping, before gesturing toward the parking lot full of cars, the ridgeline and crimped tassels of cloud behind it. "It's all, just, out there," he says, then turns to leave me in the wake of his newfound wisdom, baguette bobbing from side to side, snow squeaking under his boot soles.

As my exhaled breath meets the cold air, I stand outside the grocery's automatic doors considering what lies beyond my stunted field of vision—constellations spinning invisibly behind the blue late afternoon sky, countless moments, preexistent, that will come to light regardless of my level of preparedness for them. After shopping, I walk a few hundred yards downhill to stand above a slough off the Clark Fork, the food cooling in my hands.

Evening wanders in without wind. In the clear, day-warmed shallows a rainbow trout chases miniature *Diptera* off the bottom toward the glassine surface. Rising, too, emergent pupae wriggle through the water column and, breaching the surface, sprout gray, light-collecting wings. Once airborne, the hatchlings peel skyward, where Bohemian waxwings ambush from a nearby red osier dogwood. As a bird retreats with a midge pinned in its beak, the breath from its wings forms a swirl on the water that bears close resemblance to the swirl formed by the topside-charging trout.

I snap to. It's nearly dark and Mary must be starving by now. But with the insects ascending and the birds falling and the trout flying off the slough's dark bottom, it's hard to find any semblance of direction.

⤙

River: from the Middle English, "ryver."

Old French: *riviere*, which sounds like "reverie" to me.

From Proto-Indo-European: *to tear or cut.*

When I leave the river's company for extended periods of time, I feel like I've been torn from it, missing it the way a young child might miss a cherished pillow or plush animal. Which is not to say that rivers are gentle teachers: What are they if not infallible authorities on gravity, force, and obstacles?

When I first arrived in Montana it was early summer and the freestones were charged with runoff, a dynamic hydrological process that largely precludes productive angling, but one that I eventually came to regard as invigorating. To look skyward as the ranges—the Pintlers, the Bitterroots, the Flints, and so on—relinquish their six-month-old snowpack revivifies this oarsman, even if rowing against the river's best for a few straight weeks is nearly more than his aging shoulders can endure. What was on Monday a mile-wide snowfield lacquered with sunlight is, by Tuesday, flowing underfoot. Every molecule of water that didn't rise as humidity or wasn't absorbed by soil or vegetation joins other molecules to form rivulets, rills, creeks, and streams that wind through osier-choked bottoms before offering themselves finally in tribute—gifting volume, oxygen, cool temperature—to the main stems glinting along the valley floor thousands of feet below their beginnings.

Fed by channelized snowmelt, our public, navigable, unowned rivers begin to rise by the inch and then the foot, steadily covering gravel bars and eventually swallowing islands, even wetting the undersides of bridges. Every fifty years the Clark Fork swells so large it tickles sandbags laid in panic, flooding housing developments as well as pastureland. During peak flow, the West's freestones become navigable only by the nimblest paddlers. And even when runoff begins to subside, a river like the Blackfoot is a veritable creature, a beast to which the ultimate respect must be paid. One missed oar stroke, one gunnel edge dipped into the wrong wave, can mean a swamped or flipped boat, and quick. An illustration for the mathematically inclined: during late August, the river flows at roughly five hundred cubic feet per second, but it might crest—in June, in a brimful year—at 15,000 cubic feet per second, leaving high-water-mark flotsam in the branches of bankside trees.

Then, on an afternoon that smells of duff and pollen, when snow lingers on only the steepest north-facing peaks, the rivers begin to drop, and the waters shake off their respective stains. The North Fork trades its glacial, ashen hue for a fairly penetrable blue; the Yellowstone goes from chocolate-mousse brown to sake-bottle green; the tannin-rich Big Hole turns from tea-with-cream to a briefly steeped Earl Grey. As flows continue to recede, the rivers begin to "take shape," an idiom I've always loved for its suggestions of formation and rebirth. What was just days prior a brown blob squirming primordially down from Rogers Pass is suddenly the very fishable Blackfoot, its musculature apparent and alluring.

A beloved client of mine, a retired pharmaceutical financier whose multiple research companies funded many successful products, most notably a small blue pill prescribed by doctors to reinvigorate a particular male appendage, once said to me, "If this were bottle-able . . ." He closed his eyes and spun a three-sixty in the front seat of my raft as I anchored near the base of a rapid. I assumed he meant: if there were an equivalent psychiatric treatment to the annual hydrological process of runoff and the ensuing riparian symphony. "If this were bottle-able," he continued, "a reasonable percentage of big pharma would be rendered obsolete." A dual PhD in neurobiology and biochemistry, he sat lost in thought for a moment, not only taking in our full surround but clearly ideating, exploring the actual potential for such a product.

Shipped oars under my knees, I imagined the water under the boat running from a fettered person's frontal lobe to their occipital. The list of potential patients, including myself, was unlimited. CEOs deadened by the continuous abstraction of numbers, military veterans traumatized to a state of stupor, insomniacs gone decades without a sound night of sleep. What new levels of clarity and practicality could be reached in our travestied Washington via this revolutionary notion, this throttling possibility?

I closed my eyes and listened. While I'm stimulated to no apparent end by the sight of rivers, it is their audible reverberations that strike the deepest chords. This must be what a monk feels when he hears the temple bell ring, I thought; this is the note the earth is ever sounding, calling me back to my wildest name.

To occupy myself during the winter weeks before Mary announces her pregnancy, I cling tick-tight to what I've declared my craft, the writing of poems. Presuming that my work habits, if not my cosmology, will forever be altered with the birth of our first child, and hedging that a child's entry into our lives might render tertiary the pursuit of an art form, I work with blind obsession. In my daybook, I quote the masters with diligence, believing that my gleanings apply to poetics and the discipline of writing poems—"Form is never more than an extension of content," says one—but for a student of literature, I am embarrassingly oblivious to the dramatic irony at play.

Of course I think about the precious cargo that Mary's blood nurtures, as she lurches through each morning, sick behind the closed bathroom door, later appearing in the living room with a strange smile of satisfaction stretching across her freshly washed but sallow face. Though not a word depicting my nagging anxiety appears in my journal, I have begun to worry incessantly. Having long clung to Teresa of Ávila's assertion that "words lead to deeds," I try not to lend the fears much ink. But there is constancy to my trepidation, like breath, or the downbeats between breaths. We are fortunate to be employed, yes, but we scrape by at best, working several jobs between us, paying the proverbial "mountain tax" in a local economy where wages and cost of living are grossly unbalanced. Where will we find money for baby backpacks and bike trailers, I wonder, let alone eco-conscious diapers and organic baby food? While some of our friends started college funds for their children before entering the delivery room, the "glint in my eye" is one edged with fiscal unease.

Revisiting the long history of alcoholism and manic depression in our families renders my worries even more potent. Will these genetic tendencies resurface? And what of the world into which we plan to bring a child? Above my desk, I keep a picture of a young US-missile-struck Iraqi boy bandaged from head to amputated knees. Ali Ismail Abbas. His arms are stumps as well, and a white salve covers his trunk, his missing limbs taken by the same weapon that killed his father, brother, and pregnant mother in their sleep. I repeat his name each day, a mantra, a kind of spell against the deranged "conflict" we are engaged in as a country, which steals more and more innocent lives each day.

This is the milieu, the maniacal moment, into which you've chosen to bring a life? How can you justify such a choice? I ask myself at first light while cross-country skiing up Hellgate Canyon, a steep opening on the north flank of Mount Sentinel named centuries ago for the stench of dead bodies that collected beneath the rim (first the Salish fought off marauding Blackfeet here, then the tribes defended their land against the whites). Over the round mountain to the east, the sky hums with subtle light and the horizon comes in sharp, the wind-stripped ponderosas on the ridge like teeth on a comb. Then the rising sun cleaves the canyon.

Across the river to the north, the red neon sign of the Thunderbird Motel glares against the water, and the water returns a muddled version of the sign to the sky. Years ago, Ernest Hemingway's estranged, transgender child made lengthy stays at the Thunderbird. I wonder if this view of the canyon afforded them any escape from their personal struggles and troubled family history, their own complex sexuality decades away from becoming even remotely accepted by society. They stayed on the first floor, as rumor has it, where a single window is lit right now. I lean forward against my ski poles, my warm body casting steam, and survey the lightening skyline above the motel, the tawny, wind-exposed winter browse. Somewhere up there, the elk are bedded down, their warm bodies melting snow into a slick cast. By mid-morning, they'll crest the knoll and depart for the south-facing slope, a straggler-tracking predator likely not far behind. I turn around instinctually: nothing but the trail my skis creased, the pockmarks my poles left in fresh snow. With no mountain lion stalking me, no ghost of a father's suicide, I have relatively little to fret about. I'm a middle-class, straight white guy, after all, who has—imagine the freedom!—chosen to pursue art and a life on the rivers, whatever the trade-offs.

And yet it's palpable, this chest-fever of worry.

Later in the morning, with the sunlight bright on thawing streets, we drive across town for Mary's first ultrasound. While the nurse weighs and takes the expectant mother's measurements, I mill among the weeklies, tissue boxes, and aquarium-bound tropical fish, staring out the waiting room window at a large flock of waxwings that orbits the courtyard before filling a mountain ash tree. Landing, the birds elide the tree's robustly berried branches, then, stirred by some shared instinct, flee en masse, spilling into the sky like beads of mercury freed from the thin glass of a thermometer. I search the air for the cause of their flight, expecting a harrier to arc across the snow-covered field, but the sky is vacant. When the birds alight again, the snow beneath the tree is showered with bright red berries.

Is this a sign, I wonder, *a harbinger of miscarriage?*

"Hey," Mary says, tugging my earlobe. "Do you want to hear the heartbeat?"

How such machinery operated by latex-covered hands in a sterilized room can produce a sound so primal—eerie, interstellar—baffles me. On the monitor, a small illuminated form squirms, somersaults, contorts, and we lean toward the device's speaker like two kids sharing a headphone to hear the cosmic wash. Is that its face? Bright,

forming bones like the skull Hamlet held on the cover of
my father's weathered copy. Am I going to be a father? Is
that its blinking heart: How can such a tiny thing make
such immense, otherworldly drumming?

DOSTOYEVSKY'S KOAN

Several pounds of peeled potatoes boil in a ten-gallon steel pot. Covering kitchen duty at the homeless shelter where I'm employed part-time, I take another potato from a burlap sack and begin to peel. My cooking partner, a drifter named Carl who's made his way to Missoula from Wyoming and speaks in the staccato cadence I've come to associate with the displaced, stirs the pot with a wooden spoon. His dizzy spin downward, he informs me, began with a harmless bar fight. Carl's hands look heavy and his face, under a mantle of stubble, bears a grin of staunch recalcitrance. After that night, he says, he posted up for a few weeks in Cheyenne.

"I tossed this skinny rig-driller around. Broke a table and a few pool cues is all," he says, brushing a stubborn yellow shaving from his forehead. "Went back to pay down the damage but I was short a hundred. Owner said he'd let me work it off as a bouncer, while I was in arrears, is what he said. One night Chris LeDoux walks in. The country music star. Chris LeDoux. Had a big million-dollar spread in the valley. Some cowhand gets shit talkin' his music, whole thing dusts up. I yank LeDoux outta the fray and flatten the cowhand. Next day he offers me a job working security at his shows."

"Who does?" I ask.

"LeDoux. But my ex erased his number from my phone. She was pissed her cousin sent me a dirty text, and went through my whole contacts just deleting. Otherwise I'd be there running personal security, boy. High-hogging it. Vegas Strip."

After dinner prep, as the residents and guests shuffle red-cheeked through the supper line, Carl and I sweep the floors along with Sonja, a frequent visitor to the shelter whose weathered way of appearing simultaneously eighteen and forty-eight years old always disarms me. By way of a greeting, she offers that she was just released from County for stealing video equipment from one of the big box stores out on Reserve Street.

"First offense," she continues, stripping her hairnet off and rubbing at the indentation left by the net's elastic band. "First time they caught me anyway. Reason they released me out after just four days is 'cause I'm breast-feeding. I've been walking out of there with garbage cans full of stuff for months. I just borrow my girlfriend's fur coat and walk in that store like a rich woman. Plop a fifty-gallon Hefty can in my cart and fill it with anything I can sell. CDs, VCRs, nightgowns. Go to the back of the store and put the lid on tight, pay for the can with a twenty. Feed my kids off the haul till the first."

"How you gonna feed kids off shit you stole?" asks Carl, shaking his head and handing me a stack of wet food trays from the dish line. "These people. Wish I had some bus fare. Or a goddamn horse. I'd ride tonight."

I fit an aluminum tray onto the stack, pondering to what end I would go to provide for a child, and whether all children weren't, in some small way, my own. Despite the fact that many people in the world feed their children off crimes of one ilk or another—blue collar, white collar— there's a warped mythology in the West that imagines each individual striking out level on the same green pasture and eventually hitting pay dirt. In reality, like everywhere else in the world, the cards are stacked against the less fortunate.

"*These people*," Sonja says, pursing her lips. "You wish in one hand, cowboy, pick turds with the other. See which fills up first."

"I'll show you my hand right now—you want to see it?" Carl says.

"Hey" I say, trying to stop the chippiness from escalating, for their sakes especially. "You know if staff has to come in here and break this up you'll both be out of a bunk tonight. Let me cover your dish duty, Carl. How about you hop in line?"

Carl yanks silverware from the receptacles, grumbling something about fascist yuppies under his breath.

Along with its yuppies, college students, recent transplants, and gritty longtime residents, Missoula sports an increasing population of folks who have found themselves without a fixed address. Caught in the pervading wave of gentrification, many downtown businesses, especially the popular bars and eateries that prefer inebriated patrons to downtrodden panhandlers, are lobbying to have the shelter moved out of the city's business hub. My job as development director involves casting a light on a largely marginalized and dehumanized population by writing grants and letters of appeal that advocate for the practical needs of said population; the supper-line shifts and the shared meals help me give voice to the residents and their journeys. To that end, I sit down next to Carl and chat him up about the fishing in Wyoming. I tell him I have a good friend ranching near Crowheart, but Carl is sore at me, I can only assume, for letting Sonja have the last word. Guilty as charged, I fork into my mouth some browned lettuce got from the expired rack of a local supermarket and soaked in Italian dressing donated from the same, struck by how dystopian my utopia must appear—nearly fifteen percent of Montana residents live below the poverty line—to some of the shelter's clients. I look out the window toward the river. Nearby the Clark Fork slides glassily by the abandoned Burlington Northern trestle, beneath which, in the midsummer shade, a healthy pod of native cutthroat trout often rests—as does, just ashore, the occasional person *sans abri.*

The only way to make sense of the suffering of others is to assume responsibility for them, my dad once said, quoting, I'd later learn, Dostoyevsky. He used the line in a dogged argument with my mom about whether he should be allowed to continue teaching classes at the high-security state penitentiary in Jackson, Michigan, where he was earning credit toward his master's degree—and where an inmate-on-inmate murder had recently occurred. The walls and doors of our old apartment were thin, and when the yelling finally subsided, I gathered that my dad had yielded to my mom on the matter. This dispirited me because I knew he took pride in his service, but also because I thought him tougher, more masculine, for his work at the prison.

The eldest of three, he formed his sense of familial and social responsibility against the odds of his upbringing. His own father, Roman, had followed General Patton into the Battle of the Bulge and returned home to Detroit with a stitched-up chest wound and a profound fondness for vodka, which he self-prescribed per generational norm as a painkiller. Later, Roman worked as a journeyman pipe fitter and fell so irretrievably far down into the drink that he abandoned his wife and three children for another family a few towns away. He died an impoverished alcoholic.

I think of my dad's inevitable fears of parenthood, which must, somehow, be conflated with my own. Given the trauma of abandonment and abuse, both physical and mental, that he'd experienced at the hands of his own father, he couldn't have been completely at ease with the notion of becoming a dad. And yet he stepped into the stream. Previous genetic lines, with their potential to transmit latent psychological and physical calamities, have long struck me as compromised, polluted feeder streams that downriver lines can't help but absorb. How if ever can these tainted headwaters be reconciled when it is said that trauma experienced in a single generation requires three generations of healing before it can disperse, on a cellular level, from the genes?

To his credit, my dad rarely tests, beyond the occasional beer, his hereditary tendencies. He shaped his own journey, to say the least. After obtaining conscientious objector status vis-à-vis the conflict in Vietnam, and following two years in community college in Detroit, he moved seventy miles west to finish his studies in another flagging automobile town, Lansing, where eventually I was born. Though we could never afford cable TV or more than one pair of new jeans per year, my childhood was peppered with volunteer hours at soup kitchens and detours into grocery stores to purchase food for someone on a street corner who had asked for help.

In a stable childhood, though, perhaps it's de rigueur to desire the pop heroic in one's parents; in my case, I longed for my dad to be Lance Parrish, catcher for the Detroit Tigers. What I've just begun to glean of his example, though, is that to lend everyday help to an everyday human being requires the exertion of a less glorified muscle, the brain, specifically the anterior insular cortex that allows a human being to relate empathetically to the experiences of others. After years of study, he earned his doctorate and became a psychologist specializing in repairing broken families and, whether intending to or not, made empathy his business. As one of my dad's graduate school advisers, well versed on his background, remarked, "You're trying to change the course of a river. Be patient."

After clocking off from the shelter, I walk past the Depot Bar and the Silver Dollar, past the graffitied railcars and old granary turned office space, and turn, teeth chattering, toward home. I trace the river's slightly downhill trajectory through the valley, the floor of which was once, fifteen thousand years ago, that of a glacial lake. Some mornings, when fog envelops the floodplain, one can imagine the vast and frigid body of water that covered roughly three-thousand square miles, engulfing all but the highest elevations. At the end of the last ice age, when the Cordilleran Sheet shifted and a twenty-story-high ice dam finally caved, the river flowing from the outlet toward the ocean—a twelve-hundred-foot-high wall of surging water—was equal in volume to fifty Amazon Rivers.

Over centuries, this dynamic geological process repeated itself dozens of times before, as the climate warmed, the ice dams stopped forming and the lake floor began to stanch. The floods left few remnants beyond fossilized seaweed and billion-year-old mud, and as the subsequent glaciers carved through the land, honing peaks and sculling valleys, life was scarce. Geologically speaking, the four-legged creatures were soon to follow: ground sloth, mammoth, short-faced bear. By several centuries these and other mammals predated the initial bands of northwardly advancing humans, tribes of hunters. Later, the first people to reside permanently in this valley, the semi-migratory Salish, cohabitated in teepee camps near the confluence of rivers and, except for the occasional scrape with neighboring tribes, lived largely unperturbed, subsisting on plants and berries and camas root, on deer and moose and elk, and on stores of bison they harvested on their annual excursions to the prairie. Apparitions, helixes of dust, notes of blurred relief on the horizon, a succession of advancing Europeans soon focalized: first the largely amiable French-Canadian fur trappers, some of whom intermarried with the tribe; then squads of diligent, self-important, state-sponsored explorers; then the cavalry-backed settlers, the claimers of land.

For going on two centuries, the West has been fraught with what one writer called "the hallucination of innocence," the flawed view that vast parcels of undeveloped space, access to prolific wild game, and troves of wilderness simply conveyed a sense of freedom, constituted a blank slate. Of course, such a notion ignores blatant appropriation, waves of displacement, prolific bloodshed, and the ghosts of violent conquest: the lingering truth of what we don't always acknowledge but nonetheless navigate like a moist, heavy air.

The last light winks out above the Bitterroots as I close in on our new house, a bungalow on the industrial side of town for which we swapped our foot-of-the-mountain rental. Like our old digs, this simple craftsman build has two bedrooms, but we can paint the baby's room whatever color we wish because we own it, or pay toward the note, as the saying goes. When we signed the mortgage, our loan officer asked if we didn't want to "tack on an equity line, bring home a little extra cash" to fix up the kitchen, adding that, with home values escalating in the valley, we'd be able to refinance the house in six months easy, absorb the credit line "no prob."

His name was Rob, and since he responded to each of our queries and requests with that phrase, we nicknamed him "No Prob Rob."

"Sure," we answered with matching wide-eyed looks: *What expecting parents with a new house payment and substantial student debt wouldn't want some breathing room in an otherwise airtight budget?*

"How's five thousand?" he asked, pausing to mute the ringer on one of his two buzzing cell phones. Clearly he was born to negotiate the current boom in real estate; if he had been born in 1860, he would have been selling timber, in 1910, stakes in mines. "Or we could make it ten? Hold on, I have to take this call."

"You can do ten?"

"Hold on," he said to the caller, placing his palm over the phone, then said to us, "Of course. No prob."

Accounting for the more dependable contribution to our collective income, Mary teaches kindergarten. Like many folks in the booming New West, where the cost of living is rapidly outpacing wages, and where underemployed master's degrees abound, I work a few jobs after the guide season comes to a close, teaching composition classes at the university, working as a poet in the schools, and writing grants for the shelter. Although we swapped our monthly rent of seven hundred dollars for a nine-hundred-dollar adjustable-rate mortgage and traded the mountain trailhead at the end of our old street for a convenience store, we were soon endeared to the broadened view of Mount Jumbo, the weathered northernmost slope of the Sapphires some local in the 1800s named for its resemblance to Ringling's famous pachyderm.

Covered in a fresh skiff of snow and lit by a waxing crescent, the slope is remade in miniature in our bed as Mary's sheet-covered hip. She reclines to read, hand on her stomach, the picture of contentedness.

＿～

There ought to be some type of backwoods reagent, some earthen intelligence like a divining rod with which one might test for maternal instincts. Clearly not all humans are naturally suited to the multifaceted vocation—some swoon at the sight of an infant, while others shrink away; some relish curating a bodily space for an unfinished accompaniment, while others loathe each minute of the carrying. From across the living room, I watch Mary gravitate toward our friends' infant son, Taro, and his mother, Amelia. There is a noticeable deference paid by expectant to nursing mother: *May I?* offers the former with a mere dipped shoulder and a glance at the babe. *Impeccable timing*, implies the latter with a weary smile, and clasps the flap on her nursing bra. Two vastly different hormonal cocktails are coursing through their bodies, I conclude, but they are both clearly buzzed.

My mom tried for six years to conceive her first and only child. With my dad in graduate school, we lived in low-income housing until I reached third grade, and while not spoiled with material goods I was doted on as only a first-and-only can be. To hear my mom tell it, I walked at nine months, spoke in full sentences at a year, hung the moon, shined the stars, and so on. As a parent, her protectiveness was legendary in our apartment complex, feared by even the most hardened ne'er-do-wells, this disposition the product, I surmise, of the unsettled home she came up in.

Her biological father was, like my dad's, largely absent. A trinity of women raised her: mother, great-aunt, and grandmother, the latter of whom adopted her for a time. A lacuna in family lore: did my mom's mom leave Detroit to find work? Or did she break down under the stress of a troubled relationship, leaving her two children under the care of their grandmother? Versions of the story vary, though each retains like their protagonist a stubborn ambiguity.

At age eighteen the woman who would become my maternal grandmother was set to graduate Hazel Park High near Detroit when she met a handsome man a few years her senior, got pregnant, dropped out of school, married shotgun-style, and nine months later gave birth to a son. The union was tenuous from the start; the newlyweds smoked, caroused, and consumed copious gin martinis. A year later she divorced the man, or he divorced her, after which point she raised her son as a single parent while attending night school to complete her secondary degree. But the relationship with the man was tempestuous and a few years later she was pregnant by him again, this time with a girl. They remarried, or they didn't—again, few facts remain. During an argument about the pregnancy, he struck her, not for the first time, and she left him for good. In her mid-twenties, after giving birth to my mom, she settled into a job at a travel agency in Detroit.

Today in her mid-eighties, Shirley Burns remains striking, and I imagine that in her prime she sold more than a few vacation packages on magnetism alone. Like too many resilient women, Shirley endured waves of abuse and trauma at the hands of men who claimed to love her—sufferings she shares with the western landscape. Last summer, she visited the little sliver of Montana we work hard to call home, and was quickly taken by the landscape and our proximity to open spaces. Since the entire left side of her body is weakened by an aneurysm, I showed her the surrounding country not by hiking trail but via the four rivers that conjoin near Missoula. To this oarsman there is nothing quite as riveting in the riparian corridor as confluences—holy places, I might say, were all places not so endowed—and so I chose our floats accordingly, so that she could see the locations where two bodies of water, previously thought of as separate, interpenetrate.

One morning, we launched on the Blackfoot just upstream of its confluence with the Clark Fork, two rivers named, respectively, for a Native tribe and a soldier of manifest destiny, just another line item in the long litany of ironies perpetually underfoot in the West. There the Blackfoot dashes out of its lowermost red rock canyon to gallop alongside towering cliff walls specked with lichen and the white droppings of eagles. It was early June and the bank-full river ran brown, the color of coffee spiked with Baileys, Shirley's favored morning beverage. Current rattled the willows, shaking empty salmon fly husks that clung to the branches. I explained the stonefly's two-year-long emergence cycle to her—the airborne females dropping eggs that fall through the water column to seat among cobbles and gestate into nymphs, which then feed on detritus for twenty months before migrating to the shallows and eventually hatching into winged adults—but she didn't so much as glance up.

"Watch where you're going," she pleaded, gripping the seat with her good hand. We rounded a bend beneath a hundred-foot-long deadfall ponderosa that the current had wedged, weeks earlier in higher water, between two sedan-sized boulders. I pointed it out. "The river put it there." She took a peek. "No kidding?" I had always seen her as a thrill seeker, the carpe diem type, but she hunched within her life vest, silent for the remainder of the float.

Later, over a Cutty Sark at the Milltown Union Bar, she said, "Sheesh, Danny"—following multiple aneurysms, she often called me by her son's name, my uncle's, when flustered. "The whole ride, I thought the boat was going to—" she made a flipping motion with her left hand, and then waved her Benson & Hedges at the bartender. "I'd better have another belt." Two fingers for a double.

I asked if she didn't want to let the first drink settle before doubling down, what with the elevation gain and all.

She laughed me off and downed the fresh pour, after which she fished a twenty from her fanny pack, set it on the bar, and nudged me toward the door. Arm in arm, we waddled past the taxidermied mountain goat across what the young couples, with the help of the digital jukebox, would soon turn into a dance floor. Outside, we stood awhile in the tall Montana twilight suffused, as it is that time of year, with young greens from the hills, blues from the pines, and roses and pinks from the lingering fields of snow. A barn swallow swooped through the shadows, on the hunt, a-chitter. Shirley leaned heavy on my arm—from exhaustion or the liquor, I couldn't tell. I told her we could easily adjust tomorrow's float if she found herself needing an extra hour or two of sleep.

"Oh, bully. The air's so fresh here, you could never get a hangover," she responded. "And you can still smoke in the bars. You can't ever leave."

As I mulled her gravelly voiced commandment, she lit a final cigarette, its ember planetary against the darkening sky.

As the weeks pass, I try to work away my pre-paternal anxiety, to fend off with sledge and pry bar the dire hypotheticals between which my mind peregrinates. My catchphrase is "sweat equity," which draws hearty laughter from Mary, who reminds me with a wink that I can barely tell a screwdriver from a hammer. With the help of a few contractor friends, though, we manage to Sawzall out a new window, cut a wall in half and top it with a breakfast bar. Paddlers, climbers, and river rats themselves, our carpenters agree to shave a substantial amount from the bill in trade for future float trips and hand-tied trout flies. The crew's constant banter makes for easy work: the new wave among them gushing over the wealth of outdoor recreation opportunities, the old guard talking constantly of town's encroachment on the few remaining accessible parcels.

"Twenty-five years ago," one of the latter says, lifting the brim of his ball cap with his carpenter's pencil, "I used to hunt pheasants about three blocks from here. Just past the trailer park."

Shouldering a load of demoed rebar, I long to someday be able to wield such an ethos-laden introductory clause.

One unseasonably warm February morning after a jog along the river, I come home motivated to vacuum some lingering sheet rock dust and to prep a new wall for paint. With a Shop-Vac borrowed from our new simpatico neighbor couple Laurie and Spurgeon, I begin to suction the powdery particulate, working the nozzle down the baseboards, coughing a few times at what the hose stirs up—finely ground gypsum processed in Detroit, according to the label—and recall the day I once spent underneath that city with Shirley on a tour of a gypsum cavern. As our guide's headlamp splintered the translucent walls of pinkish rock, I relished our hiddenness beneath the bowels of those loud streets, the screeching tires and newspaper hawkers a few hundred feet above us but muffled by the subterranean distance.

Though physically proximate, Mary's body hides plenitudes these days, and our worlds seem increasingly disparate. As the Shop-Vac's exhaust stirs dust that obscures the far wall, I wonder what pre-parental anxieties she harbors, or if the increased hormones coursing through her body are providing a constant liquid courage. After standing for a moment in the powdery cloud, I strap a ventilator over my face and settle in to finish the job, trying my best to hold my breath.

I awake the next morning quaking from head to toe, the violent shuddering rousting Mary before her alarm. After a shower and a cup of tea, I pull on a wool hat and two down coats, but I can't shake the churlish cold from my neck and arms. I zip myself into a sleeping bag, drape our comforter over my shoulders for extra warmth and bay for Mary, who's just hopped out of the shower, to turn on the bath.

"The hot water's gone," she says, and after quickly dressing for work, she pushes a thermometer under my tongue, pursing her lips with an appropriate level of decorum. The youngest and scrappiest of five children—whose brothers often rolled her up into an area rug along with the frenzied house cat—Mary lacks nothing in the mettle department. "One hundred two, just over. Try some Tylenol? You'll kick it."

At noon, I haven't stopped shivering and, with my ribs shaking free of their moorings, too delirious to determine whether it's a prudent move, ride my bike to the hospital.

"Definitely pneumonia," says my friend the ENT. Dr. Gardner, or Phil as he insists I call him, is a fishing partner who generously doubles as my general practitioner since I carry no health insurance beyond catastrophic. He holds an X-ray of my lungs up to the illuminator board. "Hard to say. Could be particle-induced. You had a little cold, the drywall raked the cilia out of your lungs. Most likely. The question is whether it's bacterial or viral. We won't know that until the blood work comes back."

As Phil begins to push my wheelchair down the hallway's polished white floor, I recall the day we met; it was early in my guiding career, on a dubious float where, due to a moment of carelessness on my part, I almost flipped my raft and drowned in Rock Creek. The canyon wrens were particularly raucous that June morning, and Phil, who'd sacrificed flies and tackle to my error in judgment, declared in the aftermath that he was twice as interested in identifying birdcalls as he was in catching trout, a gracious comment to offer a chagrinned guide. Later, when

I mentioned Pablo Neruda's bird-watching ode—"How can this throat, narrower than a finger-width, gush singing waters?"—Phil proceeded to detail the intricate, flute-like construction of the songbird's throat, to answer anatomically this would-be poet's rhetorical gesture. Our kinship was instant. Specializing in restoring the so-called goose's foot nerve—the nerve that allows a face to smile—he regularly donates his services to underprivileged children that were in accidents or born with deformations. All of which is to say that my lack of health insurance doesn't bother Phil in the least. My visit is free because Phil, quite free himself, says it is.

As another blurry figure in a green coat plugs me into an IV, Phil leans in and takes one final listen to my lungs.

"It reminds me," he says, pulling the earbuds from his ears, "of listening to my mom's eight-tracks. Neil Diamond never sounded so good. We'll get a serious antibiotic called in. While you're here, Trish will take good care of you."

For the next several hours, a nurse as poised as an orchid feeds me slushed orange juice from small plastic cups, which helps to shave my fever down from 105 to 102. Sliding in and out of delirium, I am returned to boyhood, tended to by my mother, who once, when I was ill and the apartment's tank ran cold, boiled pots of water and carried them to my tepid bath. The moth-soft kiss of a mother. Beyond the hospital windows the snowy Bitterroots put on their evening blush, and I regain modest sentience. Even in a hazy state this much is clear: I am my mother's son, not my spouse's; Mary's task is to attend to her well-being, and by surrogate the well-being of the tiny life inside of her, placing me, by fairest rights, a distant third.

The door to the room opens shyly and a nurse asks if I'm hungry—not now, I respond, but thanks—a small reminder of how lucky I am to be receiving such excellent care. Just a few blocks north at the shelter, where I would have been working tonight were I not tethered to this bed by an IV, folks are lining up for supper, chatting about bed assignments, and surveying the menu. If it's a typical night, someone in line looks feverish, or is breathing noticeably labored breaths, or can't stop coughing—someone in line is likely more ill, more vulnerable, than I am now. A hospital bed is a strange place to comprehend one's privilege, but it nevertheless hits me, along with the requisite level of responsibility, daunting and inimitable as a family line.

VISITORS

The doorbell rings, snapping me from a fever-induced reverie, and from the couch I wave in my friend Adam. He totes a worn green internal frame backpack, which smells of campfire, snowmobile exhaust, and something unidentified but unmistakably mammalian. As we exchange pleasantries, he digs from the pack a bottle of Clamato and a six-pack of Hamm's.

"Too early for a red beer?" he asks, referring to the Montana brunch favorite that combines tomato juice and pilsner.

"I should pass," I say, nodding toward the pile of used tissues and the thermometer resting in a teacup. I stretch into a rare shaft of late-winter sunlight that spills through the window onto the blue down sleeping bag I keep wrapped around my shoulders. Following my hospital visit, I explain, I've spent the past few pneumonia-wracked weeks propped up with couch cushions, my back inclined so I don't further aspirate dense sinus drainage. "I feel like I'm carrying a bag of birdseed around in my chest."

He launches into a litany of synonyms for "soft," until one of my rib-rattling coughs raises his eyebrows. "Fair enough," he says, tucking the cans into his pack with slight secrecy.

A fellow Michigan native and old college dorm-mate, Adam is fresh off a long stint in the Selway-Bitterroot Wilderness where he works as a wolf biologist in an unwalled office that spans a hundred or so miles along the Idaho-Montana border. Wild country: nearly as wild, in fact, as it was in 1855 when territory governor Isaac Stevens, taken by the Bitterroot Valley's temperate climate and potential for agriculture, jettisoned a previously mapped border along the Continental Divide in favor of further westward expansion. This decision initiated the expulsion of the Salish people, inhabitants of the land between the Sapphire and the Bitterroot ranges from time immemorial. A treaty would follow, of course, the shoddily translated Hellgate Treaty signed on behalf of the Salish by Chief Victor with a conspicuous letter *X*, but "not a tenth of what was said (at the meetings) was understood by either side," estimated one Jesuit observer. Ceding 19 million acres to the US government, the tribes retained only 1.2 million. Over the next fifteen years, the First Peoples' forced migration northward would lead them onto what came to be known as the Flathead Reservation.

Adam raps a knuckle on the book I've been reading, E. O. Fuller's exhaustive history of the Salish from their initial encounters with French fur traders through 1972, when they, by then known as the Confederated Salish, Kootenai, and Flathead Tribes, successfully sued the US government for reparations. "The Flatheads, huh?"

That name came from French trappers, I explain, who had heard stories of coastal Flatheads using boards to flatten infants' heads; when Salish pressed their hands against their ears to indicate that they lived "between the mountains," the misnomer took root. "Most of the events in this book took place where you're running your snow machine right now," I add. "Bitterroot Divide."

"Penrose would be curious," Adam says, referring to a vaunted history professor we shared back in college. "But he'd want to see your sources."

"Par-for-the-course colonialism," I say, adding that the Salish were feared warriors, not par-for-the-course anything. It was said that five Blackfeet would turn tail and run from a single Salish warrior. "The tribe didn't leave the Bitterroot because they lacked courage. They were a peaceful people. When the Nez Percé were running from the US Cavalry, he tried to enlist the Salish too, but Chief Charlo, Chief Victor's son, said he wouldn't lend his tribe's help, that white blood would never be shed on Salish hands."

"I bet Charlo regretted not joining," Adam says. He fiddles with the cord on his backpack, loosens the toggle, tugs it tight again. "But then again Gibbon did ambush the Nez Percé at Big Hole. I guess the Salish would have been massacred too."

We nod, both aware that in 1877, near what's now known as Chief Joseph Pass, Colonel Gibbon told the cavalry to "shoot low," before first light, "into the tepees." Almost a hundred dead, sixty-some women and children. To examine this history as a white person, even on a surface level, is to become aware of one's complicity—distant but nonetheless existent—in the dynamic of colonial tyranny.

"Every now and then," Adam says, fidgeting with his backpack strap again, "I get a sense of the sheer number of bones I'm walking on. Reminds me of that Rummel print you like so much."

I picture the refrent, *When First Unto this Country*, is a 1980s Jay Rummel piece that hangs in Charlie B's, a downtown bar that we frequent. Three feet wide by two feet tall, the black-ink image indebted to mural composition and psychedelic poster art depicts a mountain range comprised of creatures such as bear and elk and wolverines, followed, from the peaks downward, by Native humans, then Hudson's Bay Company fur trappers, and then white settlers, culminating in a valley floor made up of cowboys and vagrants entering a saloon. The work illustrates an alternative to the "time lines" we were fed in elementary school, and suggests a more concurrent view of history, wherein the occurred is still occurring.

Once, with a week's worth of tip money in my pocket, I offered bar regular Eric, who had consigned the print to Charlie's, half of the thousand-dollar asking price. At the coin-scarred bar, he leaned into his whiskey neat surrounded by his fellow regulars—contractors with beer pints, a city councilwoman with her gin and tonic, a former Greenpeace rabble-rouser with his rum and coke—and answered with a sigh that accepting such a low offer would be an insult to the artist, an old friend. Though Jay Rummel went on to gain serious acclaim in the San Francisco art world, he struggled to make a living in Missoula, where the galleries wanted dust-raising horses and pastel sunsets. Several of his etchings hang in Charlie B's because Rummel liked to drink whiskey, and, lacking cash, was often forced to get liquid with his art, frequently selling it off to his friend, the aforementioned Eric, who was, for impeachable reasons, fairly flush back then. When Eric later fell on hard times of his own, he finally off-loaded or put on consignment most of the Rummel prints he owned to the bar, to cover a succession of substantial tabs.

"You still thinking about buying that print with the baby on the way?" Adam asks, rubbing his thumbs and forefingers together to make the universal sign for money.

Employed by the Nez Percé Tribe in Idaho, Adam spends his days hiking, snowshoeing, or snowmobiling into the backcountry with radio telemetry devices, monitoring the movements of several wolf packs across a harsh, roadless terrain trafficked by few two-leggeds.

"How many packs did you pick up this time?" I ask.

"Twice as many as they say exist up there," he replies. "Capital *T* they. No one wants to account for wolves once they're on the Divide. That's no-man's land as far as state governments are concerned."

Beyond the government cubicles, at watering holes across the West, wolf sentiment swings on a wide-arcing pendulum. For every wizened hunting outfitter who complains there aren't any more elk to hunt because the wolves have thinned the herds, there's an enviro-thinker asserting that the whole ecosystem has been revivified thanks to the return of the prodigal apex predator, avian life having rebounded because the aspen trees have as well, because ungulates like elk couldn't freeload unmolested in riparian areas anymore. And so on. If you want to wreak havoc on some jovial conversation down at Charlie's, just poll the bar on wolf policy.

"I've yet to see a wolf," I admit to Adam. "Heard them a couple times in Yellowstone."

"Give it time, you'll see one," Adam says, explaining that by his estimates each drainage will likely support its own pack within five years. "Now mind you, I'm not saying good or bad. I'm just saying *is*. That's the way it's going down. The politics slay me. Rarely do the folks involved actually care about the wild animals more than their own bureaucratic advancement.

"I just try to get far enough into the backcountry to leave that crap behind. I want contact. Day before yesterday, I was near Painted Rocks on snowshoes, five miles from the snowmobile when I found a fresh kill. Elk calf. Pretty clinical, pack-style execution, from the tracks in the snow. The way they do it is to cut a weak calf from the herd and run it until it collapses. Then they rip its backstraps out, maybe the hindquarters if they're hungry, and quit the country altogether.

"I turn on my transceiver since we've got the alpha male collared: not even a beep. Standard operating procedure. Probably not even going to put it in the logs. But then I follow some track, find sign of another tussle, and see a cow elk bedded in the aspens. Only she ain't sleeping, you know?"

I shrug.

"She's a goner," he elucidates, "almost rigor mortised. Except I can't find a deep wound anywhere on her. Got nicks all up and down her forelegs, and a few gashes in her haunches, but no fatal wounds. So I roll her over and slit her open with my knife, up to the rib cage."

Having field dressed plenty of ungulates over the years, I can picture the stomach like a bag of grain, the uncoiled brain of intestines, the improbably dense red lungs, then the dark-purple muscle behind it all, hard as a pitch-heavy knot of pine.

"Slice it down the middle," he says. "Right away I see what happened: burst ventricle."

I imagine the vital muscle's dense weight in my hands, like two halves of a grapefruit, and picture the inroads of tissue and flesh, the gullies, all the canyons intact except for one whose hot river burst through its banks.

"She just keeled over, heart attack, while watching her calf die. The wolves barely touched her after that. I know, I know: anthropomorphism, all that shit. Dude, I'm a scientist."

"You don't have to convince me," I say, surprising myself with a sudden rush of energy. I look past Adam to the window, startled to see my own grin reflected there. Across the street the rooftops steam and the eaves drip melted frost.

Adam lifts his eyebrows and nods.

"What did your boss say?" I ask.

"I could get in trouble for this," he sighs, "but I didn't report it. The guy's a total desk jockey. He wanted to name one pack 'NP-8,' like some stupid sports car. No wonder people don't give two shits about wild country."

I ask Adam if he took the ivories, the valuable molar-like teeth of the elk, a set of which might sell for a hundred dollars at Broadway Pawn and Gun.

"She died in the line of duty," Adam says, finally reaching all the way into the blue backpack at his feet. "So it didn't seem right. Plus I couldn't have someone saying I abused governmental privilege down the line. And if you ask me, the land has eyes of its own. But I did bring you a souvenir."

He rummages around for a while and finally proffers a large, sweating ziplock bag filled with ice that surrounds another smaller plastic bag containing something deeply maroonish in color and twice the size of my fist. He draws the dripping inner bag out from the melting ice of the outer bag. "Lunch."

"Elk heart?"

"Stomach too weak? Get some oil heated. A little butter. Small pan is fine. I have a mind to bake this ticker with olive oil, garlic chunks, and sage leaves tonight for this wrangler I'm trying to impress up the Blackfoot. But a couple of slices won't be missed."

By the time Adam's rinsed the plastic bag and picked a few stray elk hairs from the silver-skinned muscle, the olive oil's snapping; when I add a pad of butter, it slips across the skillet following the tilt of the un-shimmed house. He sharpens the beveled blade of the chef's knife against the hone, rinses it at the tap, then slices several coin-thin layers from the outer edge of the organ.

"Tinfoil?" he says, with three slices pierced by the tip of the blade. "Wrap these and put them in the fridge until Mary gets home. Same recipe. Iron's good for the baby."

As I follow his instructions, Adam lets the remaining slices fall into the pan, where they curl away from the heat and begin to trade magenta hues for ochre. He grinds pepper, shakes salt, and then stabs the slices with a fork.

"As close as you'll get to eating aspen leaves and drinking spring water seventeen miles up Blue Joint. Not that that's where I was."

The slice singes my fingertip. We hold the pared muscle to our mouths like shots of liquor. *Nostrovia. Salud. Chin-chin.* A feral toast to mothers and their calves. To visitors just beginning to sense their small cameo in the long story of this place. The meat is dense and leavening and tastes of timberline air just after a rain. So hot it twitches.

We chase it down with water.

~

While walking the downtown alleyways early on a Friday morning, you can study the frescoes of vomit on the pavement and consider the intense physiological transformations required to transport a body from pleasantly buzzed to raucously drunk to stumblingly pummeled to puking to, presumably, somewhere out there, wretchedly hungover. I empathize with whomever lost their lunch last night, but I feel better today than I have in a month. An hour ago, Phil tapped his pen against an X-ray sheet and put a stethoscope to my chest for a listen, quickly determining that he liked what he didn't hear. From the alley, I duck into the curio shop for a celebratory cup of tea.

Through the high windows of the long, tin-ceilinged room, ribbons of sunlight stream, refracting through large mason jars that line the walls. Several tiers of shelves house roots, petals, leaves, and spices; Darjeeling, turmeric, ginseng, bloodwart root, *ras el hanout*—words that saturate a mind worn dry by illness. One jar filled with saffron kindles like an ember that wants to go out but is stayed by a gentle breath. Behind the register, a gray-haired barista with a stringy goatee holds up a finger: one moment. In front of an older gentleman known ubiquitously as "the Octopus"—for his ability to play, and win, up to eight chess matches at once—the barista places a pot of tea, and next to the pot a napkin on top of which they set a spoon, and next to the spoon a red saucer on top of which they place a red cup.

"What would you like?" they ask.

The list is long, but I spare them. "I'd like one of those, with rose mint."

"A pot of rose mint tea?"

"Yes, please."

They turn and spoon into the stainless cylinder a mixture of dried mint, rose petals, and rose hips, then shoot steaming water into the basin of the pot, lid it, and place the accoutrements in front of me precisely as they'd placed the Octopus's in front of him. "If you're looking for a holy word," reads the three-by-five card taped to the espresso machine, "try routine."

"A dollar twenty-five," they say.

"A dollar twenty-five," I mutter. "That's all?

We're bombing schools in Baghdad by the city block, leading non-convicted detainees around Guantanamo by leashes, mindlessly assembling "islands" in the Caribbean out of our discarded plastic water bottles, and this pot of rose mint tea still costs a mere buck and a quarter?

I slide my change into the tip jar, a brass Ganesh statuette, reminded of a wise man's notion that a bucket, no matter how large, can be filled drop by drop.

Some years from now, while attempting to grade a student paper and concurrently feed a bowl of rice cereal and pureed prunes to one of our children, I'll invoke the Octopus, a kind of walking, albeit disheveled, postmodern reincarnation of the elephantine Hindu god with myriad arms. But for now, I sit down next to the local chess wiz and pour myself a cup, breathing deeply from the steam.

"It used to be a drugstore, this place," he says, without looking up from the classifieds, which he has brought to within an inch of his nearsighted eyes. He wears a gray-and-yellow cardigan, threadbare at the elbows, and has set upon the bar an oily lensed pair of horn-rims. "Peterson's."

"I don't remember that."

"Well, it was," he says. Sipping with audible annoyance from his cup, he points to the white tile floor beneath our chairs, into which is inlaid, in broken brown tiles, remnants of the store's former name. "Whether you remember it or not."

When, late in his life, a local novelist of some repute was asked by his publisher to consider writing an autobiography, he replied that he had gotten "too old to harbor any delusions of reality in nonfiction."

Such a response will haunt anyone attempting to make music that tracks against the ticking of the clock. My fear of memoir is that the mind-set it demands often removes its maker from the all too fleeting present inhabited so exquisitely by the flora and fauna, and fixes him in the past tense's "vise of stone." Further, I wonder if the task doesn't beg the author to live recklessly, to seek out danger or suffering for the sake of subject matter when danger and suffering abound in the most ordinary lives, wherever we deign to look. Often in the genre, the arrow of culpability points outward, is aimed at exposing this or that ill, societal or familial, whereas I fear that most of my important arguments are with myself, to steal a phrase from another poet. I agree with one indomitable practitioner of the form who said, "It is difficult to undo our own damage, and to recall to our presence that which we have asked to leave."

Perhaps this burdensome catalog of reasons should cause the aspirant to toss the notion aside altogether, but I'm nagged by a voice, a quiet but insistent one that suggests standing in flowing time and casting one's memory upstream might help one better comprehend, and stand upright in, the present.

⌒

Light, the day's last, renders the moments-ago clear river eye-searingly opaque. A little wind on the face, cold water shackling the ankles: these elemental blessings should be birthright, I think, among the first a body receives. Hesitant, my feet test the cobbles and my joints gauge the weight of my frame. It's early March; the river has shed its skin of ice, and I wade the Bitterroot beneath a heron rookery, a collection of nests the size of papasans, feeling a little bit reborn.

Very early this morning I sweated out the last of my illness, shook it off the way a dog would water, and have emerged in a mild state of reverie. It's my birthday, and while I'm a bit too young to take stock of my meager accomplishments, I'm also too old to ignore the reckoning of sorts that awaits. Some uncomfortable math: if I live until I'm sixty-two, the age of my grandfather when he died, I'm nearly middle-aged. I still feel too naive to be a father, too friendly with the convolutions of youth and my perpetual adolescence, but I thank the river that the twenty-five thousand or so child-forming genes inside Mary's womb don't share my traits of indecision.

Perched on a bankside fence post, returned from parts south, a male meadowlark—*Sturnella neglecta*, overlooked little starling—sings one of the seven songs in its repertoire, a combination of notes that mimic the moving water's unpredictability, the melody of an otherwise invisible composition. A pileated woodpecker arcs across the river letting go its high-pitched staccato cry, the maniacal laugh of an escapee from winter's prison. On leave from the nests, which he takes turns guarding with his mate, a male heron stalks the warming shallows where tiny midges stake out slicks behind boulders and skate in dizzying circles; where underwater stonefly nymphs cling to cobbles a few feet from shore; where a trout, rainbow, just rose.

The inevitable elation that follows catching the year's first fish is often coupled with instant, distinctly sexual melancholy. Some élan of expectation has been erased, a mystery, something previously imagined, made manifest. As the angler releases the trout back into cold water, most of him wants to catch the fish again, which of course is not immediately possible. He pulls wet fingers into jacket sleeves and leans back against a deadfall's weathered trunk to watch a just-hatched stonefly dry its dun-gray wings. After leaving its exoskeleton, the insect will spend an hour, what will amount to a large fraction of its remaining life, preparing to fly. The angler peels flaky shuck from the log and holds it in his palm, wondering which selves he's shed over the years, which ones he clings to too tightly.

The insect that inhabited the husk lived for roughly twelve moons along the riverbed, clinging to detritus and the underside of rocks, fleeing sculpins and baitfish, avoiding the downturned snouts of whitefish and the wide white mouths of trout. Now the newly incarnated adult must dodge terrestrial dangers myriad and not the least bit metaphysical: swallows, robins, even early arriving Lewis's woodpeckers will eat a stonefly on the wing, and near shore ouzels abound.

Metaphorically speaking, we seem born into a world that's trying to kill us daily in multiple ways. Does the smiling stork that wings us home in swaddling clothes morph effortlessly into the same bird that will one day pluck us from this life? A year ago, when my mom wrote to ask when Mary and I planned to have children, I penned a cryptic answer in verse: "The great horned owl / statued in the maple / peers through the neighbors' / nursery window."

Thinking myself clever, I showed the response to a friend over dinner, a father of three, who blurted incredulously through his Scotch.

"Aside from your image being stock, you answer your mother with *fear?*"

I answered him with inarticulate silence.

This evening as the door between winter and spring peeks open, I wade out to my thighs in search of a more proper answer. I've long been fond of the commonplace angling term "reading the water," which can be summarized as the brief study before casting a fly, the examination one makes of the river in hopes of deciphering what lies beneath its surface. The resulting cast, then, is a measured guess at the tack and pace of the current, and where it will likely carry the angler's offering. To learn the language of rivers is the task of many lifetimes, more than the single one I've been afforded, but this evening as a squall builds over the mountains and the water grips my knees, I seem to translate a single word issuing from the riffle: *deeper.*

Up to my waist now, I tuck my fly rod under my arm and let my bare hands dangle in the current. Gradually the cold water makes the tips of my fingers throb then burn, and, closing my eyes, I envision touching small hands.

Mary has turned away from me in bed and placed my hand on her belly, its subtle but noticeable elevation and placental tautness. We've been talking about names for the baby, girl names, and not connecting, not coming close. I suggest the name of a great-aunt she admired. Goodness no, she says. I try the name of the heroine in a favorite novel of hers. A sigh. Mulling her silence, I think of how all bodies of flowing water relinquish their name by the time they hit the ocean. Rock Creek and the Blackfoot and the Bitterroot—all three drop their names at the Clark Fork, and hundreds of miles downstream, the Clark Fork repeats the gesture when it meets the Columbia.

"I'm sure I'll come up with something suitable," she says.

Looking up through the skylight at the half-moon, I feel a small flick in my palm, like a trout's investigative tap at a current-swung fly.

"I think I just felt it," I say.

"You did."

"I thought I did."

"It's odd, but yesterday I missed the baby."

At the switching yard a few blocks away two railcars clack together, a thunderous coupling that startles us both.

"Do you ever wish, just sometimes," she asks, "that you could carry it?"

"I do wish I could carry it. On my back."

Sometime in the middle of the night I dream vividly of a meteor shower.

In the morning, with no previous knowledge of the actual solar system or current occurrences therein, I learn from the newspaper's headline that such a celestial event occurred as I slept. As I turn the front page, I feel a nudge, the slightest reminder that the earth and the cosmos are in continual conversation with us, even if our ears are mainly stoppered to such talk.

SEEDS

"Have you done your homework?" Mary asks, referring to the reading and journal exercise I was to have completed before we attend our second birthing class tonight.

She's entered the kitchen, her hair still dripping after a shower. The session starts in half an hour, and I suspect she's trying to lighten my attitude toward the curriculum, to sand down the noticeable chip on my shoulder. I did after all accuse our otherwise well-respected instructor of "prenatal fascism," following her contention that all children not born under natural birthing methods, preferably home birth, were fundamentally deprived. To agitate her I falsified a "recent study" that proved the true determining factor of psychological health in children was the mental disposition of one's parents at the moment of copulation and subsequent conception, which was at this point well beyond our control.

I relished her dumbfounded glare.

Mary bends to her left so as not to soak her shirt collar and fits the pin of a small silver hoop into her right lobe, while holding the other hoop between her lips. "Well?" she says, out of the open corner of her mouth.

"I've forgone the reading in hopes of remaining faithful to my own particular brand of genius," I say, borrowing an idea from Walt Whitman. "Besides, 'everything we are taught is false.' Rimbaud."

"How do you keep all these quotes in your head while consistently forgetting to make the car payment?"

"Baseball is to blame. Al Kaline hit 399 home runs. Ty Cobb had 4,191 career hits. My best friend Levon Porter's phone number was 332-3485. I could continue."

She gives me a sour-lipped look, chased with a dash of bemusement. Her body has begun to show slight proof of her pregnancy, and not even my childishness can dampen her happiness. I reflect on two years of babymaking attempts, on her mourning the arrival of each menstrual cycle. Books and magazines pored over, doctors called on, diets altered. Sperm killers, like tight briefs and hot tubs, outlawed. Vaginal fluids were closely monitored: rubber-cement sticky meant wait a day, but something closer to egg white meant engage in immediate intercourse. Since becoming a father still topped the list in my private catalog of fears, I felt a secret relief each time the conception boat didn't drop anchor at our house. True, it meant more monitoring of body temperature and ovulation fluids, but it also secured another month of sex with abandon.

This secret relief was a minor infraction compared to the twenty-first century's primary act of emotional impotency: failing to offer a comment during a birthing class as your partner earnestly engages the instructor's questions. One could argue for more damning failures, sure, but this one breaches the top ten. At least I have a cohort, other fathers-to-be seated cross-legged in the basement of our instructor's home, sprawled out on the shag carpet and stray pillows—a doleful roundtable of mutes.

On notepads, guided by said instructor's questions, Mary and I eventually put down our "couples goals," the kind of naive vows expecting parents are expected to make as they close in on the wilderness of parenting. While projecting slides of landfills heaped with diapers and plastic toys onto her basement wall, our instructor impresses upon us the inevitable environmental impact our growing family is likely to have on our planet. So perhaps we have been unduly led to write that we will handcraft birthday presents and clothing, though neither one of us can sew. We will also grow, hunt, or harvest all of our own food in the baby's first year, starting with what we can tend in the ten-by-four raised garden bed we will build this weekend. And we pledge that we'll never, under even the direst of circumstances, own a minivan, feed our child fast food, allow plastic toys in the house, employ a microwave, or use day care when more than three children are present.

Okay, we'll try to grow our own kale, anyway.

Mary chuckles to herself as she draws a tiny hammer about to drive a tinier nail beside a small screwdriver leaned up against a toolbox—she nudges me with an elbow and captions the sketch in her characteristic mirthful font: "screwdriver and hammer."

The shovel's handle vibrates each time it meets a cobble rounded two million years ago by a glacial flood. It's slow going, but I clang the spade against the rocky soil I hope to transform into a garden plot, while Mary constructs a row of unearthed alluvium in the grass. A century ago, the Clark Fork must've meandered through what is now our backyard, long before ranks of municipalities straightened the river with countless tons of riprap and allowed motels and gas stations and fast-food joints to be erected along its constrained banks.

She spits on a rock and rubs in the saliva with her finger, the sandstone's drab orange constellating with tiny bright blue conglomerates. The cobble is a descendant of the Sapphire Mountains to the east, a far older range than the Bitterroot batholith, which flanks our western horizon. When glaciers receded through the valley millennia ago, they ground substrate from both mountain ranges and the resulting riverbed was roughly composed of equal parts Bitterroot and Sapphire ranges, a geomorphic yin and yang that gives the channel rich contrast.

"The Bitterroots are younger, more igneous," I say, crouching to free an angular gray piece that darkens like a whetstone when wiped clean with a sweaty hand. "And harder. The Sapphires are older. By millions of years. Tens of millions, I think. But softer, anyway."

Mary laughs, takes the small portion of mountain in her hand, and sets it in the row.

Leaning against the shovel handle, I admire the humble view of the Bitterroots from our backyard. Wherever I see sky and sloped landscape meet, I consider myself on safe footing. Perhaps a budding poet should eschew sentiment altogether, but surviving here—working underpaid in a skewed economy where living and housing costs rise sharply despite stagnant wages and few full-time jobs, to name one obstacle—earns one the right to wield a dash or two of that forbidden poetic seasoning. My maternal grandfather, whom I never met, was born in the severe landscape of Armenia. I've frequently concocted a romanticized genetic need for the rugged open spaces and vistas that drew me to Montana, but I've been guilty of confusing desire with need more than once. Besides, my three female cousins from the same side of the family thrive in Detroit and report that their collective *querencia* is Twelve Oaks Mall.

Waiting for me to wrest another rock from the ground's stubborn grip, Mary retires to the hammock to read a book on prenatal brain development. From a single bruised cumulonimbus twelve thousand feet above our yard the season's first warm rain begins to fall. Unperturbed by the rain, she tells me that the baby's nerve endings already feel pain, that its taste buds are operational, and that its ovaries or testicles have already grown. An avocado, she says: that's about how heavy it is. The large raindrops plop onto the exposed ground and surrounding dandelions, knocking the weeds' pale seeds to the grass, playing their leaning stems like strings.

"It says here," she announces as the hammock squeaks on its metronomic pace, "that the baby in the womb can already recognize your voice from two rooms away." Her frequent book reports are the sole means by which I receive biological information on pregnancy. When she chides me for not reading the books piled on my nightstand, I crib from Keats.

"Extensive knowledge just eases the burden of the mystery. Besides," I say, leaning against the shovel's handle and wiping my forehead with faux exhaustion, "the course texts are all written by women *for* women. I thought we were aspiring to something resembling equality here. Do you realize that three out of four children's books depict god-awful fathers or no father at all? I mean, look at the Berenstain Bears, for instance. That guy is an absolute buffoon."

She who taught me how to drink wine and eat steaks cooked rare leans back and spills out a red-cheeked cackle. Maybe it's the tilt of the earth and the lengthening of the days, or the rivers coming to life again after the melt, or the knowledge that Mary has delivered her freight safely into the second trimester, but I can feel my fears of parenthood lightening a bit.

"Anyway," I say, rolling up my sleeve to examine the hairy, apish forearms I hope aren't endowed to our child, "I've been reading plenty."

"Okay, lend me one factoid, then, as you like to say."

"Are you aware," I say, "that while it's not quite as old as these rocks here, that egg of yours whose walls were breached by one of my hundred million sperm is thirty years old?"

"I *told* you that last night! Have you read any of the books?"

I admit that I thumbed through the "alternative one," *Spiritual Midwifery*, a book from the seventies about a commune in the Tennessee hill country where women birth their babies at home, without aid of doctor, drugs, or devices. When a few new mothers in our circle delivered their children at home, there seemed to be a strange cultural cachet attached to the method, a vague moral premium. But Mary studied home births and decided—mercifully, for my worrisome nature—that the practice wasn't right for her.

A warm, tumescent rain continues to fall on our little backyard, loosening the sweet musk of budding lilacs. Mary stretches up from the hammock and informs me that she's headed in for a shower. How about a partner, I suggest, to which she says no flunkies, even cute ones, allowed, before blowing me a jaunty kiss and closing the sliding screen door behind her.

Using most of the afternoon I finish the job: five hours to clear a four-by-ten-foot patch of ground and bracket a couple of long fir boards to a couple of short ones. Mechanically inept as ever, I made seven trips across the street to a gracious neighbor's garage to borrow tools and wood and sawhorses. Now I lodge a whitetail antler shed against the bed's southeast corner and admire what can hardly be called handiwork. I shrug and kick a cut chunk of milled lumber through the pile of sawdust. It must be said that rather than measuring twice and cutting once, I'd not measured at all, cut anyway, and returned to the hardware store for additional lumber. At the other end of the bed, I bury some porcupine quills plucked recently from a roadkill, a prickly spirit to protect the seeds and seedlings we will plant.

⁓

Early in May as the buds of the backyard aspen venture out to test the air, I write letters to our unborn child—but a decade later, hoping to gain purchase on time passed, to sift through the metaphorical flotsam time's current has strewn upon life's banks, I won't be able to locate them.

Did we bundle them with the image of the first ultrasound and the inked print of the newborn's feet? Did we throw them out before a move? *Womb-rider,* I write, *foot-drummer. How will we prepare our world for you?*

The morels have begun to emerge in earnest, and just before Mother's Day I head into the high country in search of a culinary gift for the expectant mother. One of my guiding mates, Dixie, has the mushrooms' location pinned on the forested south-facing hillsides where last summer's forest fires raged and the delectable pyrophiles now germinate in the aftermath. Born and reared in the Bitterroot, Dixie knows by rote which stands of trees, due to soil type and

photochromatic accumulation, will hold the season's initial fungal gold. Back in the seventies, before his knees gave
out, he played catcher in the minor leagues, and returned
from the California farm system "with a few seeds," which
he planted in undisclosed coverts. Long before other full-
scale operations existed, he harvested and dealt marijuana
to Montanans in copious amounts, salting away enough
profit to pay cash for a house that overlooked Lolo Peak. By
the time I met him he had settled into his second career as a
fishing guide and was completely retired from the horticul-
ture business, but he was as full of stories as a long-seated
tick is of blood.

And he owned a pet bobcat, which, to this listener,
legitimized the yarns.

We drive up a logging road with said feline in tow on
a humid afternoon, climbing in Dixie's jacked-up black
F-150 with flames painted on the doors toward a fire-
scalped ridgeline on which we hope to discover a bumper
crop. Following a balmy three-day rain, the morels—whose
microscopic spores rested in the needles of the ponderosas
before flames loosed and buried them—should be popping
out of charred earth. Dixie's bobcat, a declawed female
named Stevie, rides unleashed in the back on the center
of the bench. Our eyes meet in the rearview with shared
suspicion.

"Take a peek," he says, sluicing some Copenhagen tobacco
juice out the open window. "But I wouldn't suggest you make
eye contact. And don't under any circumstance turn around."

Like a proverbial child told not to reach toward a
stove's flame, I can't help but swivel, and find myself staring
straight into Stevie's agate-colored eyes. There is a moment

of consideration wherein predator and prey gauge which is which, before the cat's whiskered ears twitch and, in a mottled flash, her left paw swings up from the seat to belt me across the face.

"Geezus!" I say, clutching my eye, my prey hackles rising.

Dixie slings another line of spit out the open window with a shrug that seems to ask, *Why point out a thing twice?*

I shake off the blow and focus on morels. To date this year, I have only found a handful of the coveted fungi, but I can nonetheless taste the sliced caps cooked down in butter, seasoned with salt and pepper, and piled atop a jack cheese omelet. I'm thinking: mushroom reduction over a good cut of venison. Thinking: stuff the largest ones with poached Oregon salmon and fry them, ever so lightly, tempura-style. Thinking: harvest a few extra pounds to trade with the best chef in town for a meal at his bistro, and take Mary on a date I couldn't otherwise afford. In season, morels can often be purchased at farmers markets for a modest ten to twelve dollars a pound, but out of season, specialty stores price one dehydrated *ounce* at twenty dollars. After one prolific haul last year, I sold eight pounds to a local restaurateur at seventeen dollars per.

A combination of mystique, singular flavor, and physical form—the morel's deep pores sponge up melted butter, olive oil, and white wine—elicits such bargaining leverage. At one Memorial Day feast, I watched a woman reach into a viciously sizzling cast iron skillet for the last morel, drop it sans cooling breath into her mouth, chew, lick her fingers, and after a noticeably erotic moan, declare, "My God, these morels are better than sex!" A few intrigued observers glanced over their shoulders for the woman's husband, but she stared straight at the younger male chef (who would one day become a hunter-gatherer of extensive renown on television) and asked what it would take to get a second batch of mushrooms in the pan.

And while the morel's use as an aphrodisiac is debatable, its environmental merits are unquestioned. In fact, our forests would be massive garbage dumps if it weren't for fungi, which decompose everything from decaying leaves to entire trees, breaking down matter into reusable substances. Bluntly put, to eat a morel is to consume the dead understory of the forest resurrected valiantly in a simple but heavenly sauce of butter, cream, shallots, salt, and pepper. Vital to the reforestation of blighted areas, morels also fruit in stands of pines attacked by bark beetles, providing yet more evidence that perhaps the best thing we two-leggeds can do for the planet is to (occasionally anyway) remove ourselves from the equation and let the natural world heal itself.

Trillium splash up from underfoot. We traipse over the white whorls of petals, through the maze of fire-sawed and wind-felled pines: lodgepoles oozing with sap, ponderosas shading the bones of winterkill deer. Dixie kneels to pick the day's first morel, a thumb-sized specimen I nearly stepped on, taking care to slice the stem just above its base, to knock lingering bits of soil back to the earth with his horn-handled knife. He lifts the morel to his nose and gives it a sniff before tucking it into his canvas satchel.

"One February while I was shed hunting," he says, swinging his legs over a downed tree, "I found a trunk like this still smoldering."

"From the year before?" I ask, suspicious.

"Had to be."

Scouring a forest floor the color of coffee grounds, I listen to the unhurried pace of his steps on the pinecones and soil— it's as though he's waiting for one foot to firmly touch down, then looking, just looking, taking it all in, before allowing the other foot to lift. Relatively speaking, I'm sprinting. When I reach the ridgeline several long strides ahead of Dixie, he calls me a drive-by mushroom hunter and points out—after slicing open a meaty specimen with his pocketknife to show me a dusky arion—that the slugs are finding more morels than me.

I'm still learning the high country's dialect. In contrast to moving water, which I read each season with my eyes and arms, the elevations must be gleaned by foot. I tromp across foliage that remains vague to me; I can scarcely distinguish a white-bark pine from a ponderosa, let alone identify the understory beyond wintergreen, kinnikinnick, and huckleberry. I know that true knowledge of the land, the dense and durable kind, can only be gathered at the landscape's pace— why do I expect to suddenly attain the accrued intimacy of someone like Dixie, who has traversed these ridgelines for several decades?

I reckon my haste is rooted in the fear that when our child arrives, so, too, will a crippling sense of domesticity—a hypothetical, sure, but one that scares me even more than my threadbare bank account. In lieu of a trust fund, I want to endow our child with a carnal contact with the earth—not only its creatures, but its flora and fauna too. I run my finger against a ponderosa and from its trunk peel a scorched layer of bark. Its underside is adorned with intricate galleries of pine beetles and weevils, wormish markings, the likes of which adorn the backs of brook trout. I set the scrap of bark in my sack among the morels and with my index fingertips smudge two lines of soot under my eyes. Wearing the same glistening shade of black, a single raven croaks and flies across the draw.

I point to the slope beyond which the bird disappeared and ask Dixie if he ever found morels growing there.

"Too steep. But I did find fifteen pounds of weed there one year. No buds. Back then, though, a leaf would get you high."

He gestures toward my feet. "You just stepped on one."

I raise my leg, scan my footprint.

"Other boot," Dixie says.

We make our way up the saddle and look over an apocalyptic scene foregrounded by an entire hillside of trillium, the roots of which were boiled by the Nez Percé to arouse sleeping lovers, or so Dixie says. Claims he tried it once with his partner, then lets the matter lie.

"Well?" I prod.

Wind rings the dead chimes of an aspen. At the foot of a juniper, a discarded snakeskin catches a gust and rattles audibly, the ghost of its former inhabitant.

"You see that glacier lily?" Dixie picks a white, star-shaped flower from the edge of his shadow. "They generate so much heat underground they can melt the snow, bloom right through it."

"No."

"You can eat them too. Watch." He picks one and a moment later is chewing with delight.

EMISSARIES

My teacher pointed the way west with a book. Beloved among aficionados since its publication in 1976, Norman Maclean's family saga hadn't quite hit Hollywood when my sophomore English teacher handed me his weathered copy; this wasn't long after I'd turned in a shoddy personal narrative about a fishing expedition. "Read it," Mr. Colando said, pushing his glasses back onto a shiny, large-pored nose, "and tell me what you think."

Holding the slender volume in my hands, I sat intrigued between two fellow jocks, soccer teammates whose lassitude was palpable, and stared at the faded cover's aerial photo of a mountain-flanked river valley. I opened it and read the first sentence about a family and its belief in the grace of landscape, and then I read the subsequent sentence, and so on. By the time the bell rang, I'd reached page 19. By lunch, I'd made page 30, and when practice began after school, I dog-eared page 56 and zipped the book in my duffle. For dinner after training I microwaved two boxes of Mia Cucina fettuccini Alfredo and picked up the book again. When my mom arrived home from work, I mumbled a greeting while forking a warm bite of thick processed noodles to my mouth.

"What are you reading, honey?"

I showed her the cover. "This book Colando gave me."

"Is it good?"

I took another bite and chewed. "Favorite book ever."

True, I hadn't at this point in my life read *any* literary
book from cover to cover, including assigned school texts.
Other than biographies of athletes or hook-and-bullet
stories by outdoors writers that I cherry-picked my way
through, I didn't read much at all. But as my mind's eye
contacted Maclean's sentences, the physical, mental, and
emotional sensations I had experienced while standing in
a cold stream with a fly rod were reenacted. Alchemical:
that's how I would describe the reaction today, though I
scarcely knew the word back then. And I held the book
in disbelief, dumbstruck that words could so thoroughly
transport a reader.

"Poets talk about 'spots of time,'" I read—Maclean's sentence paused at its comma, then unfurled like the loop of
a perfectly timed fly cast—"but it is really fishermen who
experience eternity compressed into a moment. No one can
tell what a spot of time is until suddenly the whole world is a
fish and the fish is gone."

And there I sat, in my own spot of time, existing simultaneously in Lansing, Michigan, with a warm cardboard box
of microwaved pasta in my lap, and waist-deep in Montana's
Big Blackfoot—a river that I would, a decade and change
later, come to call home water as a guide. Yes, I was lured
that night to the place Maclean evoked; more consequen-
tially, though, I was driven to seek a deeper understanding
of how his meticulous, laconic prose and idiom enacted the
character of a landscape. As if a tuning fork had been struck
inside me, I sat thrumming with the realization that I would
somehow have to, from this moment forward, inhabit two
worlds: the physical world as well as another, equally potent
one made palpable by the written word.

In the Mitten State, the Shakespearian phrase "winter of our discontent" is patently redundant—February lasts "thirteen months" according to one former resident—and yet I recall the winter of 1993 as a particularly dismal one from which Colando rescued me continually, pressing book after book into my clammy adolescent hands, books by writers that I would come to regard as critical to my understanding of wild places and our place in them, undomesticated thinkers who lived close to the bone, for whom the natural world was not merely a subject but a living, conscious text. He would assign me imitations and return my exercises lit up with exclamations and evaluative exuberance—stars, underlining, checkmarks, *Zow! Yowza!* Since Colando was an artist himself, an accomplished photographer, his persistent attention carried gravitas.

Often, coming home from a party late at night I would happen past his house in the neighborhood and, noting his illuminated basement window, imagine him whiling away in his darkroom, bathing prints in various plastic tubs filled with odorous solutions. Some mornings he would show our standard-track class a photo that he had developed in the wee hours, an image captured on a road trip through the Columbia River Gorge, say, a print he'd framed and sold, or one he planned to trade with another local artist. Some were harrowing portraits of the hardscrabble buildings and people of Lansing, the formerly thriving General Motors hub, images I would later come to see as influenced by Walker Evans, while others were black-and-white landscapes bearing titles like *Learning the Language of Rivers* and *All My Life I've Been Troubled by Waters*. He clocked time like a miner, claimed to love the smell of film more than van Gogh had loved the smell of paint, and exemplified the tenacity required of a working artist. It would take me years to understand that the artist's life is always, societally speaking, under siege, that most of us work day jobs to earn our time at the desk, or beneath the red-orange darkroom bulb, as the case may be. Colando planted that seed: you went to the work regardless, because your survival depended on it.

One day out of the blue, he stopped over my desk and reached into his shirt pocket. "Here," he said, handing me a cassette tape, "I think you might like this."

The writing on the spine read, "For Chris—River Songs: Volume I."

Soon my classmates' discussion seeped soundlessly into the asbestos ceiling tiles and fluorescent lights, as I read and reread the list of songs my teacher had compiled for me—"Long Way Up the River," "Marias River Breakdown," "Deep River Blues," and so on. Some were by artists I knew of, such as Joni Mitchell and Bruce Springsteen, but some were new to me, like Phil Aaberg and Doc Watson. Pining for the yellow Walkman stashed in my locker, I was at once overjoyed and befuddled: There were others, then, for whom moving water was a muse?

Over the next few months, Colando would compile two more river-song mixes for me, but of these three installments, only the handwritten track listing to volume 1 remains in my possession. After several years of steady play on expeditions in the West, the tape deck of my pickup finally coughed out the first cassette in a bird's nest of shiny ribbon; volume 2 I loaned to a young female public radio disc jockey in Bozeman whom I met along the banks of the Gallatin one evening, and who promised to drop it off along with a six-pack at my apartment after playing a few cuts on her folk show, but never did.

As for volume 3, I left that in the console when I sold the truck to a logger near the Idaho border for thirty-five-hundred dollars cash. The buyer, faintly perfumed from freshly sparked reefer, handed me a roll of rubber-banded hundreds, brushed a couple of blond dreadlocks behind his ears and asked, "Remind me why you're selling this truck?"

"Gotta buy a drift boat," I said, stretching the rubber band on to my wrist and beginning to count out the bills.

"What are you going to do with a drift boat?" he asked. He opened the glove box to check for the manual, then clicked it closed.

"Guide fishing trips," I said, beaming. "Montana."

"How are you going to tow a boat without a truck?"

"Got a four-door picked out. I'll put a thousand of this down tomorrow and get a loan for the rest."

He eyed the truck's bent antenna. The skin at the corners of his eyes was splintered like a sandstone wash. "Guiding, huh. Remind me what you do now?"

I was writing for a regional newspaper, I told him, the sports and outdoors section, though I neglected to specify that my beat was semi-professional hockey.

"Well, I hate to tell you," he said as he pantomimed a cast with fairly decent form, "but westerners already know how to fly-fish. We don't need guides out here."

That night on a half-deflated air mattress I slept fitfully, the wad of bills in my pocket and an aluminum baseball bat at my side, wondering in my waking moments whether fly-fishing guides were indeed superfluous in the West.

After guiding many fruitful seasons in Montana, I still lend occasional credence to this dreadlocked logger's assertion.

~

It has taken me years to learn—I'm still learning—that a trout is a finger pointing to the river, an emissary, if you will. And I envy these emissaries their full immersion.

During my first summer in Montana, while wading a tributary stream I refuse to name, I attempted to share a holding lie with a trout. It's not only secrecy that keeps me from naming the creek, but also the notion that the creek remains nameless to itself, and two decades ago offered a visiting angler the privacy of dreams.

I was knee-deep. The current ushered dusk down a box canyon. The red rock had stored the sun's rays and alternating winds drew warm drafts from the crags, cool drafts from the deep shade of willows. Sunflowers splashed up from the bank, their seed-heavy heads bowed toward the water, by turns a mirror held to the cirrus-streaked sky, then circus glass morphing the reflections into mesmerizing forms. Delicate, anonymous to fish that gorged on them but called by anglers *Sulfur, Cahill, Pale Evening Dun,* yellow mayflies clung briefly to the moving water, then poured into the sky like snow falling in reverse.

Disturbing the slick eddy behind a boulder, the nose of a large trout appeared and vanished. The water repaired itself.

I made a single instinctual cast, hooked the trout—it leapt high, knocking caddis from the overhanging willows—and fought it to the shallows flecked with granite and pyrite, small particles of the mountains I could not see but whose peaks I knew stood some miles away, severing land from sky. Holding it loosely underwater, watching its flaring gills stir the pebbled streambed, I saw the fish as an elemental composite of its entire surround. Wildflowers dotting nearby hills had rebloomed in the red spots along its cheek; righting its form, its caudal fins mimicked the movements of a hovering kestrel's wings; and the bluish white of its inner jaw reconstituted the hue of the first, barely noticeable star dawning in the east.

Not large by Montana standards, the trout was nonetheless immaculate as it shook free of my hands and made for the depths. Anatomically, we shared little, save for our eyes, mouth, and teeth, stomach and intestines. I knew I could only momentarily enter its world, could not survive long in the element that sustained it, and yet I desired a deeper connection than our hook-and-line dance had allowed for. I stowed my fly rod and vest in the osiers, shucked my fish-slime-soiled shirt and, wading back into the creek, sussed the depth of the hole. I porpoised, stroked hard for the bottom, and embraced a boulder.

When my breath ran out I surfaced. Though I was miles from the truck and any semblance of society, I looked around to make sure there'd been no witnesses, a bit embarrassed by my strange rite. Walking to the truck in the dark I was consoled by a thought: perhaps the most authentic ceremonies are the least planned.

Oddity notwithstanding, I celebrate the anniversary of this literal immersion each year with a figurative one by embarking on a two-month-long string of guide trips just before the summer solstice. The physical work of rowing against the river's best for several straight weeks is nearly more than my aging shoulders can endure, but the gauntlet helps me to place a finger on the pulse of this landscape as its charging freestones begin to clear and charge hard for the tall Rocky Mountain horizon.

⁓

June is a song I don't really know the words to, its melody too fast to follow, but am humming along with anyway. How the longest days of the year become the briefest is a conundrum I mull on a rare busman's holiday—my first day off in three weeks—while watching Mary ply Rock Creek's currents with a stonefly imitation. Whoever christened this river a creek never attempted to cross it during runoff, when the flows can un-foot even the most nimble wader. Aiming her fly under overhanging bushes, Mary presses her weight against the burly liquid force, testing her footing and my nerves with each step across the algae-slickened boulders. Watching her fly land and speed downstream, I gauge how fast I'd have to sprint over uneven riparian ground to catch her pregnant body if she fell in: impossibly fast.

From the limbs of river-shook alders, female stoneflies the size of ring fingers part from their nocturnal mates and pour forth into the air, forming a dizzying congregation of ovipositors. With clusters of black eggs the size of huckleberries attached to the rear of their abdomens, two bugs collide and sputter to the water's surface. Immediately they're swept downstream. The largest of aquatic stoneflies that flourish only in the healthiest riparian ecosystems, *Pteronarcys californica* lives two years—nine-tenths of its life—in nymphal form before migrating to the shallows to emerge when water temperature and aspect of sunlight reach optimum levels. When an airborne female can't shake free of its egg sac midair, it will often use the tension of the river's surface to aid in the release, a technique that makes them vulnerable, if not irresistable to opportunistic trout.

Mary points her rod toward the aftermath of a trout's slashing riseform and begins to work her way to it, casting a hand-tied fly, its foam body held up by a wing of *cul de canard*, the oily, water-repellent duck-rump feather, plucked from a mallard harvested last fall. All hull, no keel, she still looks barely pregnant from behind, and more surefooted than she truly is with that growing midsection throwing her off-center. Carrying high noon in its whirring wings, a dragonfly buzzes downriver, turns on a dime, and lands on the strap of Mary's blue tank top, pausing, still as a tattoo. Intent on presenting her fly, she doesn't notice the visitor. Thigh-deep, as deep as one should ever wade into Rock Creek, she feeds line and stretches out her right arm to extend the rod, lengthening the fly's drift, but the fish rises again just out of reach.

She yells something over the roily currents I can't make out, but I take it to mean: I'll need the boat to get to it.

Obliging, I reef up the anchor and shove the oars into the oarlocks; the port oar settles perfectly, but starboard slides over the U-shaped lock and laces into the ankle-deep shallows. I drop anchor, leap from my seat, and give chase, hollering over my shoulder for Mary to hold tight. For twenty yards or so the oar seems within reach, a mere stride or two away as I thrash along the bank, but gradually I lose ground. Downstream, an island channelizes the river into a slow meander and a cliff-straightened chute. The oar veers right, doubles its speed and rides the thalweg. High-stepping, I leap a juniper, bust through a fragrant clump of sage, bloody my calf against a beaver-whittled willow, and draw a bead on the oar—just before it catches a kicker seam and speeds off into the glare.

I rip off my ball cap, swing it through the air and look back at Mary.

Even over the rushing water I can hear her careening laughter; she knows we have a spare oar to help us reach the landing several miles downstream. Gasping like a fish held up too long for a picture, I stand resigned to the loss beside the wash of Rock Creek, thinking about horizontal time and what gets lost to it.

BEGIN, O SMALL BOY, TO BE BORN

The manifold radiance of an expectant mother: hips widened to the hilt, abrupt, pear-like slope of the belly, cheekbones staunch with strength, skin lambent as if lit from within. Perhaps it's unbecoming, libidinous of a partner to stare at their bikini-clad pregnant spouse for extended periods of time in public, but I'm loath to look away. I watch Mary ease down into the chill currents of Rattlesnake Creek and recline against a boulder. Nestled against granite, with the water flowing over her shoulders, she holds at waterline a pencil and the birthing journal that our doula Colleen urged her to keep. When she licks the pencil's lead and begins to write on one of the heavily thumbed pages, I shimmy over with the current for a look. She turns the covers inward, though: a schoolgirl with her diary.

It's a swelteringly hot afternoon in late July, the air choked with forest fire haze. From Lolo Peak to Chief Joseph Pass the Bitterroot Valley burns like a seventy-mile-long wick, and consequently Missoula's barely habitable airshed is filled with humidity and flurries of ash. How strange it feels to live with water, to move atop it daily in the boat, and return in the afternoon to a landscape riddled by drought. For weeks the closest we've come to rain is the sound of parched pine needles falling from their branches onto our roof. For now, most crops are surviving thanks to small-scale irrigation, which I'll abide; large-scale irrigation of the old school type saps rivers of volume, and shallow rivers warm rapidly, which taxes the wild trout—a resource that can be stretched much further than cattle farming and dry land crops. Guided fishing trips, for example, bring in an estimated $400 million per year to Montana, a figure eclipsed only by lodging, fuel, and food purchases in the state.

On the creek's shore, a canvas bag shades what remains of our modest farmer's market haul: two huckleberries from a high-priced pint we otherwise devoured; the butt ends of four dispatched cucumbers; a bushel of unwashed carrots sold by a former student of mine, a third-generation Hmong farmer named Kuoa; and a cantaloupe selected from the reposing angle of Dixon cantaloupes that spilled across the bed of a green Dodge pickup. I pick up the pimpled melon and take a fragrant whiff off the blossom end, gauging its size against Mary's midsection. A slice or two would no doubt quench my thirst, but to partake now seems weirdly cannibalistic. I offer a carrot to Mary, who declines without looking up.

"What are you writing?" I ask.

"A list."

I snap the carrot with my canines and chew, savoring the rain the carrot is made of, the bright sun that drew its sugars out. I sense Mary's growing desire to communicate with fewer words, or perhaps with none. How long has she been trying to express this, I wonder, while I've been oblivious to her desires? She's drawn into herself of late, and carries herself with a new poise.

"A list for what?" I ask.

"So I can have everything packed in case we leave in a rush."

The first and only item on my pre-delivery list: a white pillowcase for waving out the window of the car while speeding to the hospital, "a possible" whose value my ever-thorough but semi-neurotic mother has impressed upon me numerous times. "An officer of the law will not pull you over if you do this, no matter how fast you're driving. I used one the time you sawed open that golf ball and the liquid gel inside shot into your eye. I don't know if you remember that?" Few moments from my youth, I told her, were more indelible.

Placing my hand on Mary's taut belly, relishing the tide-like movements in my palm, I bow to my own mother's protectiveness, her grizzly-sow guard, and sneak another look at the journal.

"What could you possibly need a mirror for?" I ask. "You don't need any makeup."

"No peeking," Mary says. With the pencil she draws a black bikini strap from her shoulder blades to her deltoid, to avoid tan lines I assume. Two warblers call back and forth across the riparian corridor at uneven intervals. A magpie squawks in staccato. Eventually she answers, "To see the baby's head. Before I start to push."

Turning away, I slip under the water once again and watch pearlescent bubbles of oxygen peel off my bare skin and loft toward the surface. As soon as we are able, I vow, I'll bring the baby here so that its small form can be held by the water's strong hands. Cutting through the thermocline, I surface to a view of Mary's incomparable shoulder. It's a location I'll revisit later, another of summer's sweet indecencies: not the suntanned skin of a beloved, but the pale skin the suit covered, a landscape to be mapped by the lips.

A few days before Mary gives birth, a three-year-old boy wanders off from his family's wilderness campsite in the nearby Ninemile Valley wearing only flip-flops, a pair of shorts, and a pajama T-shirt. On foot and on horseback, with helicopters and rescue dogs, the authorities search diligently. They even dredge the small lake beside which the boy's family is camped, along the shore where he was last seen. After three full days and nights of searching, with all stops pulled, with nighttime temps in the low forties, with humidity high and hypothermia a distinct possibility, they grow resigned to the loss and call off the search. His mother and stepfather plead from the newspaper cover. After public outcry, authorities are pressured back to the task and redouble their efforts, though again they come up empty-handed.

Watching the television news that night, a local man, a custodian at a fast-food chain, decides to investigate the country early the following morning. He has no children of his own but as an elk hunter has pitched annual camp in the Ninemile since childhood, not far from where the boy was last seen, and he can't imagine spending an entire season traversing the steps of a missing boy.

After the driest summer in decades, the creek alongside which the man walks is barely a trickle. Like a forty-three-year-old Hansel, he drops candy wrappers every hundred paces in case someone—the boy, he hopes—were to come upon them. Horseflies orbit the sweaty mesh of his ball cap. He considers a mid-morning nap but chides himself:

How will you ever pack out a bull in this lazy kind of shape? Thoughts boomerang like this for the better part of the morning, but eventually burn off like dew when he's walked long and hard enough. The trail he follows is too well used by ungulates for him to decipher recent track from old, but a scattered rose hip – skin broken, seedpod scattered—perks him up. A few steps later a second seedpod stops him in his tracks. All kinds of game animals ate rose hips, but none he knew regurgitated the seeds.

Just then a ruffed grouse flushes from the trail, the explosive whir of its mottled wings breaking the stagnant air, starting his heart. He mounts an imaginary shotgun as if to fell it and tracks the bird's line of flight through alders and into a clearing. And there, on the other side of the meadow, seated atop a knoll near a logging skid trail, is the boy.

"Hi," the boy says, once the man has huffed the meadow and reached him. "What are you doing?"

"Looking for you," the man says, out of breath, a little surprised that the boy didn't flee, and marveling at how alert and unaffected he appears.

Above the trail a grasshopper ascends a snowberry bush, hopping from one white fruit to the next, waiting until the first has ceased its swaying before venturing another leap— the way a body might cross, boulder by boulder, a swift and shallow stream.

"Is my mom looking?" the boy asks.

"She sure is. We're all looking for you. Here, you must be starving." The man empties his pockets of Werther's, unzips his hip pack, and proffers a peanut butter and jelly sandwich he'd made and wrapped in tinfoil well before daybreak.

The boy opens his small fist to reveal a sweaty palm filled with rose hips.

"My aunt told me if I ever got lost in the woods, I could eat the skins off these. The leaves too. But don't drink the water 'cause cows poop in it."

"I bet you're thirsty then?"

"Yeah. Really thirsty. You got a Mountain Dew?"

⁓

Mary strikes the lighter but it throws only sparks. She smacks its base against the desk several times like a gavel, strikes it again and angles the flame toward the votive until the wick catches.

Above Mount Jumbo, one day from full, the big moon rises at perigee. It won't come any nearer to the earth this year, won't pull any harder than it pulls tonight on the oceans' tides, on the child that wants to come out, wants to stay. Mary's people, the Celts, called it the Dispute Moon. The Moon When Chokecherries Darken, the Moon of Running Sturgeon, Green Corn Moon, the Moon When All Things Ripen: over the centuries, many groups of people have named this August moon. But as it banks through the skylight—a stone paused mid-skip over a deep lake—its immensity renders me mute.

Mouth stoppered with nerves, I kneel beside Mary's body rubbing her shoulders. She exhales frantically, snuffing out the candle. I light the wick again, offer her a sip of water, tilt the cup toward her mouth. Beyond stock encouragements, though, I'm unsure of my next move. I stick to the script. And while my remedial purview readied me to measure Mary's contractions, to identify their intensity and duration, nothing prepped me for her sharp tooth biting my knuckle—I jerk my hand back from her mouth as my stomach tightens. Amid the flux, two unmovable truths: I couldn't begin to endure what she's enduring; and for nine naive moons I failed to consider that my beloved would morph into my heroine.

I push myself up and recheck the packed bags at the door, pace between the bar and the couch, pat down my pockets for keys and wallet, repeat the routine. Open the fridge, close it. Then from the bedroom Mary lets go a yelp so loud I'm convinced it will chase the baby out of the birth canal and back into the womb. "I need to walk," she yells. That's all the discomfort she voices. When I reach her side she doesn't appear the least bit agitated, recalling instead some mythical huntress who, finding herself deep within an impenetrable forest and sensing the unseen, passage-preventing beast nearby, says, "Okay. So this is the place."

By the time we step outside the moon has swung to its descent. "Breathe" is the only word I can muster as we step tentatively down the quiet street.

As if she might forget.

I pick a hard pear from our neighbor's tree and pass it to her. Days from now I'll find it ripened in her overnight duffle and note where her nail prints pierced the skin.

In the birthing room our doula Colleen says what I said an hour ago—"Breathe"—but speaks it as though it were a spell, settling Mary.

Soon, between flights of breaths, they are discussing with surprising casualness a documentary film that Colleen showed us a week ago, about a band of traditional Russian women who deliver their babies directly into the Black Sea. Remarkably these just-birthed, open-eyed pilgrims navigate a cove's secluded waters with the efficacy of seals or fish. Just recalling these strong post-labor women and their children moments after "conscious" birth—their hair flowing in the tide, swimming, still attached at the umbilical to their swimming newborns—has fortified Mary, she says. And as she sinks down into the birthing tub in the delivery unit I note relief in her face, and fluidity in her movements, for the first time all night.

While Colleen copilots, whispers encouragements, I'm happy to play flight attendant, bring ice water, squeeze hands, wipe sweat, rest a palm on a bare, shaking knee. Otherwise, I stand numbly stage right with my silent plea that the four strong and utterly capable women in the room will soon deliver a breathing, wailing child into Mary's arms. I don't want to miss a moment of the spectacle, but I can understand why so many men of my father's generation—then erroneously considered the stronger gender—forwent this moment of turbulence and milled around the waiting room with unlit cigars in their coat pockets. Despite prevailing social trends, my dad was present at my birth, of which I obviously remember nothing. First memory of him: two years old, I am zipped, my entire frame save for my nose and forehead, into his high-fill goose down red parka on a frigid night as he traverses the Niagara just upstream from the Falls.

Kneeling at Mary's side in the delivery room, I am snapped from my reverie when a nurse announces that the contractions are three seconds apart. Then, without warning, Mary is calling for the mirror and someone is smiling confidently and holding the polished glass between her straining legs and telling her to touch her child's head, which is covered in the uncountable hopes and fears, in the ruthless survival, of generations; in tissue and red matter and black hair; in the invisible traces of stars; in a mother's triumphant cries.

Arrived, he gasps, and we yelp praise at his first earthly breath, his open eyes. Their fathomless, oceanic blue.

WINDFALL

In May of my eighteenth year, I hired on to paint cabins on a ridge above the South Branch of the Au Sable River near Grayling, Michigan. A wealthy downstate furniture distributor who owned the old trout camp paid me by the hour with no mind to timetable, evidenced by the sole brush he provided, a single, six-inch-wide horsehair that made for slow going, especially when coupled with my penchant for the occasional unsupervised break. Napping one afternoon as a coat of dark green latex dried on the cabins' shingles, I was awoken by a loud crack. I stirred and, assuming the wind had slammed closed a shutter, drifted pleasantly back to sleep under the washing hardwood canopy. At a second report, though, I sat up straight to regard a beaver-chewed cottonwood angled precariously over the river that shaded a favored fishing hole. Warblers, the rare Kirtland's, made their way in and out of the understory, and brook trout chasing emergent caddis splashed at the surface of the riffle. Then a wind washed down the drainage, a susurrus that dappled the water and altered the posture of the leaves, and with two more shotgun-blast-like cracks the trunk cleaved and plunged into the water. The little valley held its breath. Waves sloshed up both sandy banks. Then the first warbler pipped, and the flock reconstituted. The trout, I imagined, began to re-situate themselves in freshly formed lies, as the water stained with tannin from northwoods cedar swamps continued its gradual descent down the floodplain, its course albeit altered.

⌐

Much like that wind-felled cottonwood, a newborn comes crashing into one's life.

Even the most obsessive, proactive, meticulously prepared parent could not have imagined the suddenness of days measured in diaper changes, in the amount of meconium-laced fecal matter swiped from a wrinkled bottom each day. Intricate theories conceived months prior are obliterated, pages of ideology ingested via parenting books put to reality's test. Advice is laughed at or forgotten. Preconceived boundaries become permeable, the most staunchly held cosmologies all but throttled. Thou shalt not cave in to disposable diapers yet, the uninitiated parent tells himself, though the cloth diapers schlepped off by the pricey washing service clearly rash the boy's sensitive skin quicker than the sample Pampers sent home by the hospital. A bit modified, Newton's third law of motion applies; every present-day action—"Let's try the pacifier tonight"—proposes an equal and opposite paranoia about the future—"He'll need braces for certain someday!"

Induced by a loss of sleep, time assumes an elliptical quality. How long can two adults survive on REM-less dregs, the new parent wonders, having lost count of the times the boy has woken tonight alone, his body between theirs in bed, baying for breast milk. One night, worried at the odd silence of a soundly sleeping baby, the new father wakes himself to assess the situation. His son's breathing confirmed, he ponders the strange geometry of their triangulated bodies.

What strange equation supports this irregular isosceles? How to solve for its hypotenuse? There is a lesson here, but it lies just beyond his grasp.

All told it takes a few weeks to shake off the impact, after which a potent period of ecstasy follows. And after the ecstasy, as the saying goes, the laundry. He stands at the kitchen table folding it: the smallest shirt he's ever held.

A huff of breeze against the shutters, brief wash of leaf shade across the wall: that's all the light morning affords before the rain once again begins to fall. It's been raining since the day Luca, "bearer of light," was born. Weeks-long steady rain, soil-spattering, drought-ending, fire-snuffing rain—rain we were pining for all summer and that pounds presently on the roof like hooves and rumbles headlong through the gutters. Lulled by the sound, drowsy with the oxytocin coursing through her veins, Mary nurses Luca, whose flushed cheeks twitch with the efficacy of a hummingbird lapping nectar from a blossom.

As soon as his belly is filled, she will be famished, so I step into the kitchen and begin to prepare an omelet with basil, spinach, diced tomatoes, paprika, Muenster, a dash of garlic salt. When she unlatches his mouth from her nipple—audible pop!—he wails momentarily. I take his warm body to my chest and snap him into an ergonomic carrier called a Baby Björn, a kind of modern-day marsupial pouch fashioned with plastic snaps and padded fabric, the inventor of which should be awarded a Nobel. By the time the cheese has melted atop the bubbling egg, Mary is asleep and the boy's cries have withered.

His face squishes against my ribs, nose turned to his left, eyelids fluttering, fluttering, and then falling, like old stage curtains, closed. Looking down at his pulsing fontanel I'm frightened once again by my proximity to the body's most complex organ, a mere scalp and still-ossifying skull one-eighth as strong as an adult's protecting the billions of neurons that teem beneath his dark thatch of hair. I've been told that infants are sturdier than they appear—their bones, for instance, still pliable—but I can't stop handling our son like a model car I longed for in my youth and that, upon receiving as a gift, I was afraid to remove from its box. Steadying his flimsy neck, I lean over to eat a forkful from the omelet. A bite of tomato falls behind his ear.

Once he's slept for a few moments, I check to make sure that his airways are free, not compressed against my body or muffled by the folds of my flannel. His ample, yet-to-be-washed hair is oily and hangs over his ears. His warm neck smells of uncut wheat a day before the harvest, of his mother's inner elbow. With my knuckle under his nose, I wait for his lungs to expand with air and, after a pause, feel his nostrils emit a tiny, tremulous wind.

If he came here to kill me, per Freud's assertion, it's proving a sweet end to suffer.

Washing the pan, I listen to Luca's bowels working, to his Olympian metabolism. He grunts a few times in his sleep and works out a movement that I soon smell. I should have more couth than to speak scatologically, but such tangible muck conjoins father and son where words cannot. Esteban warned me that changing soiled diapers made him so queasy he initially wore a bandana over his nose. But like field dressing birds or fish, it's a ritual I'm taking to. I grab Luca's ankles in my left hand and raise his bum from the changing table, swipe toward me, making sure to wipe clean the folds of skin, crumple the used wipes inside the soiled diaper, then wrap a clean diaper around his undercarriage and secure it with the tape. Holding my breath, I kick open the waste bin and put the dirty cloth diaper inside with the others.

Back in the kitchen I pull the unwashed dishes from the sink and draw Luca a bath in the enamel basin. Drowsily, his eyes open as the water touches his toes. The visual world comes slowly into focus for a newborn, or so I've read while peering over Mary's shoulder in bed. Any two things in stark contrast seem of utmost interest to him: our shadows on the fence, raisins in my oatmeal, two crows rowing through a gray sky. As the moon wanes each day, his attention span seems to wax. His expressions are myriad—stately, gravely pained, unfettered—dated within the hour.

What's that? his huge eyes seem to ask at present.

That's the clock. It tells time. There's not enough of it.

Outside, the deluge has stopped and my blue raft cradled on its trailer glistens with rainwater. The mismatched oars shine with droplets too, and for the first time in months I recall the oar that evaded my outstretched hand on Rock Creek. Where did it end up? Most likely it is lodged in one of the root wads three hundred yards downstream from where it first slid past the oarlock, the current and current-carried particulate eating at the grains of wood. But it might have ridden the length of Rock Creek and washed into the Clark Fork, continuing on through the EPA Superfund site of Milltown Reservoir, slowing a bit in the largely stagnant, arsenic-tinged water before tumbling over the century-old dam. For all I know it could have shot straight past Missoula and surfed the rapids of two gorges on its way to the Columbia. Maybe it miraculously passed the turbines of Bonneville Dam and eventually washed up nine hundred miles downstream from Missoula in Astoria, where a child on the beach is using the dinted blade to construct a sand sculpture.

I reach back into my memory of the past several weeks, hoping to grasp something tangible. Where have those thousand hours gone? Vanished like the vestigial umbilical clipping that fell from Luca's belly button in the middle of the night—last, or was it the night before? Did I leave it on the folding chair that doubles as a nightstand, or is it tangled in the bedsheets? Who said you must lose your life to gain it? It's late September and on the foothills a sudden light from the first star teases out the tide lines and corrugations from a prehistoric flood.

I rub my eyes: Mount Jumbo hasn't moved.

⌒

October is a hawk resting on a thermal.

With something resembling valor it arrives, absolving whatever weather sins the rest of the year committed. A foxed hillside bears the impossibly long shadow of a lone juniper, an hour hand that barely turns. Huge cumuli the weight of a hundred buses loft above the valley. The wind arrives leisurely from the Pacific and forgets what it came for. Framed by fledged grasses the mountains wear the light as a garment. Yellowed, aphid-bulbed, long-stemmed cottonwood leaves fall windblown into the creek and float on the gunmetal currents, shuffling among themselves for a spell before collecting and stacking vertically between the rocks like the pages of a book.

And we have larches!

Freckling the otherwise deep green, pine-laden elevations with cadmium yellow, they ignite the forests with color that accumulates by the day and passes gradually over the mountainsides like a wave of lighter flames held aloft in an encored concert.

October's grandeur is enough to turn anyone into a gaper. And domestically, that's largely what Mary and I have become, patrons at the living museum of Luca, free admission. We are too tired to do much else, as good sleep is of course the great hypothetical horizon, an oasis the new parent keeps walking toward, toward, toward, but never quite reaching. We lean into our areas of growing expertise. Mine: standing in for his mother with a bottle of pumped breast milk, a trade he vehemently opposes early this morning.

"What?" I ask, as he kicks his stout legs with surprising force and screams, spits, pressing his tongue in fundamental rejection of the bottle's rubber nipple. "You don't prefer cold latex to your mother's warm breast?"

Sensate experience, I note, is grossly heightened during the wee hours: the refrigerator's light blinds, a diaper heavy with the scent of urine waters the eyes, a hungry cry sears the unready eardrums. If I had warmed the bottle in a saucepan on the stove to trick him into thinking the nipple belonged to his mother, we might have endured several more minutes of wailing while the water heated, forcing Mary to suffer the same audible torture I was—how chivalrous!—attempting to spare her from. Mercifully, Luca finishes the bottle. I swaddle him in a waffled cotton blanket, tucking his arms into the folds, and rock him in the glider toward slumber.

Though not far enough.

There's a shushing rhythm that he prefers, a meter that settles him, which I can't conjure this morning. Is it anapestic (short-short-long) or trochaic (long-short)? Does he prefer it whispered into his right ear or his left? Outside the newspaper clunks against the screen door, yanking me from the cusp of sleep. In the rocker with me, Luca is überalert to my rapidly diminishing serotonin levels, but I place him gently on the crib's mattress with one last shush. The sleep experts, pediatricians with ghost writers who target the most vulnerable of markets, suggest walking away from one's sleep-resistant child without word or gesture. Not a second after I attempt this board-approved technique, though, Luca's head pops up. I look down at his all-eyes face, wondering if our warped version of a heaven-hung patriarch scanning earth for wrongdoers isn't merely a reconstitution of just such a moment: a father staring wearily down into a crib.

I have to guide in a few hours, so resign myself to the idea of a reinvigorating river swim this afternoon. Cradled in my left arm, Luca looks curiously as I fix oatmeal, tracking my three-scoop garnish of rhubarb crisp from baking pan to bowl. Breakfast and baby in tow, I step out onto the porch and plop down in a plastic Adirondack, then buckle Luca into his battery-powered vibrating bouncy seat, a thrift store purchase he prefers to the expensive wooden high chair made in Sweden. I look across the street and nod at Laurie and Spurgeon, silently thanking them for the rhubarb crisp made from the stalks grown in their garden. Their living room lamp is on, Spurgeon no doubt already engaged in some form of elite exercise, a dozen or more trail miles logged behind his headlamp's beam. With my big toe I bounce Luca's chair, the extent of my workout, and let the chunks of rhubarb burst in my mouth.

I consider my zinging taste buds: the fruit is exquisite, but a splash of heavy cream may be required to cut its tartness. Hold tight, I tell Luca, giving his chair one more nudge to keep it in motion. I'll be right back. Inside, I open the fridge: no cream. Milk will do, then, even skim. No luck there, either. Between the mayo and Dijon, though, a glass baby bottle is tucked. It contains the only milk in the house, pumped maternal fossil fuel saved for the next inevitable 3:00 a.m. emergency: I couldn't possibly. Through the open doorway I hear Luca give out one fussy cry, then a second one loud enough to wake the neighbors. I peek at the breast milk again.

The smell is sweeter than expected, with nutty hints on the nose. Into my rhubarb I pour a shot's worth of the world's most precious fluid, which turns the red chunks of cooked stalk pink. Outside, I give the bottle a shake, and offer the nipple to Luca. Previously inconsolable, he sniffles and steadies the bottle with all ten of his tiny fingers. With my left hand I spoon bites of milk-drenched rhubarb into my mouth. His grimace slackens, and soon we are smiling at one another, mutual keepers of this rich secret.

⁓

I've never considered guiding an escape from "the real world" so much as a way to wrap myself in life's entire cloth, a means of resolving the many-ness that seems a prerequisite of postmodern existence. Of course, I didn't start out thinking that way. I simply enjoyed fishing and revered the locations my quarry inhabited. I ignored the repeated warnings of an early mentor—"Becoming a guide might just cause you to hate fishing"—reasoning that the adults I knew weren't utterly in love with their jobs either. The authority figures around which I was reared worked as insurance brokers, accountants, realtors, salesmen, secretaries; in other words, there didn't exist in my suburban milieu some fast track to adventurous outdoors-based occupations. Wasn't it better to take a chance and find out if you might eventually hate something, I wondered, than embark upon a path you already disliked?

This crisp late morning under a sheaf of blue sky I'm rowing my longest-standing client, Peg, down the Clark Fork just upstream of the Alberton Gorge. An ebullient retired music teacher, Peg first fished with me in the company of her then husband George, the aforementioned mentor, who was a decorated Korean War hero and Michigan district court judge before he retired to take up guiding and river conservation in northern Michigan. When I moved to Montana in the mid-nineties and began to guide, they booked my services for a week and brought as their guests George's brother and sister-in-law. The Alexanders made a ribald quartet, equally dedicated to the art of angling and irreverent in respect to its often annoying decorum, and plans were quickly formed to reconvene the following summer.

That winter, though, the indefatigable George elected to undergo double knee surgery in rural northern Michigan. A hale seventy-two, he still cut a swath wherever he went and said he would trade his Navy Cross for one more pain-free season in the riverboat. Despite her best efforts, Peg couldn't convince him to simply hobble around for another decade or so, nor could she persuade him into waiting until the spring, when more reputable surgeons downstate could be booked. Although the surgery was a success, George contracted pneumonia as he convalesced, and died within the week.

Much to my surprise, Peg arrived the following August with brother-in-law Chick and sister-in-law Mackie in tow. The trio fished tirelessly, in a piscatorial elegy of sorts. Whenever someone suggested taking a day off, though, Mackie threw up her arms in exasperation. The ovarian cancer she had been fighting for several years had progressed, and her oncologist's recent stage-four diagnosis had her convinced that this Montana trip might be her last. There was little room for argument. Despite twice-a-week trips to a Bozeman hospital to receive chemo treatments, Mackie often fished well into the evening.

One night on the Ruby River after a caddis hatch had waned and the cottonwoods' shadows had congealed on the river's surface so that the water twisted through the bottomland like a lucent skein of cobalt yarn flecked with threads of red, Mackie waded upstream past my parked truck, where I stood grilling dinner on the tailgate. As a result of the previous day's chemo, her hands shook violently, which made tying a small fly on to a thin tippet nearly impossible. Calling across the water, I asked if she wouldn't like a little help getting rigged, a set of magnifiers, perhaps, or maybe a pair of nippers to cut a cleaner edge on the tippet, thereby helping it to thread more easily through the hook's miniscule eye. She looked at me like to haul hell out of its shuck: *You want to help, young man? Stay ready with the net.* In time, she seated the knot—I watched her exhale deeply—and continued upstream, fishing until dark, intent on leaving a part of herself in a place that she cherished.

After her funeral the following February, Chick called me to detail Mackie's last days: the tapering of a body so resilient that the University of Michigan Medical School asked her to donate her organs for research; the brief repose she had been afforded after the chemo treatments ceased; the flurry of final visitors; and then the shared knowledge of the dreaded calm that was to come. On her last night she sat up in bed listening to Chick spin tales in his near-falsetto voice, until eventually he got to talking about how desperately he missed her already, at which point he delaminated. She took his hand and placed his index finger over his lips.

"You'll have to be quiet, my dear." She waited until he had finished sniffling. "I'm going to fish the Ruby now."

Any reader of fables will be aware that only two characters, Peg and Chick, remain in this humble digression, and will have at least a hunch as to its denouement. A year after Mackie died, two years after George had passed, and several months after spending an awkward summer together in Montana, widow and widower became bride and groom. Rigorously they kept the Montana summer rite for several years and, with my grandfathers long absent or dead, Chick became a surrogate of sorts, and someone who taught me how potent the river's medicine can be.

"Sawdust doesn't seed" is the kind of thing he used to exclaim as my drift boat neared a patch of forest denuded by overaggressive logging, adding that his father had run a timber business in Pennsylvania and he possessed authority on the matter. He spoke few phrases that weren't somehow poeticized, adorned with his particular backwoods originality and bequeathed to us, his angling constituency, with a continuous strain of episodes featuring the loveably troubled, unpolished characters of the county in Pennsylvania over which he presided, in keeping with the family trade, as judge. His tales adhered to a unique comprehension of time, one more braided and fluvial than measurable in our dross durations. He would often call me midwinter to quote passages from *Shane* or the Sixth Amendment—he was instrumental in developing arguments for Families Against Mandatory Minimums—or to discuss a particular fly selection we had made during the summer, an offering refused by a memorably large trout, and one that he had determined, in retrospect, questionable. With a .22 rifle he could shoot a hole in a dime tossed high into the air, refused to step onto a boat without at least one safety pin superstitiously pinned to his vest (I never saw one otherwise employed), and was, despite all he endured, one of the most fair-natured humans I've rowed down a river.

But when his fifty-two-year-old son Jimmy developed advanced renal cell carcinoma and died, Chick ventured into a dense existential forest from which he never fully emerged. His favorite cousin died shortly thereafter. Adding up the family deaths, he told Peg he felt like "the guy in the book with the gilded pages. I won't say his name but it rhymes with 'robe.'" At the subsequent wake he opened the eulogy, "Well, Big Fella, just who do you plan to take next week?" Two days later his sister died of a stroke. Peg tried to draw him back into the physical world by planning their next trip west, but he slumped with what he called "irony of survival," finally buckling under the weight of the stories he was now sole teller of. While sitting in his deer stand one late-November morning, he suffered a massive brain hemorrhage and died almost instantly—and providently, as he had harbored a rabid fear of hospitals since his brother's death.

"Someone like us," he'd told me after George's passing, "damned sure shouldn't die in a room."

"So, just when do you and Mary plan to start pitching squealers?" was a question Chick often asked, and one I recall with a tinge of melancholy as I ease the boat down a slow bank draped in grass, their seed heads tanned and hanging heavy. I pull hard on the oars, feel the current tension cede to the cut of the chine. The boat moves upstream as if greased. I'm giving Peg the best shots possible at the scant shady lies, but since launching the boat we've gone an hour without a fish, a horse-collar I ignored during my elegiac mental hiatus, but one that currently has me growing anxious. As the sun ascends and spills its syrupy glare across the water, the difficulty level of our fishing will only increase, as our imitations become more obvious to the discerning trout. The risers we've located have been sipping on Tricos, tiny, black-bodied mayflies with translucent wings that rest spent upon the water, dead-still, not twitching like many aquatic insects do. Large trout seek out these imagoes, a dozen of which would cover a dime, in the thin, slick shallows where angling mistakes are magnified.

I tell Peg she's placing the fly at all the right angles, that not even her guide could deliver a cleaner presentation, but I know my encouragements offer little recompense.

She has always taken personally what the river gives or doesn't. I try to laud her for her courageous spirit, for making this solo jaunt west so soon after Chick's passing; rather, I hedge toward the gesture but come up with half a consolation. Mercifully, she changes the subject to our fishing prospects, concluding that she's been to enough funerals in the past year to last a while and is still here, so far as she can tell.

Currently *here* is a table-flat, calm-before-the-rapids reach that harbors a decent population of rainbow trout, a reductive name for a fish, to say the least. Were I a more inventive naturalist, I might forgo the accepted moniker derived from the typical spectrum of colors that adorns the species' gill plates and give each rainbow a more befitting name. Cosmetically speaking, there are few spectacles in the freshwater angling world quite as striking as the star-white belly of an otherwise weed-colored fish that frequents shallow sloughs along the Bitterroot, or the polished-apple-red cheek of its current-fighting cousin. The nose of a Clark Fork rainbow feeding on mayfly duns at last light in November glows like the underside of a polished spoon. While the milk-blue back of a Blackfoot rainbow caught in June, when the Blackfoot runs high, reminds me of a shade Rothko invented for one of his sparest canvases.

Their temperaments differ too. Blackfoot rainbows fight the hardest—Norman Maclean asserted that only grizzly bears were more ornery. A twenty-inch chrome-nosed Clark Fork hen hooked on light tippet will give the angler a few token headshakes before running to the precise center of the river and banking for the Puget Sound. Locals are fond of saying that a sixteen-inch brick-shaped Bitterroot rainbow will "give you your money's worth," but I think such efficient creatures have earned their divestment from our convoluted economic web. Unlike other western states, Montana doesn't stock its rivers with hatchery-bred trout, relying instead on habitat improvements to curate increased survival rates in fisheries, so any rainbow trout caught on the Clark Fork is a wild one, a survivor like Peg.

All of which is to say there's no such thing as an "average" rainbow trout, but if there were it would be a fourteen-incher aged three years and weighing roughly one pound, what guides often call a "cookie-cutter fish," the likes of which Peg has caught hundreds. So I'm a bit stymied when, after hooking and playing such a specimen to net, she begins to gawk. At first, I take her muteness as base-level relief that a fish has finally come to the boat, but when she raises the dripping rainbow from the water with her long arthritic fingers, her fuchsia-painted nails accenting its cheek, she begins to gasp, then folds over at her torso as if the fish were solid ore, as if its weight were drawing her into the river. As she unhooks it, her eyes moisten.

"This is the last place we fished together while Chick was still—while he was well," she says. "The exact spot. I remember leaning against that boulder while he waded out to the drop-off. A big fish was feeding on some stage of mayfly he couldn't match. He dug through every box in his vest, changed a dozen flies, muttering to himself the whole time. Completely entertained! Just like a dog with a ball. I think he liked it more that way than if he'd fooled the fish."

Underwater, Peg slackens her grip and the revived trout drops through the pool and out of sight.

"I've thought of this place all year, not every day but a lot of days. This place." She points toward the bank. "I know that boulder better than my pillow. Do you know what he told me that evening, before we went back to your boat?"

I shake my head.

"He said, 'If I kick over dead tonight and wake up somewhere tomorrow, it had better be here.'"

NEIGHBORS

Parents turned grandparents arrive. Photos are snapped, the first curly locks of hair scissored gingerly from the brow. Advice dispensed. Heirlooms passed down. A brother turned uncle rides his motorcycle from Chicago through a prairie snowstorm to meet his nephew, sleeps on the couch, wakes at the morning feeding, then turns around and rides home. From a coffee mug a grandmother pours warm water over and over onto the infant's bare belly, eliciting uncontrollable squeals of joy. With hands crippled from an aneurism, a great-grandmother holds her first great-grandchild.

What can memory hope to shore up against the horizontal surge of calendar time? What does the lead goose in a southbound V of migratory birds, with visual acuity eighteen times greater than our human own, see when it cranes its neck to look down at two-leggeds walking through a snowbound field? These are two equally unanswerable questions to ponder as November's cold strikes like a club, and overnight the geese spill southward.

We wake to latent calls and a foot of eider-light snow on the ground. In the gray of early morning, with Luca snug in the Björn, I traipse along the Bitterroot not far from its three-pronged confluence with the Clark Fork. For a mile or so I hear little more than the sound of my boot soles flattening snow; when Luca finally begins to fuss, rutting against my chest as if he might find milk, I'm startled by his presence. I remove my hands from my mittens and with my fingers warm his taut, cold-bitten cheeks. From a bowed rose hip branch I scoop fresh snow and drop it into my mouth, pressing it between my palate and tongue, the element that fell through the sky last night now mingling with my saliva. I pinch more snow into a small disk, and sneak it into Luca's mouth.

He starts with a squeal, feet kicking against my chest, steam rising from his mouth.

"Snow," I say.

By and by the sun muscles through a tight scrim and the untracked field before us flashes blindingly white, reminding me of my happiness, a recent concern. What is there to say of happiness that doesn't evaporate before it hits the page? They say it can't be written of: Because an author in such a state finds no reason to write? Or because depictions of happiness are too light to provide contrast, relief, on the blank page? While I haven't abandoned my writing practice, exactly, I'm certainly more concerned with mastering the proper way to toss our two-month-old son into the air to elicit spasms of laughter than I am with how to engender, say, tension in free verse poems via heavy line enjambment.

Contrarily, Mary seems runic of late, inaccessible. I know that her body has been glacialized with physical trauma, and that the adrenaline following the monumental act of giving birth—after forming hair and teeth and eyeballs and organs!—has months ago worn off, but I hadn't expected the onset of winter to wrest her so thoroughly from her early, well-earned maternal bliss. She seems weighed down of late, sleep-deprived, sure, pumped full of hormones, of course. For some time I attributed her downturn in mood to post-partum depression—a birthing class lecture had warned me of this inevitable bout with malaise—but when I asked if her ache could be blamed on late-onset postpartum, she assured me that such a phase had largely passed.

"There would seem to be nothing more obvious, more tangible and palpable, than the present moment," Milan Kundera wrote forty-some years before I transcribed the lines into my journal this morning. "And yet it eludes us completely. All the sadness of life lies in that fact."

Driving home with Luca from our hike, I consider offering the Kundera to Mary as a nostrum, but when I arrive home I find her seated on the bed clutching her knees, facing the buttercream wall, as if my ruminating on her mind-set had placed her there. The look on her face says: now is hardly the time for encouragement couched in existential philosophy. In a wide arc, I swing Luca's car seat back and forth to keep him napping and inquire as gently as possible about her current state of mind.

"I just can't do it," she says, looking out on the backyard, where an electrical wire casts a thin gray shadow between the gutter and the electric box. "I can't leave him. He's only three months old. I can't go back to teaching."

"Yet, you mean. Right?" I ask. "How long have you been feeling this way?"

"A while. I didn't want to bring it up. I know we agreed I'd go back to work after Thanksgiving. But it's eating me up every time I look at him. I know we need the money. I know we planned on it."

I offer to bring Luca to her classroom every day, for lunchtime breast-feedings. It's only three weeks, I say, fifteen school days, from Thanksgiving to winter break.

"That's not it," she says.

"What then?" I press, frustrated to have come full circle.

What she wants to express, what she can't seem to articulate, what I'll deduce after we've fought about the lack of money and budgetary failures and shared responsibility and gripped our anger in suffocating solitudes for most of the evening, is that the thought of caring for *other* children, of giving her energy to them instead of to her own child, is what's breaking her spirit.

Maybe it's worth asking the school director for an extended unpaid leave, I suggest. If there were more guide trips to be had, I would take them, but the season is long over, the boat stowed until March.

An annual epiphany recalled immutably from childhood: Christmas cleanup after the presents have been unwrapped and the living room scattered with torn paper and boxes—at some point, no matter how well you fend it off, the reality of raising a child amid financial and societal pressures sets in. Suppressed threats rise to the surface and, because it would be a biological failure to question the life you've helped create, you begin to question your partner. I try to imagine what it might be like to rear a body inside of my body from the size of a grape seed to the size of the being currently straining my right elbow joint.

"Okay. I'll see about picking up a few extra hours at the shelter," I say, determined to use what's left on our home equity loan to make up the line-item loss in our budget. We may regret it later, I think, switching the swinging car seat to my left hand, but severing the figurative umbilical still fusing mother to child is not a cut I'm willing to make. I look out the window. I am not certain of my next move here, but I know it isn't furthering this discussion. Next door, behind drawn shades, our neighbors Frank and Dotty can be seen moving slowly in silhouette. They shift a few steps to the left, a few to the right, then shrink into the center of the room. I wonder if they're rearranging furniture, a coffee table perhaps, some item a pair of eighty-somethings could move with ease.

Or they could be dancing: a knock-kneed, cumbersome waltz.

⟋

Certain flavors of life, of peach, say, of apricot, are not lost from generation to generation, wrote Ezra Pound. "Neither are they transmitted by book learning." The flavors of the elk and the duck and the pheasant, among others, are what we are hoping to transmit to Luca, via breast milk for now. A week before Thanksgiving our neighbor Laurie is fortunate enough to harvest her first bull elk—she would correct me, saying "shoot" instead of "harvest"—and with the main course accounted for, we start planning our appetizers around her credo: "Wilder food, wilder life." After some menu discussion, Mary and Laurie charge me with providing appetizers of smoked duck breast, smoked whitefish dip, and smoked pheasant.

"Remember the way you did it last year," Mary hints, "with that porter and orange-zest brine, and ginger? And the smoked whitefish flaked into the whipped cream cheese with chives. I think you served Emmentaler with the duck breasts."

"I can grind elk sausage for stuffing the bird," Laurie offers.

"We have a pile of dried cherries for that," Mary adds. Since our decision to keep her home with Luca several days ago, her spirits have been buoyed. Food is an additional balm.

"Aren't we long on appetizers?" I ask.

Mary takes Luca from her breast, touches his lips gently, and hands the tightly swaddled boy to Laurie, who has lately become a kind of neighborhood godmother. "There is no such thing as too many appetizers," Mary says.

"That would be like too many huckleberries," Laurie says, running her hand gently down the blue waffle blanket, beaming at Luca's post-nursing gaze. "Or too much sex."

The latter taps a tender bone—Mary and I dodge each other's glances—as we have not, since Luca's birth, regained our otherwise robust stride. A perpetual but vague state of desperation surrounds life with an infant, a new parent's urgent desire for sleep or sex or recreation mirroring his young child's desperation for milk. The boy wakes in third-watch panic, wailing because he can't yet fathom that his lactating mother sleeps a mere ten paces away. *Will I ever taste breast milk again?* he would scream if he possessed words. The new father experiences similar panic after waking from a dream of migratory ducks, wondering if he'll ever sit in a waterfowl blind made of cattails and willows again, or if he should simply sell his camouflage and decoys.

In her youth Laurie hunted with her father and harvested many animals, always relishing the fair-chase pursuit of wild game in good country, followed sometimes by the nourishment of organic—though no one called it that back then—elk and venison. But only as she matured did she come to believe that the pinnacle of the sport was to harvest an animal, a small portion of a renewable resource from a landscape she works hard to sustain. Now a conservationist in the university's Wilderness and Civilization program, she espouses Aldo Leopold's land ethic: that we can be ethical only in relation to something we can see, feel, understand, love, and otherwise have faith in.

While many of our friends hunt for their food, Laurie remains my favorite lobbyist for wild game cuisine, the most articulate advocate for its nutritional and environmental benefits. If society were forced "to eat only animals grown wild on the land," she offered the other night at an otherwise benign potluck, "wouldn't we care a little better for the land our food came from?

"Plus," she said, pausing to point at her partner and our friend Spurgeon, who was unwrapping a package of store-bought bratwurst and, as ever, smiling. "Only a physical freak like Spurge can process that injected-with-who-knows-what shit and get up in the morning for a twenty-mile run."

A former college football player turned elite mountain athlete, Spurgeon's graciousness is exceeded only by his list of physical accomplishments. These days he works as an X-ray tech, powering through his seven-on shifts so that he can spend his seven-offs hunting, skiing, or running ultra-marathon in the backcountry. In nothing short of legendary fashion, he once rode his motorcycle ninety miles to compete in a double-marathon trail run, ran the race, finished first, rode back to Missoula, and closed Charlie B's. His quiet fierceness and routine summiting of peaks I merely admire from the valley floor should leave me feeling insufficient, but he's so humble I end up buoyed in his company rather than shamed.

To her point, Laurie was implying that with game meat you don't only avoid the hormones contained in most store-bought meats; when you eat game, you also fill yourself with more potent fuel, the upgrade not so much unleaded to premium as unleaded to jet. She turned to me with an appeal to my artistic side: Wild game smells stronger, and its tastes are foreign, nuanced with each animal and cut, adding with finality that wild game "is everything you say you want art to be. Unmanufactured. Spurgeon says I talk about food too often, but can we really over-prioritize it?"

Who could argue? Archaeologists tell us, after all, that the planting of crops preceded the construction of cities by five thousand years. We were what we ate long before we believed we were what we owned. There is a new generation of hunters increasingly less focused on "the kill" than on the enhancement of habitat, a generation aware of the fact that wild food not only nourishes our bodies but also restores our proper relationship with the food web. Perhaps the most cynical, if anthropocentrically informed, among us, the ones who spend the most time poring over the dismal statistics, might also be readying ourselves for a day when we'll be living off the deer in our backyards.

It took some time for Mary to ease into the idea of living in a hunting household. The exotic nature of wild game didn't bother her; she grew up eating headcheese and pâté and escargot that her mother, an accomplished cook with French roots, prepared. But "the dead things" did. I recall the first duck I shot and brought home, setting it proudly, if conspicuously, on the back lawn, where I planned to butcher it on some newspaper. It was a cinnamon teal drake, the likes of which frequented a pond near her childhood house.

"I don't know if I can eat that," Mary said. "He was just swimming out there with his buddies."

"Some would say it also becomes us who eat it."

"And that's consolation? To whom?" she asked.

"Both parties, I guess."

~

In front of me on northbound Route 93, a Winnebago sporting forty-two of fifty state magnets labors up Evaro Hill. Fidgety, scanning the mountain-elided radio stations, I ride out news of an embassy bombing, flip past a crackling sonata, find an oldies channel on the AM and turn up Sam Cooke, before eventually shutting the music off. I seek solitude, I remind myself, not voices careening in and out of my head. While one purpose of hunting is to feed my family with game whose habitat I have traversed—whose own food I've walked through, or in the case of berries, eaten—another is to return home empty-headed. When the voices of the ego ebb, I often find myself wandering in a primal fashion. I might say "crow" or "waning moon" aloud, or "grouseberry" or "bull thistle," but I'm just saying what I am seeing, uttering my way through the world, practicing a verbless religion.

After crossing a river named for a French fur trapper, I turn onto a county road and crest an agriculture bench, then drop in along a two-track, the truck's tires shifting in the gumbo, and aim for a creek the early white lawmakers named "Mission" for the building they—is it more appropriate to say *we*?—built beside it. Incarnadine with evening, the snowcapped Mission Range looms to the east. To the west, the wide, sun-struck Flathead River backlights the pines, and I accelerate down the rutted road toward the river until I'm slowed by a herd of livestock milling near a fence gate. Somewhat famously, Montana hosts more cows than humans, a stat that seems implausible until you find yourself stalled on an otherwise deserted two-track by eighty head of lowing Black Angus crossing from grazed land to fresh pasture.

These days most ranchers in the Mission Valley run Herefords or Galloways, but only a hundred and fifty years ago the ten-million-acre short-grass prairie that spans from present-day Evaro to the western shore of Flathead Lake teemed with Salish horses. Arriving in the early 1800s, French-Canadian fur traders were surprised to discover that some Salish warriors owned as many as three hundred head, and they estimated the tribal herd of horses at several thousand all told. Historians contend that these mustangs of Spanish descent originated from stocks brought across the Atlantic by de Soto and Coronado and that later traveled up the spine of the continent from Mexico via trade with and theft by other tribes. On the heels of the Homestead Act, as settlers introduced non-native grasses and crops to the region, most of the Salish herd was vanquished. A few horses of the original strain still dwell on Flathead Lake's Wild Horse Island, a pristine, two-thousand-acre parcel once used to shelter herds from raiding tribes, and now owned by the state of Montana.

This spare November evening, two paints swish their sparse white tails and regard me from a nearby pasture. The creek is not far off. I load my gun and shoulder my vest and begin to push through a rattling patch of chin-high bull thistles, among which I soon discover a roost filled with fresh pheasant droppings, along with several circular dusting sites where birds cleaned mites from their feathers. The swaying tassels of the brittle plants knock loudly against one another, a sound that must alert the birds to predators, including the occasional human hunter. I part the stalks, searching for a place to cross the barbed wire fence, and hear the distinct footfalls of fleeing pheasants, of webbed feet ticking across dry undergrowth.

Though I can't tell precisely what type of fencing the neighboring rancher employed, it resembles the commonly used "Ford's Kink and Double Twist." Fencing options are endless and evocatively named. Blackmier's Strip and Tack, Barnes's Fluted Ribbon, Carpenter's Serpentine Wire. Some variations remind me of Christmas tree decorations, while others look like concertina wire strung around prison walls. In the 1800s, pronged impediments made their way west from southern Illinois, and it's estimated that hundreds of millions of acres in Montana are currently cordoned off by one barbed strain or another. Much of what is fenced nowadays is land white settlers originally appropriated from the Salish in the 1904 Flathead Allotment Act, land that was originally deeded to the Tribes in 1885.

As the old cowboys sang, "They say that Heaven is a free-range land,"

Goodbye, Goodbye, O fare you well
But it's barbed-wire fence for the Devil's hatband
And barbed-wire blankets down in Hell.

Last year for Halloween a friend of ours came dressed in a tight black leather dress with fencing wrapped around both biceps, calling herself Barbed Wire Woman, "new superhero of the West,"; her superpower, she said, was ridding the landscape of straight lines and sharp edges. Needless to say, she won the costume contest. Despite its inevitable inconveniences, though, barbed fencing often serves to alert human visitors to the mammalian company they keep. I scan the top rung left to right and spot, snagged on a barb, an oily tuft of bear hair. It's impossible to discern what species it belonged to—grizzly or black—from ruddy coloration and texture alone. I consider tucking it into the small pouch in my vest reserved for totems such as vole skulls and curious rocks—at home I could use it to fashion a classic crane-fly imitation called a Brown Bear Brown—but I feel the sudden ominous need to ask some sort of permission. I hold the coarse fur a moment longer, then let the wind lift it from my fingers.

For the next hundred yards or so, I try to convince myself that the fur was left by a black bear, but when I come upon a huge pile of scat, skillet wide and loaded with apples, my optimism withers. Only a very big bear, very likely a grizzly, could have left it. Normally in grizzly country I would announce myself obnoxiously, alert bears to my presence so as not to sneak up on them, but I've prioritized stealth and, more inanely, a would-be pheasant harvest over my own safety. As I walk, the knowledge of recent bear attacks weighs heavily. Not far from here a young sow with cubs grabbed an unsuspecting pheasant hunter, a guiding mate of mine, and dragged him for fifteen yards by the ankles as he entered a thicket of redbuds. Several miles to my north, an eight-hundred-pound boar charged a duck hunter in his blind. And just a section north from where I walk, an old sow's gaping maw was the last thing a hunter saw before he wheeled around, smelled her sour breath, and fired, his load of peppercorn-sized number 4 steel shot felling all nine hundred pounds of bear directly on top of him, her mass bending his gun barrel's forged steel.

Although these encounters have locally begun to carry the air of myth, they remain legitimate warning: I should not be traversing such territory solo, nor moving with such stealth.

But the narcotic of the country eclipses my wits, and I continue on. Stepping down off the calving bank and into the creek, I stop to admire the steeply pitched headwaters of the robust body of water I'm about to ford. While I stand shin-deep in its meanders, there, several miles up the valley, it also exists: the waterfall of it, plunging down the mountain's black scarp. A thoroughfare between the stark mountains and this rather fertile bottomland, the drainage serves as the bear's passageway between two distinct environs. It's humbling to travel the same road, to cross paths even for a few steps. Proximity to feral neighbors quickens me. More present and alive from the encounter, I'll bring something of this place home to my family, and my untamed but domestic neighbors, creatures all: dependent on the land for sustenance and inspiration.

FIRST FALL

Mary has that dreamy, post-breast-feeding, oxytocin-infused look in her eyes as she slides up to the bar and takes a sip of my red wine. Jerusalem couscous simmers on the kitchen stove, and a gutted and picked pheasant, seasoned with thyme, salt, pepper, cayenne, and lemon juice, marinates in a baking dish on the counter. I plan to brown the entire bird in a skillet, then remove the bird from the cast iron and fill its cavity with a halved lemon and several sprigs of thyme. After I drape a butter-soaked cheesecloth atop bird and baking dish, I'll put the entire assemblage into the oven at 275 degrees and set a timer for ninety minutes, or is it two hours?

With a whoop, Laurie enters through the front door bearing brussels sprouts, yams, and a softball-sized purple onion. She is anxious to trade an armful of root crops for warm infant, and without further greeting, rolls the vegetables across the counter and, reaching toward Mary, takes Luca in a football carry, his neck braced soundly in her hand, his chubby legs straddling her forearm.

"Where'd the pheasant come from?" Laurie sniffs.

"Closer to here than there, but not too far from you know where," I respond. Describing the hunting ground, I obscure the actual waypoint in the grand tradition of hunters everywhere, not because Laurie hunts birds and would horn in on my spot, but because any hunter worth their salt is reasonably more protective of their coverts than their banking passwords. "Is Spurgeon on his way?"

"He's getting cleaned up from his hunt. Still got the horse collar. The old bagel. The schneid. The zilch. The nada."

"Has he come to terms with the fact that the only elk meat in the freezer so far is yours?"

"Not in the least," she says, without taking her eyes from the infant in her arms. She makes a goo-goo sound at him and tweaks his nose. Looks briefly back at me. "You're staying out of those creek bottoms, right? Those bears are still weeks away from denning up."

"I made plenty of noise," I lie. With a wedding-gift Wusthof, I slice an onion in half. I watch its exposed spiral core bead with moisture and envision the ground I traversed earlier today: the union of two springs and a tangle of hawthorns, a nearly impenetrable creek bottom choked with bushes and vines that hosts a variety of berries still fragrant on warm evenings and hoarded by bears before hibernation. I sniff and blink away the onion tears. "Whenever I got near the cover I started crooning some loud, off-key Dylan. *If you're travelin' in the north country fair . . .*"

Mary cringes at my version, and Laurie fires her *don't-be-so-stupid-in-bear-country* double-barrel at me.

I don't mention the tuft of hair I found in the barbed wire, or the massive pile of scat, but instead inform them that the bird's feathers smelled of sap and that its crop was filled with what I thought was bison berry.

"Did you save it?" Laurie asks of the crop, adding that she's brushing up on her botany for a foraging course she is teaching next semester.

"Of course," I say, and trade Laurie the knife for Luca so that she can begin to dice a head of parsley.

Instead of discarding the crops of birds, I usually place the digestive pouches on the windowsill in the garage to dry, creating an admittedly macabre installation of forage that ranges from grain to snails to watercress. Outside with me in the sudden cold, Luca hews to my side. I wonder if he'll want to hunt; he's certainly got the early waking part down. My father has never hunted, except for a single blue jay sniped with his BB gun at age seven, a kill he mourns to this day. Conscientious objector to Vietnam, antinuclear protestor in the 1980s, he earned an FBI file for marching in several controversial rallies—he's a pacifist, in other words, who has never expressed any displeasure over my affection for the hunt, but who must think it a bit strange that his child, raised in the postindustrial suburbs of mid-Michigan, feels unassailably alive while walking around the woods with a firearm.

In the cool garage, I place the crop of the pheasant we're about to eat in the center of a white salad plate. For the hunter with limited daylight and legal days to pursue their quarry, much of autumn is spent trying to prolong experience, to nourish the latent Pleistocene-biped side of their brain. At its apex, hunting is an occupation that adds time to one's life rather than taking it away, or so said the Spanish philosopher Ortega y Gasset. Feral rites such as saving crops bring us closer to our quarry and help us squeeze each glorious drop out of the season. In much the same way, we hope to wring out the nourishment of each creature we harvest. So we make elaborate meals of the flesh, stock of the carcass, and trout flies with the feathers and tails.

Seated at the bar holding a full bottle of Smirnoff by the neck, Spurgeon, all spiffed up for dinner in a black Pendleton button-up with pearl snaps, points to the plate I carry. "That is quite the presentation. You've got a fallback option if the rivers dry up."

"Looks like a dangerous unit," I say, nodding to the bottle. I hand Luca to Mary so that Spurgeon and I can bro hug.

"I've got some fierce elk sorrows to drown," he says, and cracks the bottle's seal. "I feel like Elmer Fudd out there."

I crack the seal on the Smirnoff. "The Russian nurse can help."

"Short glass and a couple of ice cubes, please."

I grab a glass from the freezer and knock two rocks from the ice tray, swing back to the counter for the bottle, and pour a four-finger belt. The cubes cleave audibly in the glass. Sipping, Spurgeon pokes at the muscular extension of the pheasant's esophagus with a butter knife. Our meal-to-be had been feasting: several crab apples, one still stemmed, a single snowberry, a couple of watercress leaves, and a pile of seedy berries the color of polished garnets.

"Bison berry?" I ask.

He swallows. "Grows on vines, in clumps?"

"They look like miniature Roma tomatoes," Mary says while leaning over the plate and guarding Luca's head from the counter. He reaches toward the bright gathering of berries with his tiny hand, the nails of which Mary still trims with her teeth. She sways her torso so he can't touch them.

Spurgeon scratches his arête of a nose, then snaps to attention. "That's nightshade. Birds can eat it but it's totally toxic to humans."

With a gasp Mary steps further back and checks Luca's fingertips to make sure they haven't come in contact with any pulp.

"Red means stop, boy-o," Spurgeon says. "Remember."

When Luca was born, the attending nurses checked to make sure his "nine gates" were open and functioning—eyes, ears, nostrils, mouth, and the two below the belt—making certain that the world would be able to find its way in, as well as out. Now as his primary custodians, Mary and I negotiate an awkward give-and-take; over and over we must decide whether to allow exposure to experience or to provide protection, whether to protect him from the ills of the world or toughen him to its inevitable onslaught.

Perhaps my lingering anxiety stems from my occupation: the guide's number one responsibility is to avoid potential dangers and deliver guests safely to the dock at the end of the day. *Watch your head on that branch. Keep your legs in the knee locks. Don't wade any deeper than your thighs.* Of course, the domestic doesn't preclude danger. My grandmother often recounted the story of a breakfast during which my uncle attempted to swallow a whole ice cube. When it lodged in his four-year-old throat and his breathless face turned blue, he slapped the table and tried to gag; hearing him, she whirled around from doing the dishes and instinctively poured her mugful of hot coffee down his throat, singeing his tongue and gums but melting the offending cube in an instant.

"Every gun," writes a beloved poet, "is loaded and cocked."

❧

Geologists call Lolo Peak a "high-angle down-to-east" but from the north the mountain looks to my impressionistic eye like a heron that has folded its wings and tucked its long beak into downy chest feathers. Through our south-facing picture window I watch the dun-blue distances of pines recede into more blue distances, watch the mountain as I do each day, in keeping with N. Scott Momaday's credo that one should look upon the same rock ritually, the same landform in all weather, from all angles. Nine thousand feet in elevation, named for a French fur trapper killed by a grizzly and buried on the mountain's flank, Lolo can be seen from nearly every vantage point in town. And thanks to former city planners, from every side street and alleyway too. Though its apparent stillness above our thoroughfares seems to stop time, the mountain is still growing due to tectonic shifts, rising in elevation even as it erodes and weathers: a confounding geological fact.

In the corner of my eye, I catch sight of Spurgeon bow-leggedly ascending our front steps with a card table under one arm and a growler full of dark beer under the other. I usher him in. We exchange Happy Thanksgivings, snug his square table against our round one, snap open a blue gingham tablecloth to cover them both, and set places for five. Laurie, he reports, is just about to throw the main course on the grill, and he has been instructed to grind horseradish for a dipping sauce. He looks around the room, like a dog sniffing for old scent.

"It's quiet in here."

"Yeah, the boy's sleeping."

We're relishing a long moment of nothing but refrigerator hum when Mary and her best friend Beth burst into the living room. They've been bowling all afternoon at an alley a few blocks away and smell of cheap pilsner. I high-five Beth, then embrace Mary with a curious sniff.

"Don't worry," she says, rolling her eyes. "I pumped earlier."

Sudden as a grease fire, Luca is up from his nap, wailing in the nursery. I gather him up and shush him and wing open the fridge, then grab his bottle from between the stuffing and the cranberry sauce and get the cold faux nipple in his open mouth before he can see Mary, recall the superiority of a real breast, and become further undone. Red-faced, he drains the bottle with frantic desperation, takes a deep, gasping breath, and—after I thump the small of his back with the palm of my hand—lets out a formidable, five-count belch.

While Spurgeon and Beth share greetings, Mary tromps out the appetizers: smoked duck breasts thinly sliced and covered with shavings of Emmentaler; cured flakes of whitefish stirred into whipped cream cheese, topped with finely chopped chives and capers, and slathered onto crackers; and the pheasant, sliced onto chunks of fresh baguette and surrounded by grilled vegetables.

"Tuck in," she tells Spurgeon.

"Ladies first," he says.

"Beth's a vegetarian," Mary explains.

"From Portland," I add.

"But I'll try a little," Beth says. "Maybe later."

Spurgeon spreads some whitefish dip onto a cracker, dots it with a caper, and pops it into his mouth, lifting his eyebrows approvingly as he chews. I suggest the duck, which he hoovers and washes down with a frothy gulp of beer. Finally, he pairs a forkful of pheasant with a pan-fried brussels sprout dressed in balsamic, spicy brown mustard, and cayenne. That's the stuff, I say. But he bites down—square, I gauge from his wince—into one of the number 5 steel shot I fired at the pheasant several weeks ago.

"Did you get one?" I ask, embarrassed. "You didn't crack a filling?"

Mary explains to Beth that while cleaning the bird I'd missed one of the BBs.

"Oh no, I'm fine," he says, smiling as he works the shot from the meat with his tongue. He plucks it from the chewed meat and drops it on the uneven table, where it rolls onto a platter. "Just a little closer to my food source."

We set the table: green beans sprinkled with goat cheese and walnuts, roasted brussels, elk sausage stuffing with dried cherries, garlic mashed potatoes, and fresh sourdough. In short order Laurie appears in the doorway wearing red oven mitts, cradling a baking dish. I open the door and take the dish, inhaling deeply the aroma of the elk backstrap she harvested and cooked. While the prime cut settles under foil, Laurie begins to tell the story she's been hoarding from us for a few weeks, the tale of how she felled the elk we're about to consume—all but Beth, of course, who will subsist quite well on the veggies, provided she's not converted. Which is to say we won't starve, we can wait to pass the sides, but there is something in this mealtime pause that recalls an elderly uncle clearing his throat for effect in the middle of an already prolonged grace.

"I tracked it over the mountain and found it in a south-facing bowl bedded under a ponderosa, with six or seven cows," she says. "The wind was blowing straight at me and even at that distance I caught a whiff of musk." Spurgeon smiles and refills Laurie's glass. Foam settles into beer the color of a bull elk's cape. A few weeks ago—when she crouched down in the bunchgrass, leaned her pack against a sage bush, lay down on her belly, and, prone on her knees and elbows, rested the barrel of her .30-06 on the backpack and took aim—she and Spurgeon were on the rocks, reportedly over Laurie's unwillingness to share the location of this particular hunting spot she currently describes. Spurgeon has since shot "his elk," as the saying around here goes, and the two have reconciled, but for a few weeks the relationship was, hear tell, in the balance.

"They were still sleeping," Laurie says of the small herd that rose and fell in her rifle scope's reticle. The final elevation gain had been covered quickly and now her prone body heaved as she tried to keep the breath inside her chest cavity.

I gulp from my wine and picture her squeezing out the air through her nostrils, dimming her pulse to a low glow, a hum.

"You had to be coming out of your skin," Mary says, rocking Luca's bouncy chair with her foot.

"Could not hear a thing but my heartbeat," Laurie says.

After she had rested the crosshairs on the bull's front shoulder for several seconds, she tells us, she slipped the rifle's safety off. The sun was cresting the hill behind her, making the elk's coat shine. She could not see the big animal's eyes; in light this keen, she wagered, even at this distance, two hundred or so yards, she would have been able to see them if they were open, a wink of light in the drab browns and greens of surrounding foliage.

Shooting the bull in his sleep, she explains to Beth, would mean less suffering, not to mention less adrenaline coursing through the animal's veins, and by result, less spoiled meat.

With no small tinge of jealousy, I take Luca from the bouncy seat and begin to joggle him on my knee, ready to storm out the front door, pack boots on, Luca strapped in the Björn, and ascend rugged terrain to gain proximity to a bull elk in its wild environs.

"I tried not to think of how many days I hunted last year without finding even a single elk," Laurie says, "let alone a viable shot. Nothing last year, nothing all this season. Then the wind changed. Time was up. 'Just give me this gift,' I said. And settled into my shot."

To what had she addressed her appeal, or to whom? The mountain, or herself, perhaps the creature, or the landscape entire. Wanting her to expound, wanting her to say what she meant but not wanting to play the part of annoying listener who ruins a story's momentum with cosmological questions, I rip a hunk of sourdough from the loaf and dip it in the juices collected on the serving platter. Everyone at the table sans storyteller stares at me with the same shaming, accusatory eyes: You're not seriously going to eat that before she's finished, are you?

I set the saturated pinkish bread on my plate.

"I pressed the trigger," Laurie says—the frozen scene would have shuddered as the stock punched her shoulder and her ears rang. "Racked in a second shell and settled back into the scope."

Now the half dozen cows were bolt upright and astir, she explains, stamping, shuffling briefly up the hill, retreating, and eventually vanishing over the rise. Calculating, she kept the hairs trained on the animal that lay now at a slightly different angle.

"Maybe the bull stood up at the shot and went back down when it hit him. I saw his eyes open and wondered if I should put another round through his front shoulder, but then you're wasting good meat. He inched forward on his knees, made to stand, and—".

Laurie dropped her chin to her collarbone.

I look to see if Beth's complexion has paled with Laurie's last detail, but she hasn't glanced away.

Spurgeon is glowing. He looks out the window at Lolo—umber now in the dusk—and nods, his glacial-blue eyes full of pride.

"I'd helped Spurgeon clean an elk a few times," Laurie says, pinging him a proud glance back, "but field dressing that animal alone—that's the real work. Solid start and end point, distinct series of moves along the way. The first incision is always the hardest, putting a blade into the still intact body. When all the remorse comes flooding in. But all along the way I'm thinking about what cuts and pulls are going to get all those innards out in the cleanest way."

Laurie peeks under the tinfoil and deems the backstrap properly rested. "Do the honors?" she asks Spurgeon. The thin cuts fold juicily onto themselves as Spurgeon layers them neatly with knife and fork. When he's finished, he raises a glass to Laurie's tale and suggests that we share a small gratitude before we eat. You first, we insist. With apologies to John Muir, he responds he's already had enough happiness for a dozen lives, a sentiment we heartily second, third, and fourth. Luca squirms and dry cries in my lap. Beth adds that she is very grateful to meet Luca and would be even more grateful to taste a single bite of elk.

"Just a slice," she says, extending her plate to Spurgeon. "What did you do with the horns?"

Many hunters would have mounted the bull's skull and six-foot-wide rack of antlers in their living room above the fireplace, but Laurie didn't have much use for the trophy, and gave it to her elderly grandfather, who plied the Colorado high country before his hips went bad. "I did keep this," Laurie says, drawing out a pendant from the neckline of her sweater.

One of the elk's ivories hangs on a black string of leather. Laurie unclasps the necklace and passes it across the table to Beth. She admires it momentarily before placing it in Luca's hands. Between his tiny fingers he fumbles the blunt vestigial tusk and leans toward the charm with his open mouth to gum the feral pacifier. A sound issues from his lips then, not a word but a distinctly communicative gesture we all huddle toward, as if trying to decipher.

⁓

When this babbling child is nearly five, Spurgeon, telemarking alone on Lolo Peak, will be caught in an avalanche of rain-rotted snow at the base of a steep couloir and die almost instantly of severe head trauma. I wish it were otherwise. I wish I didn't have to mention this now, on such an otherwise festive occasion. No matter how hard we try to marshal it, though, a river will occasionally slip its banks.

A week before the summer solstice. No cell phone, no avalanche beacon, no helmet: a list of items suspiciously missing from among Spurgeon's things, as anyone who ever joined him in the mountains knew him as a thoughtful, responsible, overly attentive companion. He will come to be memorialized by friends as a truly singular character, someone who maintained a raw relationship with the landscape, who pushed his body and being further than the rest of us dared, and who didn't so much visit as inhabit the backcountry. Who courted the wild and was indentured to the land. Over the years, the high-angle down-east peak on which he left his body will by turn come to serve as a kind of memorial stone survivors can't help but visit, with our eyes anyway, in all but the worst of weather.

His attire—T-shirt, no gloves—will suggest repose, a lack of concern for danger. After skinning up and descending backcountry ski routes, he often swam in a basin's alpine lake before taking a nap. When the news arrives, I'll drop my cell phone in the front yard next to the sputtering lawnmower and, in the midst of my numb shock, picture him like that: head propped up on a sun-warmed slab of granite, dark curls still wet from his swim, dozing under nighthawks that stoop from invisible precipices, their wings audibly sawing the ozone.

THE RIVER OF REAL TIME

Mary tousles Luca's hair and swivels to smile at him but he is racing, chased by a giggling friend, quick on his surer-by-the-day legs, one day shy of his second birthday.

Indeed, two years: you ship the oars, look back upstream, and the distance you've covered—accounted for or not—is indisputable.

"Times like these," she tells me over the din of the beer-cheered Saturday afternoon crowd, "I could use a leash for this boy."

We are gathered with a crowd of sixty, craving the shade a white canvas tent casts across the griddle-hot, late-August parking lot, here to partake in a fundraiser I organized for the shelter, a fishing tournament that began as a pipedream but came to fruition as an exemplary braid of our community's generous nature and resources: anglers paid entry fees; fishing guides donated time and expertise; sandwich shops provided lunches; a brewery gave India and Scotch pale ales; and a restaurant served free barbeque, some of which I rub from my chin as I attempt to gather guides and anglers for a group photo to commemorate the event.

"Let's circle around the boats," I say, ushering an armful of folks away from the major traffic artery that flanks our festivities, my instructions drowned out by the dull hum of intersection traffic. "Light's wrong for the pic, but it would be nice to keep Orange Street out of the background. The traffic's a bear."

I whistle for the stragglers and, in the brief lull of the moshing crowd, hear Mary's voice, stern: "Luca, stop!"

Through the pastiche of legs and sandaled feet I catch an obscured glimpse of him running from his friend, the pursuer's bob cut flapping like wings above a chubby, flushed face. They are laughing so hard I can almost hear them over the welter of voices and the bluegrass band that has begun to play "Columbus Stockade Blues." Someone asks if I've tasted the cold-smoked barbeque sauce. Someone asks if we can get the mayor to join the pic. You still have sauce on your nose, someone tells someone else.

"Okay, are we ready?" the photographer asks with measurable fatigue. "On the count of three, say—"

"Luca!" Mary yells, her voice panicked, shrill. "Stop!"

The crowd stills and in unison turns to see Luca—his friend has halted at the last command—gut laughing now, accelerating, gait propelled by solid hams and ever-bruised knees, on path for the traffic. Without braking he shoots a puzzled look back at Mary, which causes his strides to elasticize just long enough for me to bellow his name in an already mournful voice, a voice I hope never to use again.

I don't know how it is mentally possible to note each of the following nascent thoughts the instant before the shiny black Volkswagen lurches to a stop and Mary reaches into traffic and the cacophony of screeching brakes and belting car horns to grab our son by his small left shoulder blade but—unmistakably, in the course of a millisecond—I register: *So this is how our lives will change again forever / they'll all feel so sorry for us / hold his sweet body / what grace he's been a perfect boy*

He entered the street from behind a shrub. That the car's driver could have seen him coming strikes me as implausible. Perhaps they noticed the crowd's commotion through the car's tinted windows, or felt the energy wave of a hundred eyes shifting in unison, or heard, however faintly, the ignored commands. Bless you. *Why weren't you fiddling with your radio dial, or turning up the air conditioning, adjusting the vents, or looking down to find your ringing cell phone? I don't even know what you look like, let alone your name. You spared our son's life and drove on, your heart doubtlessly pounding as rapidly as ours.*

Driving to the river after the fundraiser with the raft in tow, we have to whisper to keep from waking him. Snug in his car seat, surrounded by board books and discarded cheese puffs, Luca sleeps soundly in the afterwash of adrenaline. Staring out the window, Mary talks about—what would we call it?—the incident, the near tragedy, the likes of which observers will recount to us for years to come, in great detail, as if we had not witnessed it but had only participated in it as actors do a scene. She riffs practical, then philosophical, metaphysical, cosmological. Clearly Luca is growing more explorative, adventuresome, and agile by the day; without squelching these qualities, we'll have to train our eyes on him again, teach him that danger casts a wide net, does not play favorites, nor cull cute children from its catch. Then without sequitur, she begins to heap blame on herself for what didn't happen.

"I watched it all," I argue. "You sensed he wasn't going to stop unless you stopped chasing him. So you stopped. You would have dived in front of that car, but you knew you couldn't catch him. Your instincts saved him."

She looks out the window and says nothing.

Intermittently sprawled along the highway's shoulder lie roadkill deer and raccoons, unseen flies congregating around eye sockets and nostrils. With every animal shape we pass, I can't help picturing Luca's small body mangled by the black sedan. What would have become of his dimpled elbows, his hobbit-like feet that seem to be growing a toenail's length each day? Is he, are we, this near to mortal danger each day? Driving in the haze of this hypothetical cross-examination, I give passing vehicles a wide berth, keep watch for magpies rising from carcasses, even run my wipers to dissuade the lavender butterflies from connecting with the windshield. The entire highway-scape—even the grasshoppers, lifting from the dry ditch grass only to be spattered by the side mirrors—makes me shudder with a sense of fragility.

Did it matter if we called the near tragedy a blessing, a warning, or both? If we called it "good fortune," would we offend the powers that had doubtless attended, perhaps in the form of a blade of light refracted from a northbound car's hood onto the windshield of the southbound black Volkswagen that centered the driver's attention? If we said "powers," though, weren't we faced with the fact that hundreds of children die in similar accidents each day—one every twelve minutes—and thus have to conclude such ineffability hadn't attended those who met less fortunate ends? What is it with lessons that we want them so quickly? Why the moral before the story's over?

By looking back like this, mining what's barely memory, I am ignoring the most potent of details: Luca is in our midst. Countless times in two years I have envied his ability to be fully present, in medias res. And yet it was this enviable quality—*Momma is following me fast, and I see nothing but the empty, endless sidewalk, feel nothing but boundless laughter filling my chest*—that landed him so perilously close to danger. More irony: if the operator of the black Volkswagen hadn't been equally present and awake to their task, they might not have been able to slam on the brakes and spare Luca's life.

Fear can quicken, enlighten.

Legend has it that Zen monk Ikkyu attained a higher plain of understanding when he heard a pebble strike his rake. I will never know what level of attainment Luca experienced when Mary reached across the threshold of two worlds to yank him back onto the sidewalk, but I know that once tight in her arms, he began to weep the tears of a rescued man, crying until someone slapped a plateful of chocolate cake and ice cream in front of him. He did his best then to make an old haiku master he'd never heard of proud—"One must work to achieve enlightenment and then return to the common world"—by bolting down the heaping dessert with his hands, stopping just once to sniffle.

⁓

As most caregivers do, we will come to endure other encounters as harrowing as that day's. When Luca is twelve, for instance, he will combine a lingering chest cold with a long day of downhill skiing and a soak in a hot tub's overchlorinated waters—and find himself instantly gasping for breath. He will raise his hands above his head as if gut punched and one of us, noting the panic in his eyes, will rush to him while the other readies the car and calls the emergency room. Traveling in an unfamiliar town, our phone's navigation system will direct us over and over to a former entrance of the ER that, because of construction, is blocked. Crippled with helplessness, we'll speed down the floors of the parking ramp as his breaths grow more and more frantic, each inhale catching before it can fill his lungs.

Maybe, gentle reader, you have experienced a similarly narrow escape, as enduring such seems a prerequisite of this parental vocation. Or worse. I hate knowing that worse is often true. I don't recount these close calls to suggest some exclusivity, but because such traumas, micro and macro, seem part and parcel to the shared parental experience. And also to ask how we can rightly process such events.

The next day he wakes up hungry, famished.

Breakfast is French toast.

~

Gear strapped down? Check. Oars? Check. Spare? Yep. Life jackets, tent, food, stove, sleeping bags and pads? Check. Liturgically, without a wasted word, we launch the raft and are soon floating along the confluence line formed at the junction of the nearly transparent Blackfoot and the peat-colored Clearwater. Entering from the north, the inaptly named Clearwater is a winding meadow stream that issues from a chain of lakes and cedar swamps at the foot of the Swan Range, while the frenetic, glacial-fed Blackfoot falls hard from the Continental Divide and pushes at a dizzying pitch through red-rock-tightened canyons. After the rivers merge, though, and tumble through a series of rapids, they are transmogrified, indistinguishable from one another.

In what's left of the blue hour, we pitch on a willowy island our simple camp: tent, sleeping bags, Roll-a-Table, stove. Mary zips Luca into his sleeping bag, and tucks alongside his bone-tired body a quilt that Beth stitched and sent for his birthday: bolts the color of late-season sage, of huckleberry juice, of clear August skies behind windy pines. The river rushing past our campsite slams hard into a wall of sandstone and turns abruptly before caroming through a tight box canyon.

In this cherished spot, a place we visited frequently before Luca was born, I sleep fitfully.

Before dawn in the faint light, I tend a small driftwood fire. A peregrine falcon perched high on a cliff speckled with pale bird droppings cries shrilly for its fledglings, and from a hidden nest her cast of young birds peep a response. From the rim, down a steep game trail, scree tumbles—then stops, as if something up there has paused to examine us. Starts again: the sound of pebbles tossed across a frozen pond. I hear the tent unzip and turn to see Luca, his brow furrowed, rushing across the sandbar to me. I pull his warm, fresh-from-the-sleeping-bag body to me and hold him to my chest, his rapid heartbeats hammering into mine.

He dreamt of waves crashing, he says, and loud things going by. His bare legs are pimpled with the morning cold. I rub them warm. Together we walk down to the shore for his life vest, which hangs from a willow shoot. At the foot of the cliff an eddy spins around a moving center, the way a dervish whirls ceremonially in an attempt to slip time. I absorb the sound, blood pulse of the earth, groan of the gears of the turning world, and hawk him as he walks toward the water's edge, his small feet laying prints in the wet sand beside those of killdeer and heron. He crouches for a moment, then stands and comes toward me.

"Here," he says, passing me a handful of sand, a portion of mountain and foothill ground into granular particulate.

Here: where he stands and where—how far—he's carried us.

II.

LEARNING THE LANGUAGE OF RIVERS

"In a life properly lived, you're a river."
—JIM HARRISON

BED REST

On Rock Creek last summer, I watched a three-foot bull snake drag a trout through the shallows. Or was the trout dragging the snake? I wasn't quite sure.

I hopped out of the raft, tossed the anchor over a deadfall, and, closing in on the tug-of-war, determined that the snake after striking had somehow clamped its jaws around the fish's adipose fin. When the panicked fish kicked its caudal muscles into gear, though, the snake was pulled into the river by its would-be prey. Adrift, the snake threw its ribbon of a body into a serpentine fit, dragging the fish back into the shallows, whereupon both creatures gathered their breath before the cycle repeated itself several times. Was this duel a metaphor for a subconscious struggle within the watcher, I wondered narcissistically, or simply a fish struggling to be free of a snake that had attempted to capture an outsized meal?

It didn't stand to reason that I was rooting for the trout, either, since a good portion of my livelihood stems from helping tourists dupe said species into mistaking fur- and feather-covered hooks for insects. On top of that, my favored childhood companions were not fish but snakes, turtles, salamanders, newts, frogs, and toads. One of childhood's prized discoveries, for instance, was not the flint arrowhead found one rainy day after our baseball field had been ploughed under by a developer, but the licorice-thin green snake I untangled from the bristled stalks of my mom's tomato plants. I housed it in a pickle jar with a lid of cut screen, admiring the way it coiled, lacquered skin against the glass. I anchored Herbert Zim's Pocket Field Guide to Reptiles and Amphibians under my pillow until I was of age to wonder if such reading material might frighten off potential female visitors, scarce though they proved to be.

Turtles were coveted, too, particularly young-of-the-year red-eared sliders that could be plucked from sunny logs along the shores of small manufactured lakes bordered by suburban townhouses and interstate, kept in a homemade outdoor terrarium, or sold as pets around the apartment complex for a quarter apiece, a buck for the most prized specimens with silver dollar–sized shells, a bull market until a neighbor boy was rumored to have contracted salmonella and an upbraiding band of mothers put an end to further transactions. As a consolation I was allowed to keep an adult painted turtle—the adults were supposedly free of disease—in a ten-gallon bucket tucked into the corner of our entryway. For several weeks, I changed its water and fed it earwigs, scraps of earthworms, and occasional bits of deli ham. One night at dinner we were alarmed by the sudden knock of its shell on the linoleum: it had scaled the bucket's wall, nudged away the stone-weighted screen, and fallen over the bucket's edge, its claws clicking across the kitchen floor—a sound my mom found understandably disquieting.

A requisite hard rain fell the night I was to release the turtle back into a forest preserve. I had bartered for more time, been given an extra, gravid day, but beyond that my parents stuck to their guns. My dad drove me in his blue Buick Skylark to the edge of the woodlot and flicked the windshield wipers off. Raindrops blurred the window. From

Detroit, WJR broadcast a Tigers baseball game, Ernie
Harwell's richly timbred voice washing over the state on AM
radio, an audible salve tempering the reality of our ghost-
town GM factories and skyrocketing crime rates. A Detroit
double play—"Trammel to Whitaker to a stretching Darrel
Evans"—leavened me and, grabbing the bucket's metal handle, I went into the woodlot alone.

Rilke wrote that our youthful conversations with dolls
prepare us for our conversations with the Great Silence.
Since I owned no dolls, I spoke to the creatures that I collected. We posit, project, Rilke continued, but mostly do our
own talking. A rational inkling, no doubt. Out where the
woods swallowed the Buick's high beams, though, I couldn't
muster a word and, more heartbroken by my muteness than
any letting go, I slid the turtle out of the bucket and walked
back toward the car, grateful for the rain on my face.

At the onset of puberty, fish replaced reptiles, and
though my angling pastime didn't necessarily attract young
women, it wasn't as off-putting as the presence of a scaled or
shelled onlooker beside the potential suitor's bed. One July,
though, a chance encounter re-focalized my attention.

While fishing a neighborhood pond I caught a bullhead,
a long-whiskered cousin to the catfish, which had swallowed
the hook too deeply to be revived. After reefing the well-
seated hook from the fish's gullet, I tossed its limp, bleeding
form into the shallows. In short order two crawdads convened and began to spar with nimble blue claws over the
marl-colored fish carcass. Without presage, they vanished.
From a soggy bank hovered by mosquitos, I stepped toward
the margin of the pond inquisitively, my tennis shoe sucking
down into the mud. I drew it out quick.

Then with eyes the distant blue of Neptune, a moss-dark thing hoved out of the depths: a snapping turtle with a shell the size of a school desk. Stalks of milfoil shifted as it moved to investigate the carcass. Like landing gears, its four stout legs set down, stirring puffs of sand. Then, thick as a grown man's forearm, the turtle's wrinkled neck elongated, its head jabbed out, its beaked jaws cleaved, and, lurching—the dead bullhead hadn't been in the water a minute and already the denizen had found it—inhaled the entire fish.

Frenzied, I readied a snelled hook, quickly caught a small bluegill, and baited the turtle with that fish's torn gills and innards. But it did not reemerge, and soon evening shellacked the surface of the pond with glare.

"Better watch it," my dad warned after hearing my story. "Your hand would fare better in Kowalski's sausage grinder than in that thing's mouth. Besides, a kid drowned in that pond. It's fenced off for good reason." Indeed, next to the No Trespassing sign an engraved memorial plaque hung from the locked gate I jumped each afternoon, but I ignored it citing its potential bad luck.

That night, I fell asleep imagining that I held the hissing turtle by its tuberculate tail, a term I'd learned from Zim, and the following afternoon began an unrelenting pursuit, baiting it like a huckster, hoping to glimpse its nightmarish eyes again. It could not be coerced though. Weeks passed. Summer wore ponderously on. School pictures loomed and I didn't like my haircut. Finally, on an afternoon of its choosing, the turtle reappeared—it wasn't there, and then it was—to deduct a fish from my offered row of chum.

Surprisingly, I didn't revel in that unsanctioned view of predation as I had expected to. I thought instead of all the panfish I sacrificed in such pursuits, the countless bullheads, bluegills, pumpkinseeds, and sunfish. A wise person once told me that every act stands on its own—no one act undoes another. And hearing their words, I remembered those fish, and realized it was then, on the pond's shore, that I fell in with the underlings.

Survival of the one in direst need: that's why I was pulling for the trout last summer and not the snake. Sure the snake needed food but the willows, loaded with freshly hatched, rain-numbed stoneflies, afforded protein galore. I understood that even if the trout were to escape the snake's jaws, it would likely be too injured to return to its normal feeding lie and would soon become sustenance for a larger, more piscivorous member of its own species. Still, I reasoned beyond Darwinian logic, it deserved a chance.

And I've embarked on this meandering digression, I realize, because Mary, a mere six months pregnant with our second child and just ordered to bed rest, is trying to ensure that the underling inside her womb survives despite the odds. It's Halloween morning, and we're just home from the hospital's labor and delivery unit, where we spent the sleepless night watching multiple monitors track heartbeats—maternal and fetal—and her contractions' duration and intensity. Following a day of intense physical activity yesterday that included her ritual daybreak run and an afternoon hike with friends in the hills above our new house, the contractions came on sudden, wresting Mary from the dinner table, where we listened to Luca practice the lion's roar he planned to employ with his Halloween costume.

"Babe," she said, pulling my hand to her pumpkin-round belly. "Can you feel that?"

Through a sweatshirt, Mary's uterus felt as tight as hands locked in white-knuckled prayer.

"Is that a contraction?" I asked, afraid of the word, afraid that my speaking it might usher something hidden into the daylight.

Her uterine muscles relaxed momentarily, long enough for me to ask how many contractions she had experienced, and long enough for her to consider, count on her fingers, and then answer, "a dozen or so," before—sixty or so seconds later—another gut punch arrived. She inhaled through her teeth, pinched lips—exhaled as if she were trying to push air through a keyhole, the way she had when she was in labor with the boy now seated beside us eating store-bought, mass-produced, dinosaur-shaped pieces of breaded chicken.

I didn't footle about. I picked up the phone and called Nancy, our even-keeled nurse-practitioner, who said, "Yeah, I wouldn't wait on that. Like, not even an hour." Mary rang one of my former students to come watch Luca, and after the usual chase from front room to guest room to bedroom to dust-bunnied hardwood beneath his bed, I got him undressed and into the bathroom, where I ran the water and explained that mom and dad had to go to the hospital "for a little while to make sure the baby in mommy's belly stays in mommy's belly."

Naked now, testing the hot water with his toe, Luca shot me a quizzical look.

"Remember?" I asked. "Mom's gonna have another baby and you're going to have a little brother or sister."

"Can you do lots of bubbles this time?" he said, looking at the flowing spigot.

I reminded him that he'd gone with Mary for her checkup and ultrasound recently.

"Most is, I like to get a sticker," he said. "But Nancy let me push the button and I could hear the baby. That breaks my heart every time."

"Okay, bud," I said, as the breath gummed up in the back of my throat. "Dillon's gonna be here in a second. We'll leave then. After you get into your pj's, he'll put you to bed, okay?"

He aimed a furrowed brow at me again and crouched in the bath like a baseball catcher, the warm water up to his smooth, bare stomach marred with chicken pox scars from the year before: I recalled those sleepless nights, the fever that wouldn't break despite maximum doses of ibuprofen backed with maximum doses of Tylenol, Bob the Builder DVDs playing on a steady loop to distract him.

"See you in the morning, okay," I said.

"Okay, but—" he said, sloshing out of the bath, "I gotta pee!"

Precisely nineteen minutes later, following Mary into the birthing center after speeding across town, I glanced through the attendant window of the NICU and shuddered. The miniature fingers rigged to wires and tubes, the muted cries of the tiny infants, seemed impossibly real. Dumbfounded, I stared until Mary yanked my sleeve and led me to the intake desk. There, before Mary could remove her coat, the on-call doctor wanted to administer a shot, a corticosteroid injection that would help the baby's lungs develop more rapidly in case of imminent arrival.

"You mean," I asked the obstetrician, a stand-in for Nancy, "this baby could come tonight?"

"Afraid so," he said, as the nurses quickly disrobed Mary, tied a gown around her, and patched her into multiple monitors. "She's experiencing intense contractions, and the uterine muscles loosened significantly at your first child's birth. These could be what are called Braxton-Hicks contractions, or false contractions, but they can still ripen the cervix. Even dilate it. Preterm labor is a distinct possibility. Unfortunately, there's no way to tell the difference between the two types of contractions. Bothersome is that they seem to be occurring at very close intervals."

I nodded my way through the diagnosis, my anatomical vocabulary tested.

"We'll know the baby's heart rate here in a moment, and be able to tell if it's distressed," he said, monotone. He still hadn't introduced himself. He wore a layer of gray stubble on his face; I wondered how long he'd been on call. "If this is the case, we may consider a magnesium injection to slow down the labor, but that might only buy forty-eight hours. Not a lot, but some crucial development can occur in that amount of time."

I shot a glance at Mary. Her face twitched with fear.

"Such as?" I asked.

"She's right at twenty-five weeks today." He proceeded to run down a sobering list of potential outcomes that included long-term lapses in brain development as well as a high chance of sight and hearing impairment. Then he said the words "survival rate," as in "increases from between 50 percent and 80–90 percent at twenty-seven weeks," at which point I began to hear my own pulse far louder than the conclusion of the assessment.

"What do you mean 'survival rate'?" I asked, to no response.

Without coddling, two nurses—each sporting identical outfits down to their pink scrubs, zebra-striped lanyards, and blue New Balance shoes, but differing vastly in height—led Mary to an inclined bed and strapped a belt-like contraption around her midsection. Through electrodes suctioned to her belly, a device monitored the baby's heart rate, which became increasingly distressed with each contraction, the machines beeping as the baby fended off a clenched uterus. To complicate matters, Mary was dehydrated, and despite several attempts Tall Nurse couldn't successfully install an IV. Another tech and several more needle pricks failed, and eventually the phlebotomist was called in. Monte and I recognized each other immediately from Charlie's Bar as friendly acquaintances who had never formally met but had shared a round or two. "Strange to run into you without a glass in hand," he said. "What are you having?" I said. "I'll buy." With a stern glance, Short Nurse curtailed our small talk, and in little time at all, Monte tapped the radial vein above Mary's thin wrist on his first attempt. The room let out a collective sigh.

"I owe you something off the top shelf," I said. "The Goose, if I remember right."

"You know where to find me," Monte said, and stole coolly out of the room, kit bag tucked under his right arm.

A flurry of activity ensued. A technician squirted a dollop of blue gel on Mary's belly and pressed a probe to her stretched skin. Tall Nurse whisked me out of the room to fill out paperwork while Short Nurse performed a phenol swipe on Mary, a test for the possible presence of fetal fibronectin, which is a protein that glues the amniotic sack to the lining of the uterus and thereby helps ensure fetal cushioning; if the protein was present, there was a 90 percent chance that preterm labor had begun, and full-fledged labor would start within twenty-four hours. Moments later, Tall Nurse returned to inform us: positive phenol swipe.

Six months, I thought, trying to recall the rudimentary drawings of fetal development in books I had skimmed. Which facial features had begun to develop? Even with my remedial purview, I recalled that the baby's eyelids were there, along with its ability to smile, frown, burp. It could kick its feet against the walls of its uterine world, the reverberations of which I'd already relished in my hands. Though weighing less than a pound, its lips and palate had already formed, its eyelashes too. I could picture its wrinkled fingers waving off the ultrasound's vibrations, the folds of skin stored around the wrists, ready for bones to expand, the brain inside the still-fusing skull glowing like the flame inside a jack-o'-lantern.

Silently, I sent my thoughts to it. *They tell me that you already dream. Of what?*

Tall Nurse wheeled in a cot for me and stationed it next to Mary's bed.

"If we're lucky," she said, locking the wheels of the cot with her feet and placing a hand on Mary's knee, "it'll be a long night of waiting. I'm here if you need anything."

Mary's right hand shook as it gripped the bed's steel frame. With her left, she reached toward me. She wasn't crying. I took her ever-clammy hand in my own and tried to smile. Years removed from this moment she will insist that the look I offered her that night granted her a tiny shard of courage—but she must have mistaken fear and fatigue for equanimity.

I listened to the monitor's speaker, and the sounds of channeled blood rushing in and out of the baby's heart: the sound of wind-shifted cottonwood leaves above a back-country river, the percussive currents divvied by an island on which two smitten young lovers once shared an evening picnic.

I asked her if she remembered the island on the South Fork we waded to when I proposed.

She laughed once through her nostrils. "You carried me on your back. So manly. But you forgot the corkscrew!"

"Even then, you knew what to expect," I said. I glanced over at the monitors, the momentarily stable digital lines. "You just smiled and shook your head. I did have my Swiss Army knife, though, and the underutilized leather-working awl." I pictured the two of us shivering in the cool, slipping grip of twilight, toasting and drinking from camp cups peppered with hashed cork.

"You had me gather up some kindling," Mary continued, tugging at the string on her scrubs. "Came back with an armful of sticks and there you were, kneeling in the dry wash."

"Do you remember those two kids?"

"Their faces are a little blurry," she said. "But yeah, I do."

THE CREATUREHOOD

With minimal exertion, Mary wheels herself around the kitchen in an office chair, holding what in our family passes for a budgetary spreadsheet: a calculator and dry-erase board covered with numbers. While the on-call OB told us somewhat flippantly that Mary could "probably" return to work without a hitch, "just ride out the contractions" for a few months, our trusted caregiver Nancy urged us to leave nothing to fate.

"I know you," she told Mary before we left the hospital. "And I know teachers. You work too hard. I want you to stay home and be lazy. Do you do crossword puzzles? Knit? Right. Didn't pin you as the crafty sort. But you get the gist: I want you home for the duration. I want this baby getting bored in there. Understand?"

Mary understood, followed Nancy's instructions, and with blue marker in hand began to comprehend a deflating reality: she would be forced to use all her accrued sick time and paid maternity leave before the baby's birth.

As our eyes meet, we draw dueling stunted breaths: Mary's due to the contracted uterus pressing on her diaphragm, I assume; mine caused by a sudden onset of paternal panic. Earlier this year I cut back on teaching duties at the University and as a poet-in-the schools with the hope of spending ample time at home with Luca before returning to a fully booked season on the river, where I log long days, often leaving before he wakes and returning after he's gone to bed.

Now, my naively formed plans make the fluids in my stomach churn. Time is indeed a commodity, until you try to trade on it. After full appraisal, we determine that the fear of long-term trauma and potential costs caused by preterm birth far outweigh the anxiety caused by a soon-to-be threadbare bank account. On the calendar we highlight each holiday between today and the full-term due date: Thanksgiving, Christmas, New Year's. Ten weeks until full term.

"We tried for two years to conceive this baby," Mary exclaims, "and now it's in a hurry to get out?"

Beyond the living room window a waxing moon crests Mount Jumbo, illuminating a dense swath of pines and the rounded, west-facing peak I call "the Island." According to historical models depicting this valley before Glacial Lake Missoula drained, the Island was, for a few thousand years, the only dry ground for miles, forming with surrounding peaks—Sentinel, Lolo, Sleeping Woman—a kind of archipelago. As the moon rises, it silhouettes a single tree I'm fond of, a two-trunked ponderosa that sits at what I imagine was once waterline. I'm surmising of course, eyeballing it. Regardless, the tree has a firmer grasp on time than I do.

I place my hand on Mary's belly. *Stay put a while longer, Little One, where it's still safe to swim.*

As night draws on, the neighborhood coyotes begin to call, their individual yips gradually congealing into a single fluid song, which stirs me from my makeshift bed on the rug by the fireplace's sputtering logs. I've barely slept but pop up nonetheless, crawling on all fours to the window for a peek: no eyeglasses, so the outer dark is a misty blur. They howl unabashedly, jaws cocked to the hilt, I imagine, their hunger a welcome distraction from the stirred acids in my gut, from my flaring, newly acquired ulcer.

When I went down with an untimely bleeding stomach lining last week, my doctor friend Phil came to my aid once again, scoping my stomach at no cost and, after analyzing the results, prescribing meds. The proton pump inhibitor should kick in after a few days, thereby allowing me to avoid surgery on the hiatal hernia, but due to the wicked cocktail of discomfort and anxiety I haven't slept much, a factor that only exacerbates acidity levels. Clutching my gut, I picture the pack of coyotes romping down our small paved street, a bushy-tailed gathering celebrating the blood on their tongues, and, having eaten little more than saltines of late, envy their ravenous hunger.

In our interstitial neighborhood, the savvy pack's kill could have been a well-groomed poodle or a whitetail fawn. Here the ecotone's spruce lined streets are trafficked by mountain lion, moose, elk, coyotes, and black bear (grizzlies, say biologists, are on their way). Flying squirrels, red squirrels, crows, ospreys, owls, eagles, ravens, hawks, and over a hundred species of birds have also made room for colonizing humans. And though we've only occupied this 1970s ranch for two months, we've already encountered the apex predator. Located just across Dickinson Street from us, Luca's preschool recently called to report a mountain lion sighting. The cat had been spotted a few blocks away lurking under a swing set, its tan fur and four-foot-long tail camouflaged in the wood chips. Last week a neighbor's motion-activated camera caught what was presumably the same cat, its long bowed tail glowing in the camera's flash, as it slipped across a cement patio. And it may in fact be the same one Mary locked eyes with while running just a few weeks before our emergency room interlude. A hundred yards from home, she rounded the street corner before dawn and froze mid-stride as the beam of her headlamp met the unblinking astral glance of a young lion. Not wanting to turn her back on the cat, she backtracked up the hill and toward the house, no longer in need of a cardio workout.

From the porch in the gray first light, I cock my ear to listen for the coyotes, but the fog has absconded with their noise. No cry or holler, however faint. The air is wet and dense, the clouds resting on the roofs. A few hundred yards away, the creek is loud, charged with last night's rain, the current knocking from the fins of trout minute leeches that attached themselves during summer's weary flows. John Keats— whose short life is the subject of the book I've been reading, who once placed a leech on his eyelid to decrease a bruise's swelling—would remind us that "the creature hath a purpose and its eyes are bright with it." I know Mary's prevailing purpose, and that of the child inside her, but am unsure of mine.

It's a floodlit epiphany, realizing that one's vocation doesn't necessarily double as a lucrative occupation. It should have dawned on me sooner, I guess, but for several years now since graduate school, guiding has kept me in my habit, has funded, shall we say, the writing of poems. After the boats are stabled for the season, I spend a few hours nearly every morning at the desk in the basement, covered in quilts and down coat, at work on poems. After several recent close calls with the first book manuscript, though, I have yet to find a publisher. Practicalities and affirmations aside—"poetry is a fire in the summer," wrote Basho, "and a fan in winter"—I can't abandon the practice, which has become, for better or worse, a matter of finding sustenance in language. If I'm not gathering such food, my spirit starves.

Slumping back on the floor, I return the Keats biography to my sternum, to help abate my flaring stomach acids. It's heavy, like a shovelful of soil. In addition to the ulcer and the guilt I wear for not being able to help Mary bear her current yoke, I have a career change to consider. After learning of her bed rest, Mary's father, a successful life insurance salesman, pulled some strings to get me an interview with the Missoula branch of a well-known national firm. Though I have yet to accept his offer, I'm weighing my options, sparse though they may be. I settle against the couch and discard the biography for my river journal and begin to thumb through last season's entries. Keats's "improvidently short life" is doubtless more interesting than my own, but far from a palliative for this doctor who's forgotten how to employ his own prescription.

To the earliest human inhabitants of this valley, the measure of a person's wealth was their horse—or horses, if they were flush. Now those of means compare stock portfolios and real estate holdings. If I, with none of the former and little of the latter, have learned anything about currency from my wealthy clients over the years, it is that staying outside, living at the oars instead of inside a cubicle, is a luxury that only time can buy. Viewed broadly across human civilization, and even within contemporary American society, I remain, I realize, on the relatively privileged end of the economic spectrum; any talk of having a "calling" is a luxury too, borderline romantic.

Nonetheless, I have attempted to live with place-driven purpose. My aim at the oars has always been to empty myself as thoroughly as possible, and to subsequently become infused by the immensity of this infinitely wise landscape, to let it charge every pore in my being. For better or worse, measurable success or none, writing is the record of this process, is part of that story.

"And we're in trouble," my neighbor William Kittredge once wrote, "when we don't know which story is ours."

A loss of faith, Mary tells me at breakfast, begins with a loss of ritual.

"Go hunting for the day," she says, tapping her midsection. "Your gut will feel better with some exercise."

"Yours is the one I'm worried about," I say. "I don't want to be away if you suddenly go into labor again." I butter Luca's waffle, tilting the yellow wheel of processed wheat along its rim so that each of the square recesses fills with melted Land O'Lakes, then sprinkle a heaping spoonful of powdered sugar across the oily spill.

Sitting at the table, Luca scratches his inner thigh, which is chaffed from a recent encounter with a patch of stinging nettles. These days he is all body, ever ready to tumble or scrap. When playing a game of catch, he demands passes that require him to dive onto the ground after the football rather than ones thrown directly into the breadbasket. Indoors, his preferred pastime is one of our own invention in which he attempts to run across the living room through a maze of couch cushions while I bomb pillows at his knees, trying to take him out. When he tumbles, bright laughter runs like sparks from his toes to his scalp.

"What's wrong with your belly is you're fat," he says.

I set the plated waffle down in front of him.

"I'm just bloated," I say, slapping my midsection.

"No, you're fat," he says, folding the waffle in half like a taco and hoovering a mouthful. "Everybody knows it."

From her gray office chair, Mary shrugs affirmatively. "Daddy's belly is really irritated. There's a little hole in his stomach, in the stomach lining, where there's not supposed to be a hole."

Luca noshes on the waffle and seems to consider this. "Is there a baby trying to get out. Like Mommy's?"

"No, bud. No baby."

The irony is not lost on me: agonies of childbearing versus the inconvenience of a sour gut. Mary scoffs whenever I wince while plucking eyebrows. "If men had to deliver babies. . ." she says often, and leaves this phrase lingering, not needing to connect another clause. This morning I've eaten a bottle's worth of antacids, a chalky meal that availed only rancid belches, but the pain is only alleviated when my knees are pressed to my chest or when I'm facedown, a couch cushion sandwiched between my stomach and the floor. Presently I feel like I've swallowed a handful of sidewalk-sharpened jacks that carom off the walls of my stomach and esophagus.

"Just keep your phone on and don't get further than an hour away," Mary says. She wheels her chair over to the pantry, takes Luca's Spiderman lunch box off a shelf. "If you can get his lunch together, I'll call someone to walk him across the street to school."

Slapping a sandwich together for a child's school lunch should be a simple enough task for a parent to undertake. But when there's no organic peanut butter in the pantry or when, owing to dirty dishes, said parent packs a plastic spoon with the non-biodegradable yogurt container in the lunch box, several vectors of guilt converge. It's impossible to know whether the hopefully positive impression you're making on a young human will outgain the negative one you're making on the environment. Despite prevailing sentiment, this is an unimpeachable truth. Is it possible for a family to outgain its planet-level impact, its daily contributions to the earth's demise, through the education and nurturing of mindful children?

Inspired the other day by two squares of toilet paper into which I'd blown my nose, I made some rudimentary calculations. As a fully potty-trained family, we use eight rolls of toilet paper per week, amounting to roughly four hundred rolls per year. Over the course of the next twenty years, our three-person clan alone will be responsible for the deaths of nearly twelve hundred trees. To say nothing of our detractions of water, gas, and energy resources, or the epic fuel use of airplane rides to visit grandparents, cousins, aunts, and uncles.

At this point in the Anthropocene we could use an eco-superhero, I think, zipping Luca's sandwich into his Spiderman lunchbox along with a cheese stick and a juice box. I stuff the box into his backpack, which I hang from the door handle on my way out to hunt.

Later, driving north past our local landfill, I consider how long it will take for the lunch's plastic contents (straw, cheese stick wrapper) to end up among this 98-acre, 220-foot-deep pile of waste. There's no question Luca's first Pampers are still out there, only a few years into the five hundred it will take for them to degrade. Every day, 10,000 tons of garbage ends up here from our environmentally conscious town of roughly 82,000 residents, and a $225,000 smasher runs eight hours a day to squeeze the mass of our collective complicity into one rectangular hole.

However tightly we pack our waste, wherever we ship it, however we divvy the blame, there's no distancing ourselves from the fact that the earth is in pain. By turn, so are we. Or as the cyberneticist Gregory Bateson says, "You decide that you want to get rid of the by-products of human life and that Lake Erie will be a good place to put them. You forget that the eco-mental system called Lake Erie is part of *your* wider eco-mental system—and that if Lake Erie is driven insane, its insanity is incorporated in the larger system of *your* thought and experience."

Whether we know it or not, whether we acknowledge it or not, our relationship with the earth is a psychosomatic one.

The other day while I was cleaning dinner up, Mary suggested from her rolling chair that the raging abscess on the lining of my stomach could be a psychosomatic attempt to empathize with her preterm labor, some odd physiological stride toward communal suffering. I told her she was overestimating my empathetic powers, but I would gladly accept her spin.

Certainly our parental roles are shifting: Mary's from provider-nurturer to protector of the unborn, mine from provider-protector to something far less defined. Perhaps her prenatal limbo has stirred some long-latent Pleistocene instincts. She could reasonably demand that I toughen up—take her father up on his offer to connect me with the insurance job, or go out and find another temporary position checking groceries or delivering papers, anything to abate the financial pressure—but she urged me to go for a hunt. Could her insistence simply indicate a desperate view of our situation, as in: if the balance sheet gets any worse, his hunting abilities may be more useful than his stunted earning potential?

Continuing west, I watch the gulls scatter in the distance like wads of paper, indistinguishable from the debris.

An hour north near the small town of Saint Ignatius, my eyes ascend the lank Mission Range, its young granitic peaks calico under snowfield and cloud shadow. There is a mythic association between mountains and verticality of spirit that post-Jungian psychologist James Hillman has called phallic. In my base-level paraphrase, he says that men are adept at going up and down in an attempt to, as the fourteenth Dalai Lama put it, "mate with the cosmos," but the gritty work of the soul is accomplished in the feminine vale. Admittedly, most of my emotional life has been lived between the high registers of gratitude and the bowls of self-pity. These fluctuations were once a specious point of pride, a juvenile misinterpretation of passion. I read Hillman for years with faltering comprehension before bearing witness to Mary's current level of resiliency.

Near a favorite covert, I park and let a borrowed bird dog out to pee. From the back hatch a Llewellin setter named Pearl bounds, quickly tearing through a copse of aspen and leaping a creek before vanishing into the brake.

While loading my vest with shells, I call *Come!* And Pearl's soon back at my side, chestnut eyes afire with concentration. After a stationary moment she rolls in the deep and lissome grass, wagging her entire body, and pops up to attention with a jowl-snapping headshake, a renovation of consciousness the likes of which we two-leggeds cannot begin to replicate.

Toward this complete reset and away from my mind's obsessions, I follow Pearl's strides all morning. Although she locates no pheasants, I trust her increasingly as the day wears on, placing my faith in her unassailable instincts and sense of purpose. By midafternoon, I'm so engrossed by her indefatigable casting that I nearly fall into a tea-black spring creek. I step back and stare at the water below my feet. Spooked by my shadow, spawning brook trout dart around the bathtub-sized pool, their white-rimmed fins telltale against the gravel bottom. The gray markings on their backs are a vermiculate script. Then Pearl leaps the spring and my reflection, pulling me on an invisible leash back into the hunt.

Pearl's is another way to read the world, a method that will, barring rapid advancements in science, remain elusive to humans. A dog like Pearl has 220 million scent receptors to my 5 million; a less domesticated creature, such as the black bear sow so fond of our backyard pears, has 500 million. In other words, as society has advanced through the epochs, our instinctual survival traits have been bred out of us. Some would argue for the worse. After depending on the Pleistocene brain for roughly three hundred thousand years, humanity abruptly jettisoned its deeply seated way of engagement for another mode we deemed "more evolved." Though the Pleistocene mode of discourse with the inhuman world has only been out of fashion for a few thousand years—a mere pebble-blip in the ocean of history—we have not, despite appearances, completely disengaged with it. We still feel its tendrils reaching out of us toward the earth, urging us to communicate with all that we evolved alongside.

The most evolved hunters understand that we share, along with all earth-bound creatures, a collective imagination. Expounding on Bateson, eco-philosopher Paul Shepard contends that when we sever ourselves from this imagination, as we kill off species and chew up the landscapes required for their survival, we go mad. It is self-mutilation, he says, to destroy that with which we share "a mind." Perhaps some small collective recognition of these processes explains the resurgence in hunting and gathering in the West over the past several years, and the increasing number of what Shepard calls "tender carnivores."

Jose Ortega y Gasset: "The hunter knows that he does not know what is going to happen . . . thus he needs to prepare . . . an attention which does not consist in riveting itself on the presumed but consists precisely in not presuming anything and avoiding inattentiveness." As the collective narrative in this country becomes more and more predictable and homogenous—what are we if not divided, polarized, untenable?—thoughtful outdoorspeople will continue to search for a less pre-interpreted, less governed cosmology in the physical world.

Pearl is the opposite of a being "riveted to the presumed," and I bow to her allegiance to the immediacy of sensory experience. To say nothing of her physical elegance, the way she veers suddenly toward a patch of redbuds, nose high, tasting the wind, then slows with caution in her steps, before falling into a stymied sort of point, her tail at half-mast. There is a bird, she is telling me, just on the periphery of my scent line. She is staunch but facing ground she just covered, as if she can't believe she didn't smell the bird on first pass. I puzzle over her stance but load two shells and close the over-under. Then, very slowly, slow as the minute hand on a clock, her nose dials around to the north and her tail rises and hardens with assurance.

The rooster pheasant cackles once on the flush, clears the stand of osiers, then falls to the load of bismuth shot like a puppet abandoned by its master's hands.

～

I take the pheasant from its curing hook in the garage and, on the bird-cleaning board that doubles as Luca's outdoor art table, set to butchering it. Although it has aged for a few hours above bicycles and lawnmowers, sharing space with Mary's Subaru and a sprawl of unsorted camping gear, the bird still smells faintly of the rose hips, grouseberry, and Russian olives it once traversed. Sitting on our cement stoop, I hold the dead bird in my lap, a young-of-the-year rooster with a patchy red mask and stubs for spurs, and start picking. The oily feathers make a slight popping sound as the quills depart the bird's pimpled skin, and after a while the naked legs and hip joints begin to resemble my own. Pearl, who scented the bird in a thicket, pointed it, and retrieved its limp form from tall grass, stands nearby, alternately licking her chops and snapping at stray tufts of plumage that drift by on the breeze.

Last summer, a fashion craze had many young women scrambling for the iridescent filoplumes, or aftershaft feathers, of rooster pheasants. Fishing tackle shops sold out of capes, and online distribution centers ran dry. That women were going to great lengths to adorn themselves with the rump plumage of male pheasants tickled me, I'll admit. On the wing, the male rooster looks like a dark-purple kite hemmed with red and emerald and tossed into a ripping wind, while the hen is a far more practical, mottled tan, her drab camouflage most necessary in the nesting and rearing seasons. Native to hill country half a globe away, in China, the pheasant has adapted keenly since its initial introduction to the American west in 1881, with wild populations presently flourishing in agricultural lands across the region. Visually, though, the male remains conspicuous, particularly while on the feed, when the white, priestly ring around its neck gleams above uncut alfalfa or winter wheat.

Unless you clean game birds often, you will likely feel saliva gather at the back of the throat or have to choke back a gag while raking the innards and sweetbreads from the cooled chest cavity of a pheasant. This blood-on-the-hands act is a far cry from dropping a Styrofoam- and cellophane-bound package of chicken breasts into the bottom of a shopping cart, prior to a relatively tasteless meal of store-bought poultry that spent most of its life in a crowded coop, its feathers and webbed feet soiled by the droppings of hundreds of other clucking clones. In contrast to its hormone-injected, very distant cousins, a wild upland bird's taste is unsurpassed. Sometimes when I've made a clean shot, I'll hang a pheasant or grouse for several days, the way the French do, waiting until it falls, sans head, from its hook, "perfectly aged," the meat tender and full of character.

"Eaten only three days after its death," writer Jean Anthelme Brillat-Savarin said, "the pheasant has no peculiarity, and must be allowed to be decomposed."

I tend to agree with the French on most culinary matters, but this bird is due on the table tonight. So to add flavor, I'll slow cook the meat in a ragout of sorts, with garlic, onions, red peppers, mushrooms, grape tomatoes, heavy thyme, crushed red pepper, a squeeze or two of lemon. A confession: potential recipes occasionally cross my mind during a hunt, à la Wile E. Coyote, and fellow hunter-gatherers admit to sharing this mild psychosis. It goes beyond the meat too. A responsible hunter is always pondering how to utilize the entire kill, though, even the bones, which will be saved and boiled down for stock. With the long tail feathers of this bird, I'll tie flies, wrapping the variegated fibers around stainless steel hooks to imitate mayfly nymphs, miniscule and otherwise nondescript food items that are staples of any trout's diet, particularly those that reside beneath the cutbanks of the spring creek near which this bird once lived.

It would constitute a delicious circuitry to fool a fish next summer in this very spring creek with an imitation fashioned from the tail of a bird that once roamed the banks.

I pick the last rump feather and toss it into the wind, wishing on it for luck and answers.

ROAD TO THE BUFFALO

Goblins, superheroes, pop stars, football players, princesses—
they rang the doorbell, crooned the expected ultimatum,
opened their pillowcase sacks and plastic bags, and we prof-
fered candy. In trade we received fall's leaf-snatching winds
and short evenings made shorter by the swindlers at the Bank
of Standard Time. Not to be mistaken for autumn, that "season of mists and mellow fruitfulness," true fall has arrived,
and daily we're losing light at a staggering pace.

Outside in the late-afternoon quiet, I lie on our black
cement porch in a black down coat beside the deer-gnawed
pumpkins, trying to mainline as much of the southerly sunlight as possible. Warmed by the first star's rare appearance, a
box elder bug taps against the storm door before falling to the
porch, lifts again in brief flight, falters. I look to the south past
the valley's geomorphic scoop, where Lolo Peak is backed by a
swatch of clear sky. Cumuli spill overhead like streambed pebbles then collect, as if caught by an invisible seine. Momentarily
the wind halts, the clouds' undersides darken, and the valley
dims. As the low-pressure weather system squeezes air from
the valley, I sense a similar sensation enacted on my cranium.
I recently read that while the organ constitutes only 2 percent
of the body's weight, the brain consumes over 20 percent of
the body's energy. Is that all? Oblivious to factoid and verse,
a black-capped chickadee the weight of two quarters alights
from our mountain ash, jostling a clump of orange berries,
perhaps the lighter for what it doesn't know.

I have a great many things on my mind and trying to ignore them exhausts me. I take the bookmark from the book at my side and on it write, "Early slender moon over the mountain"; then, "how to sketch a waxing crescent"; then, "fix basement toilet."

My subconscious is trying to tell me something. Maybe creative writing is just daydreaming, like Freud said, a continuation of and substitute for the play of childhood; maybe I should just grow up, cede to the inevitability of practicality and accept my father-in-law's offer, schedule the dreaded interview. A single curd of hail the size of a spitball strikes me in the center of the forehead. I open the book and begin to read with little volition. A book is a wind that blows through your life. Sometimes that wind is power-ful enough to dishevel everything it contacts. Sometimes it coasts through, altering very little. Sometimes you want to reexperience a once-felt gust or breeze but the variables have changed and thus the effect, though still elemental, is altogether different than expected. Hoping to feel blown open once again, I read a favorite poem in a cherished book but remain cloistered.

The storm door squeaks open.

"What are you doing?" Luca asks, swinging on the door handle.

"I'm reading a poem. Don't swing on the handle, please."

"What's a poem?"

"A poem"—I pause—"is a 'machine made of words,'" a heartless theft from William Carlos Williams, a poet and physician who once told an interviewer that he navigated the dual worlds of literature and medicine by way of "continual conversation."

"No. It's not," Luca counters with conviction. "It's a tractor."

Certain that children are born better poets than most adults can become, I zip my coat and pull my hat over my ears. Bested, I push myself up from the stoop, tickle his ribs with an index finger, and step inside. On the couch, bunkered by no fewer than half a dozen pillows, Mary reclines. Staunchly, she is petitioning her womb-child—*Please, stay put*—and within the squalor of worry and uncertainty that otherwise pervades the household she's made a bulwark, a little womb for herself. I check in, place my palm on her stomach, refill her glass with water from the tap, and head down the steps in search of a book she's requested. While thumbing through the stacks in my cement-walled basement office, I can hear Luca stomping loudly.

"What's going on up there?" I holler through the heating vent.

"I'm making thunder," he yells, and stomps again, a Zeusian gesture that should please me far more than it does.

The Stegner novel Mary requested is shelved beside *The Necessary Angel* by Wallace Stevens, who worked as an insurance executive. Ted Kooser, who recently won the Pulitzer Prize for Poetry, earned a living in the field as well. For a while in the musty basement cold I consider whether these vaunted poets' shared connection is a sign to take the interview with the insurance company, or just a result of my alphabetical shelving methods, but before long I am sneezing. Instantly my nose is running, and soon my head is aching; this is due, I assume, to the large patina of black mold behind the plywood, a recent discovery I've hidden from Mary.

Black mold: surely sign enough.

The following day while wearing a borrowed sport coat, I offer a strong handshake and say something about how a fishing guide is just a salesman selling good experiences to clients and fake mayflies to trout, which draws a hearty round of laughter from the crew decked out in red, company-logoed polo shirts. Before I've left the parking lot, they call my cell phone to offer me the job, starting in two weeks. I thank them and ask politely for the weekend to consider.

～

We are breaking one of our unofficial wedding vows: delving into finances before consuming a second cup of tea. After dropping Luca at preschool, Mary and I drive up the Blackfoot while volleying back and forth the pros and cons of the insurance company's shrewd job offer. But when we account for Mary's still tenuous pregnancy, our rally dies. Her contractions haven't abated so much as become a known quantity. Whatever she's doing is working. She feels comfortable on a two-hour car ride, as comfortable as she's felt in a month, she says, and plans to keep listening to her body.

Against the foothills, woodsmoke mingles with a low-hung fog as we pass the tiered hives of honeybees and the parked trucks of hunters who made their way into the woods long before first light. The regional manager offered just enough money to stop the bleeding for a few pay cycles, with the first noticeable bump in salary coming after eighteen months of commitment on my part—just after I lose my fishing clientele for good, I explain, along with my teaching gigs. I crunch the numbers aloud, the numbers adding up "to nothing," as Neil Young sang, borrowing from a Russian novelist. Mary doubtless already comprehends as much. Like water, she sees possibility, a way around. I see the steady gig as abandoning my vocations midstream. Clearly she has parsed the numbers too, weighed the pros and cons. In the end she leaves the decision to me but reminds me that I have in the past been able to work productively very early in the mornings, a couple of hours at a time, dedicating the most fecund section of the day to the craft, and offering the remains to the outside world. It's not unreasonable to think that I could establish the same routine again.

"What if the insurance thing just overtook me?" I ask, seesawing again. "If I stopped getting up early, just bagged writing altogether?"

She stares out the window toward a ridgeline where, among hundreds of deep-green spruces, a single larch tree clings stubbornly to its cadmium needles. I let my eyes carry up the contours of the mountain toward a hollow and a plume of smoke ascending from a very distant chimney. What I would give for a cabin like that, a life reduced to the elemental: the wine cup revised as the teacup, the blade that cleaned the felled grouse in the evening used to strain steeped tea leaves the next morning. There I go, mooning around again. Idealist, I used to call myself, but now I know that escapist is a more accurate word. While I romanticize, look for ways to transcend, Mary digs in like a watercourse.

"Don't take this the wrong way," she says, handing me a chunk of scone she's unwrapped from a square of tinfoil. A student's mom, grateful for Mary's work and sympathetic to her need for bed rest, baked a batch and delivered them fresh this morning.

I bite in, scenting nutmeg and sunlit bushels of wheat. A blueberry at the scone's center still holds a touch of warmth. I chew, waiting.

Mary inhales. "If you stopped writing altogether." She pauses, bites the inside of her lip. "I guess I would say that it just wasn't important enough to you."

The words hit me like a ball-peen, but I do my best to hold a poker face. Never has a truer verdict been levied by a more gracious and gorgeous judge. At the village of Ovando, where the North Fork of the Blackfoot and the main stem meet, I turn the Subaru around. I'm hungry for poached eggs and side pork at the Silver Bullet but a handwritten note taped to the café's door reads "Arizona." The town's unofficial mascot, a Peruvian hairless dog wearing a crocheted pink sweater, shivers in front of the post office. Curlicue tail spinning, it stands on the edge of the boreal, a few drainages from the Continental Divide. As the small dog grows smaller and more cartoonish in the rectangular mirror, I think of how easily you can end up with a life that doesn't faintly resemble the one you envisioned for yourself. As if the poor dog had a say in the matter.

Soon we're crossing Monture Creek, which is hemmed in by ice and the deep maroon of dogwoods; Cottonwood Creek, near which a hunter, gutting out his harvest last week, was mauled by a sow grizzly bear; and finally, the nauseating spills of Roundup Rapids. Far below the bridge the river tosses clouds of vapor into the frigid air. The Blackfoot: antithesis of cubicle. At Camas Prairie, we pass the apiary again, the ordered trays of sleeping colonies, and Mary recounts the story of my old client and the bee boxes. I've told it unceasingly at so many parties with a final cocktail in hand that I suspect she's just trying to lighten my mood.

"What did she say again?"

"We were driving across a pasture to get to the river and we passed a stack of hives. She said, 'Montana sure is beautiful, but could you explain to me why people keep throwing out their file cabinets?'"

"She didn't."

"She was well educated too." I say. "I think she'd gone to Groton."

And without further word we continue to wind slowly down the route the First Peoples called "the Road to the Buffalo," though it occurs to me that the Salish gave it that name while traveling in the opposite direction, toward their quarry.

⌒

"How come you're not sleeping?" Luca asks.

Cold air seeps through the three-decades-old window above his bed. My neck is sore from having nodded off on the lumped hood of my jacket. According to my cell phone it is 2:37 a.m..

"I'm just thinking," I say. "I figured you were asleep."

"You think easier than me."

"I doubt that."

He yawns and swallows loudly and hikes himself up with his elbows. I try to snuggle him back to sleep but can tell by the tautness of his upper body that he's going to want the story I promised before bed.

"You were going to tell me a story," he says, shifting his head out of the nook I'd made for it below my shoulder. "Remember?"

"I tried but we fell asleep."

"I'm awake now."

"You want to hear the one about Coyote, the Cedar, and the Slug?"

"That one's weird."

"I won't argue that. The Clatsop passed it down from one generation to the next from time immemorial to time present, and by rights I should probably ask an elder for permission before beginning. May the gods forgive my further appropriation. You should probably know that we come from a long line of appropriators. Actually, that's not wholly true. Only by association. Skin color. Our people on Grandpa's side were field workers in Poland turned manual laborers whose better years were eventually sacrificed to the military after they landed in America. Grandma's side is a little more complicated, but the Armenians were forced out of their homeland at the hands of the Turks. As many as a million and a half dead in the genocide."

"Huh?"

"I'm sorry, bud. Went a little stream of consciousness there. How come you're not sleeping?"

"Can you tell another one?"

"I can tell you one I've been working on."

"What's it called?"

"It doesn't have a title."

"Stories always have titles. I like 'The Two Hunchbacks.' Can you do that one?"

"Not by heart. Listen, though, this is one about the time I floated down the Yellowstone River at night without my boat. Mom's in it."

He sighs deeply, an affirmation of sorts.

"We were on an island in the middle of the Yellowstone River. We had drifted there. Mom had rowed a raft that was full of camping gear and Dad had rowed the drift boat, guiding Peg and her husband Chick."

"I remember Peg. Who's Chick?"

"He died right before you were born."

A long pause ensues during which I assume he has fallen asleep.

"When we die," he asks, "do our days start over?"

An even longer pause follows during which I consider how to answer him. After a while his head falls heavy on my chest and warm breath casts against my neck.

I close my eyes and remember floating with Peg and Chick. I had launched the fishing boat ten miles upstream from our intended camp, after which Mary launched the gear boat loaded down with supplies several miles downstream, to give her a shorter float and more daylight to pitch tents and assemble camp. When I anchored at the island with Peg and Chick, dusk was flooding the river bottom. Soon our camp cups were filled with red wine and we were recounting the day's spoils. Then Chick began to sneeze—he must have stirred up an allergen—first in a steady rhythm but soon uncontrollably, over and over, each sneeze beginning where the last one left off. No problem, he said, sniffling, I've got my allergy meds in the tent. But the medicine wasn't there; in his giddy pre-fishing rush, he had left them in the truck at the bridge, two miles upstream from camp.

"I'll just hike back upstream through the pasture to the bridge," he said, sneezing again. "Still plenty of daylight."

And off he strode. A few minutes later, I spotted his headlamp on the camp table and felt a brief flutter of worry. I turned the light on and off, then fed the bonfire another gnarled cottonwood limb, calculating that he had an hour of dusk by which to see. The Crazy Mountains were quick to close twilight into their massive basalt palm, though, and in the time it took for the fire to engulf the limb, the sky grew twilit, then dim, then completely dark.

Hoping to catch Chick on his return route, I headed upriver with his headlamp.

But the trail upstream was not a trail for long. It led through darkening cow pasture, wet with dew and punctuated by cattle-hammered mounds of dirt that made a stumblebum of me. Then the mounds were moving across the pasture in my direction, led by a constant, undulating, many-voiced *moo*, the drum rumble of cloven feet striking the ground. Bull fear, hoof fear, swinging udder fear. I moved more quickly now, tacking toward the river, soon plunging my sandal into a den of some kind. Snake fear. Badger fear. I called out a couple of times for Chick.

As a philosophical figure, I loved the notion of two men passing in the night, one looking for the other, who does not know someone is looking for him, but in actuality it stifled me. When I cleared the pasture drenched in sweat, I began to acknowledge the mosquitoes taking root in my skin. Innumerable, ravenous, far more ferocious than any I had ever encountered. Flummoxed, I found the river—cooler there, fewer mosquitoes—and began a tentative hopscotch down the riprap until my snake fear returned: Where would a cold-blooded rattler coil on a quickly cooling night if not against the warmest, heat-storing black rock it could find? I shone my headlamp on the sharp rocks. No snakes, but writhing everywhere were large, cream-colored stoneflies emerging from their nymphal shucks, traversing dexterously over the boulders though they had just moments ago transitioned from their underwater existence to a terranean one.

Now the moon had risen above the swaying trees and shone in a bleached streak on the rushing river, which made the sound of ever-new water tumbling over rocks from time's cellar.

It is good sometimes to say an invocation, to call on powers beyond one's own.

Little moon, I implored, *shine me a way back to camp.*

Shin-deep, I picked my way across the shallows that were warmer than the air until the balminess covered me to the waist. I had rowed the upcoming beat of water just an hour ago and recalled it clear of snags. Still, picturing how swiftly the sharp branch of a single deadfall could snare me permanently, it was all I could muster to wade a little deeper, to lift my feet from the riverbed. How bottomless the dark water seemed. But how it seemed to hold me too, a buoyant trout fly fastened to the most gossamer of monofilaments, cast into the thalweg. And the fish that ascended to engulf me was not the dread I had expected, but the sensation that the current carrying me through wave train, hissing riffle, and slower, moon-blanched pool was the Great Current herself that permitted and transmuted everything.

I came sidelong into shore, stood dripping in the bonfire's glow reflected beneath the cutbank, eye to eye with the big trees' roots. Muted by the moving water that still seemed to be tossing my body about, I heard three voices and clambered up the bank toward them, careful not to flatten the mass of hatching insects. Giant nocturnal stonefly: emerges after nightfall with stunted wings, or without wings at all. I had a hot steak, which I devoured, a cup full of wine, which I drained, a roaring blaze to warm me, and later, in our tent, the warm body of a beloved: wings enough.

~

It's 3:33 a.m. and beside me my son sleeps, his posture recalling mine as I drifted down the Yellowstone that night: palms up, arms open at the sides.

"Inherent in story," Barry Lopez writes, "is the power to reorder a state of psychological confusion through contact with the pervasive truth of those relationships we call 'the land.'"

Of late, I have neglected the story the river told me that night, a tale of release. Given the fiscal and prenatal variables, it seems impossible to figuratively repeat the pose—the one the river taught me—but I try nonetheless. I leave his warm bed, creep into the living room, open my phone and call the insurance company, get, as expected, the answering machine, and, rescued by my own story, say thanks but no thanks to the job.

HEATHEN

In a blue plastic sled, Luca drags our freshly felled Christmas tree, a rangy, asymmetrical bantamweight, toward the car, where Mary waits to sign off on our choice. A dusting of snow cushions our footfalls. The air is hung with the scent of our fresh-cut pine, its base already beaded with sap. From the north, a wind blows through the mountainside of pines, playing an eerie note.

"What's that?" Luca asks.

"What's what?" I say.

"That noise."

"Wind, blowing through the trees."

"Nice to meet you, wind," he says. He looks down at our tree, then back up at the windblown ridge populated by its kin. "Sorry about your friend, trees."

Back at the car, Mary looks up from her book and smiles, pleased with our bedraggled harvest. For a family of procrastinators, it's early for a tree, but the weather had us feeling festive. And she seems unburdened, lightened by my decision to turn down the job offer. The money will come, she assured, adding that she's another day closer to carrying the baby to full term and is starting to like her chances. As I tie the tree's sticky trunk to the roof, I pause to look south at the town of Bonner. On the valley floor a few thousand feet below us, the Clark Fork and Blackfoot join but are immediately impeded by Milltown Dam. Built in 1906, the dam's resulting impoundment has become the resting place of more than seven million cubic yards of toxified sediment—enough to fill one hundred football fields thirty feet deep—the result of upstream mining and related environmental abuses. Suffice it to say, no one thought to ask: To who else's valley might this river someday flow?

For more than a century, the fallout from mining and smelting in the headwaters of the upper Clark Fork gradually made its way eighty-some miles down the basin to the reservoir. Citing the dam's structural failings and potential threats to the downstream aquifer, the Environmental Protection Agency declared the impoundment a $1.3 billion Superfund site. Though the Atlantic Richfield Company procured the upstream mine only after it closed, in 1977, and hardly profited before shutting down operations for good in 1982, it was nonetheless found liable for the cleanup, as it owned the mineral rights and, by law, the ledger and tab. While the company explores cleanup options, the issue continues to agitate local political circles. "REMOVE THE DAM, RESTORE THE RIVER," reads a bumper sticker created by a local conservation organization. "REMOVE MISSOULA, RESTORE THE VALLEY," reads a rebuttal printed up by some Milltown residents. Smaller communities like Milltown are rightly curious as to why Missoula has seen $4.8 million in restoration money, while the upstream towns have seen a relative pittance.

Behind the scenes, while local politicos and nonprofits square off, some creative abatement is taking place. The Washington Companies of Montana, for example, which owns liability on several other upper Clark Fork mines, recently founded and now operates Envirocon (the environmental cleanup company being paid to restore Milltown), as well as Montana Rail Link (which is being paid to transport loads of dredged toxic sediment up the valley to the town of Opportunity). We may be more than a century removed from the Butte labor riots of 1914, or from the 1917 fire at the Speculator Mine that killed almost two hundred workers, but the fungoid profiteering hasn't lost a step.

The current abuses prove once again the paucity of historical memory in our state, where the extraction mind-set has reigned for centuries. Upper Clark Fork settlements were built largely on the labor of tens of thousands of American immigrants—Irish, Czech, German—hardscrabble workers who toiled for the so-called Copper Kings, William Clark and Marcus Daly—tycoons who repeatedly introduced, rooted, and perpetuated an arcane way of life, the results of which Montanans still suffer. Along with Rockefellers, Hearsts, and Heinzes, the Copper Kings owned the nation's largest silver mine, high-yielding gold mines, over a million acres of timber, the biggest smelter in the world, and countless human beings from all walks of life. They owned editors, archbishops, congressmen, and senators. "They even," wrote Timothy Egan, "bribed grand jurors who were assigned to look into bribery."

In its heyday, Butte produced over 9.6 million metric tons of copper, mostly for use as telegraph wires and in lightbulbs, and $48 billion (in today's dollars) worth of ore. Since 2005, though, Butte's copper has become synonymous with large-scale pollution and the Berkeley Pit, a mile-wide ecological abomination that serves as a settling pond and that stretches nearly two thousand feet underground, of which half is filled with water—that is, if a large volume of liquid registering a pH of 2.5, the acidity of lemon juice, can rightly be called water. In 1995 a migrating flock of more than three hundred geese landed in the pit and died soon after from contamination. Today a siren called the Phoenix Wailer screeches an unbearable series of tones nonstop to frighten waterfowl away.

~

In the back of the Subaru, Luca bashes two plastic dinosaurs together with loud, saliva-loaded roars. We wind our way down the logging road and through Milltown, past the company houses, their wood paneling stained yellow from smoke, and eventually turn west at the reservoir. Even if removed successfully, the twenty-eight-foot-tall dam and by proxy its sediment will cast a pall on the downstream portions of the river. Generations will have to pass before the toxic particulate, released when the river flows freely again, has been thoroughly diluted throughout the river system; even then, unmitigated upstream sites will, with each spring's runoff, re-toxify the water downstream, the previously mitigated stretches. "Physical changes made to a river conflict with natural processes, resulting in damage," writes hydrologist Luna Leopold, a bald fact our princelings of profit choose to obscure.

What biological and behavioral toxins will Luca have to dilute and mitigate from my generational line? Doubtless there is plenty of remediation needed due to my side of the genetic valley, I think, looking down from the overpass at a view of the Clark Fork. As a guide, I tend to divide rivers into reaches, stretches of water eight to twelve miles long that are floatable in several hours; but to truly fathom a river is to know it from its headwaters to its mouth, a body of water in constant arrival, an extension of everything upstream and down. It sounds overly philosophical but it's actually ele-mental: to acknowledge our generational non-separateness, our interpenetration, is to take a step toward preservation and transformation.

At home I drop Luca and Mary, seat the tree in a stand, load the car with my hunting gear, and drive toward a remote trailhead where I fall asleep in the car with my wool pants on.

On my neck, invisible hackles rise in reptilian alert, a familiar but nonetheless quickening backcountry sensation. Deep in grizzly territory, on publicly owned wilderness, several miles from an unmarked trailhead and another ten from a small outpost town, I cup my ear toward the draw and listen: no high-pitched cow elk mew, no buck grunt, no sow bear's warn-ing huff. A still dawn on the snowy Rocky Mountain Front. Laboring uphill through a pewter light I track a single deer along a sharply rising ridge, following each of its heart-shaped hoofprints toward the timberline. After several false sum-mits the tracks die out and, clearing a stand of leafless aspen, I pause to catch my breath. Stones of hail drop from the sky, ticking my upturned face. I tilt my head and open my mouth.

I'm looking for a spot Spurgeon called the Weeping Eye. He shared this reliable location with me in hopes of lead-ing me toward what he called a table deer, as opposed to a trophy, but I'm confused by his cryptic directions. "You'll know it when you see it," he said. "Then hunt your way north until you can glass both draws. From that vantage, just sit."

Several attempts at big game this fall have yielded only "tag soup," a term derived from a hackneyed joke wherein the unsuccessful hunter must boil his unused game licenses to flavor the meatless stock he cooks for his family. Esoteric musings like "hunting is an occupation that adds time rather than subtracting it" have worn thin around home, and I've tapped the bank account with zero returns in the meat department. More than once I've added up gas receipts from the season's jaunts and blushed at the tally: enough to buy an entire side of grassfed beef or bison. Pushing these calculations to the back of my mind, I press up the steep pitch, a loaner rifle slung over my shoulder.

Sudden, slicing the quiet and rushing down-mountain, a wind cuts across the scarp, rattling the scree at my feet. In a crazed grain, sunrise spills over the horizon, blinding me for an instant, then the air stills again and I stop, scenting the proximal ozone. In the day's new light, I see a hundred yards off the feature on which Spurgeon bestowed his moniker: a deep circular forbidding gorge in the side of the cliff from which a trail of sand and choss has fallen. *Is* falling. If I stand still enough and trap my breath inside my chest, I can almost hear the crumbled earth trickling down the sheer mountain face. I tell myself that the wind must have set it in motion, but any number of mammal species could have sent it cascading from the wide cave. The Weeping Eye is the kind of hollow that could house a large predator, or inside which a large predator could house its spoils undisturbed.

Though my instincts urge me to move on, out of perceived danger, a more tangible and demanding sense of astonishment shackles me in place. How many two-legged thinking mammals across the eons have ascended this ridge spine, stood precisely where I'm standing, and been rendered speechless with awe? Regarding the circumference of my surroundings, I lift my arms to the sky and shudder wildly, sensing that others once left their wonder here as well. Perhaps the ghost wash of it hasn't entirely dispersed. Yeats said that a ghost is someone who felt intense emotion just before they died, and that the emotion was strong enough to hold their molecules together for a few months after their death or sometimes longer. Not that someone necessarily died here. But could a portion of what we feel most intensely somehow take residence at the foot of what we witness, an offering of sorts to the majesty of the earth?

After a spell, I no longer feel threatened by the grotto—rather, pulled to it. It's the kind of place a hermit could live, someone like Dōgen, who in thirteenth-century Japan said, "Mountains belong to the people living there, and . . . are fond of wise people." I can't imagine being acknowledged by the land, let alone being regarded fondly. And I know I'm not wise. But I am certain that a person does not attain wisdom without access to places such as this one, places of deep, resonant quietude. Every wisdom tradition in the world contains stories of human beings retreating into uninhabited places in search of the repose and illumination they eventually carried back to society. Gautama Buddha made dozens of rainy-season retreats into the forest, where he remained in solitude for sometimes several months at a time. Jesus's forty days in the desert readied him for his gravest trials. The wealthiest of kings left large parcels of land accessible to seekers of all kinds.

The knowledge that sanctuaries like this are under siege scares me more than any apex predator. Nationally, most would scoff at Dōgen's notion. Prevailing opinion says the land exists primarily as a resource for humans to profit from and subsequently disregard. Such a mind-set explains why landscapes like this face legitimate danger. I realize that anyone hell-bent on destroying a place like this, or selling it off, or placing it in careless hands of billion-dollar corporations would say "Dōgen who?" Fewer and fewer human beings aspire to the type of enlightened relationship to which the old monk refers.

But if our wildest public landscapes begin to vanish, if they end up in the hands of corporations or the überelite, the collective losses will be of fatal consequence to us and our future generations. To lose a place like this to cynical greed or irresponsible management would be to lose a venerable elder: not only the physical body and the mind associated with that body, but also the vast and profound experience and intelligence stored within that mind. To relinquish such a location would be to relinquish a portion of what Paul Shepard called our shared imagination—not to mention a place where one (a globally privileged one, yes, but a relative peasant compared to the economic forces that threaten our wild lands) can reliably gather sustainable food and generate income. And such a loss of publicly owned land would be potentially fatal to our spiritual, intellectual, and physical survival.

I can't say how long I rant like this in my head, but eventually the existential, the philo-political, wimples beside the practical. Recalling the empty chest freezer back home and my fruitless deer hunting this season, I return my attention to the physical: in particular, the strand of spring water eking from the granite batholith near my feet. I have a full bottle in my hip pack, but I crouch down and with my open hands bring a sip to my mouth. Bright splotches of yolk lichen surround the spring, tiny thousand-year-old flares. With a layer of perspiration cooling quickly on my neck, I begin to calculate the drive time home, the hours Mary has endured alone and sacrificed to this pursuit. That's it, I declare to myself, I'll take the bagel for the season. *Nada*, I whisper. With my pack leaned against a tree, I sit chagrined, resolved to coming home empty-handed yet again. Though perhaps the discovery of this singular place will be my consolation, an inedible one.

After a good while the sun rises to that detrimental, too-revealing aspect angle the hunter dreads, and I stretch out my left leg and then my right. I stretch my arms and then my knuckles, unzip my pack and draw out a PowerBar. On the grassy slope below me I notice something, a tawny, oblong bush, leafless, that I don't recall from the hike in. When the bush begins to move, I register that it's a mule deer buck cresting the hill now broadside at twenty yards, nearly too close to shoot with a scoped, high-powered rifle. For years I've heard fellow hunters' stories of animals "giving themselves up," and found them hard to believe. And I'd always thought of the Spanish philosopher's notion of prey anticipating, on some level of consciousness, its death, as highfalutin. But here is a deer walking straight toward me.

To keep myself from shaking, I twist my torso inward and hug my right knee with the inside of my left elbow, then bring my rifle to my shoulder and stare through the scope down the reticle, placing the frail crosshairs just behind the buck's front shoulder. At the shank end of an exhaled breath, I squeeze the trigger. The deer buckles at the shot, runs five strong steps, and drops; heart shot, it begins to heave out final breaths. I unchamber the empty rifle round and finger the warm brass cartridge, place the gun on safe, and walk downhill. For the mindful hunter this is when all the consequence comes flooding in. I sit down next to the animal and wrap my hand around its antlers. Already its eyes have glazed. I touch its side and thank it, pledge to extend its life in savored meals. Field dressing the buck with shaking hands, I slice my left index finger near the half-moon in the nail, an accidental gash from which the blood flows freely.

⌒

Before Western religion and its trappings took root in the region, the geographical space between neighboring groups of Native tribes afforded a certain cosmological freedom. (Some would assert that this notion that space equals intellectual/moral freedom exists to some extent in Montana to this day.) This is not to imply that tribal coexistence was without violent conflict, of course—not for a moment—but rather that physical distance between people engendered tolerance toward, or at base the ability to ignore, differing beliefs and practices. Of course the early black robes in Montana were charged with converting a "territory full of heathens," a tragic and ignorant aim that initiated the severing of the body of a people from its collective mind, the land.

The word "heathen," rife with negative connotations, has nearly become a slur. An early definition of the word, though—"one who prays in the heather"—is one I think of often when engaged with untamed places, where I can feel the land, and what Rick Bass called "its considerable powers coming up through my feet and hands." A decade from now, when the fight for our public lands ensues, when a suit is filed with the Federal Election Commission against several Montana writers, myself included, for donating editorials in favor of public land to newspapers throughout the state—alleging that the five-hundred-word essays we donated exceeded the five-thousand-dollar limit for political contributions—I'll return to the Weeping Eye in an editorial and defend the wild place as vehemently and mightily as I can. For those who pray in the heather, destruction of church is an unpardonable sin.

BLACK RIVER, BRIGHT STARS

Christmas slips by without fanfare, then New Year's, after which we enter what Nancy, stethoscope in hand, calls the gravy days.

"Let's keep her in there until the due date, but if something comes loose and you go into labor today, everything will be fine."

Mary exhales for what seems like an entire minute, prelapsarian relief glowing in her eyes. She peels her eyes from the floor, turning in profile to glance out the window. Hands on her belly, she surveys a landscape locked in snow, the pines sugared, the ground covered in posthole snow and hardpan ice.

"Wait," she says with a jolt. "Did you say keep *her* in there?"

Nancy straightens up.

"'Keep 'er in there,' I said. You know, like 'Git 'er done.'"

With knitted eyebrows Mary stares at her nurse practitioner, who begins to thumb almost too nonchalantly through a pile of medical charts.

"Okay. Either way. I'm good with healthy," Mary says.

⸮

"Coyote was walking through the forest when it began to rain," I tell Luca, beginning a version of an old Clatsop tale as I put him to bed later that evening. "When the rain didn't quit but fell harder and colder, he hid beneath a cedar tree.

The tree kept him dry for a while, but it was the beginning of the rainy season and so the rain fell for days and then weeks and by and by Coyote was sopping wet and shivering and starving. 'This is not at all what I had planned,' he moaned. 'I will likely die a lonely, frigid death far from home. But wait: I am the wisest, most cunning animal in the entire forest. Surely I can think myself out of this trouble.'

"Just then he caught a glimpse of Woodpecker, who was perched high in the cedar tree. 'Woodpecker, about that favor you owe me? Don't forget, I am the one who made your beak so sharp. So why don't you peck me a giant hole in this cedar?' And Woodpecker did as he was told."

"Last time you told me that Coyote punched a hole in the tree," Luca says.

"I forgot about Woodpecker, but you're right, the tree was hollow last time. Anyway, after Woodpecker hollowed out the tree Coyote climbed high into the branches and scared all the squirrels into the hole, then shimmied down the tree, slid into the hole, and pounced on them. As the weeks passed, he ate the squirrels one by one and eventually curled up and fell asleep in the cedar shavings at the bottom of the trunk. You know how nice it is to go to sleep when the rain is falling? Well, Coyote slept like that for a very long time until finally a beam of sunlight came through the hole and fell across his face, waking him.

"'Ahhhhh,' he said, 'what a lovely sleep that was.' He stretched his limbs and listened to the birds singing and decided it must be spring, time to return to the forest. And so, he shimmied up the inside of the tree, and tried to jump out of the hole—but he was stuck! His belly had grown too much after eating all of those squirrels and not exercising."

"I bet he had to poop," Luca laughs.

"You know it. He pushed himself back down into the base of the tree, where he began to moan, 'I am going to die a lonely death in a hollow tree while the rest of the creatures enjoy spring.' He cried and gnashed his teeth in misery. 'But wait, I am Coyote, the wisest and most cunning animal in the entire forest, and surely I can think of a way out of this mess,' he said, kicking the bones of one of the squirrels he'd eaten. The bones flew everywhere, giving him an idea."

"This bone part's new," Luca says. "Is this when he takes his body apart? That's what I said was weird."

"Why did you say it was weird?"

"Because even when he takes his arms and legs off there's no blood."

"You don't think animals talking to one another is weird?"

"That's the same thing you said last time. Keep going."

"So, Coyote took his arms off one by one and threw them out the hole. Then he took his legs off too and threw them out. Last time you asked how he takes his legs off if he doesn't even have his arms and I can't give you an answer to that. So anyway, he popped off his ears and nose and tail, and while he's at it, he thought, he might as well take out his eyes, so he plucked them out too. And with all his might he shimmied up the inside of the tree like a snake, poked through the hole, and slid down the trunk into the sunlight. He put on his forelegs, and he put on his hind legs, he put on his tail and his ears and his nose—but just as he's started to sniff out his eyes, Raven flew over, swooped down and plucked Coyote's eyes off the ground.

"'Crawk, Coyote,' Raven called, 'I've got your eyes.'"

"Raven does not like Coyote," Luca says, grimacing.

"No, they aren't exactly pals."

"What's a pal?"

"A friend. You and Solan are pals."

"Yeah, we wrestle but we always high-five when we say bye."

"Well, Raven wanted to rule the forest, and even though Coyote begged, Raven dropped the eyes in a mountain lake, where they sank toward the bottom. 'Coyote, Cutthroat Trout is about to eat your eyes,' called Raven, as he disappeared into the sky.

"Coyote moaned, 'This cannot be. I'm doomed to die a blind death here at the start of my favorite season. But wait—'"

"I know this part," Luca says.

"And so Coyote started to slink around the forest with his nose to the ground. For days he did this. He didn't say a word to the other animals, and they started to get suspicious. Black-Tailed Deer even saw him bump into a wild rose bush, and whispered to her fawns that Coyote had gone blind. Coyote heard Black-Tailed Deer, though, and placed two rose petals over his eyeglasses. By and by—"

"How long is by and by?" Luca asks.

"You mean is it an hour or the next day? I don't know. It's just something a teller says when time passes in a story. But that's a good question. *By and by*, Coyote ran into Slug, who said, 'Oh, Coyote! It is good to see you. I've heard from Black-Tailed Deer that you have gone blind. She said you ran into her last week as well. I'm very sorry to hear this.'

"'Come now, Slug. Coyote, blind?'

"'Old friend, aren't you're wearing rose petals over your eyes?'

"'These aren't rose petals, Slug, but special glasses that help me see spirit rays.'

"'Spirit rays? I have never seen spirit rays. Tell me, Coyote, what exactly do they look like?'

"'Oh, I couldn't begin to describe them. They're the most glorious spectacle in the entire rainforest, but you must see for yourself. Here, I'll loan you these glasses for a moment. However, they only work if you pull out your own eyes first. I'd rather not hold them, for sanitary reasons and all, but just this once I'll keep track of them for you,' Coyote said.

"Slug did as she'd been told, and after snatching up her eyes, Coyote placed the rose petals over Slug's face.

"'Something must be wrong with these glasses,' Slug said. 'I can't see a thing.'

"'Of course you can't,' Coyote said, popping Slug's eyes into his own eye sockets and instantly regaining his sight. 'I am Coyote, the wisest, most cunning animal in the entire forest—did you actually think I would treat you fairly? Those weren't spirit ray glasses, but petals plucked from a wild rose bush. How could you have trusted me, Slug? For your folly you will never again see with your eyes, and will only know where you are by feeling your way around the forest.'

"And that is the story of how Coyote almost lost his eyesight and how Slug got banished to a life of blindness."

"I put a coyote in my project for school," Luca says.

Once he's asleep, I lean in on the diorama he's been working on for school, a miniature valley fashioned from chicken wire and papier-mâché that resembles our own. With a glue gun he seated a small plastic palomino horse on the green felt valley floor, and with scissors cut a winding creek from a sheet of blue felt. Real pebbles stand in for boulders, chunks of moss gathered from the backyard look like cliffs, and the tips of actual evergreen boughs make perfect bankside pines. Lamplight falls across the plastic animals he's glued to the green felt slope: horse, coyote, beaver, cougar, black bear, otter, and a plastic man.

Very early the next morning, inspired by my son's imagination, I'm hiking through a low-hung fog to the actual saddle in search of wolf sign. There've been rumors of a sighting on the south-facing bowl, and I want to see if any tracks remain in the fresh snow. I huff the pitch. At ridgeline, the wind blows chaff across ground made bare by previous wind. Winter grass trembling over snow. A tight gathering of curled, white-tipped bird droppings, left by a covey of Hungarian partridge that had roosted tail to tail. But no wolf tracks. And so, against the forked trunk of a favorite ponderosa, I recline, watching the cloud break into clouds, until my accumulated sweat goes cold and I begin to shiver. Sitting up, I am startled to see a large coyote with a ginger coat standing no more than twenty feet away. No telling how long it had stood there, breath blooming before its face. It regards me for a moment, and flashes away over the rise. That it might have, even for a moment, considered me potential prey gives me a brief flutter of fear, then a rare but distinct lilt of childlike escape.

"We live in a cage of light, an amazing cage," Ikkyū wrote. "Animals, animals without end."

The coming days sweep past like a squall shot through with arterial sunlight—grains of snow that gallop headlong across the street until the wind gives way and they come suddenly to rest on the blacktop, melting in a blare of light—and brim with more glad tidings: an acceptance email explaining that a magazine will buy an article with payment on signed contract, a rarity in the freelance world; another message notifying me that the most distinguished poetry journal in the country has accepted three of my poems for publication, offering a robust payment contract to boot; and, unfathomably, a phone call from the editor of a reputable university press with news that my manuscript, the manuscript that had been on submission for eighteen months, has been selected for publication. This means nothing for the monthly bottom line, but it is subtle validation of calling, an ornithologist's brief sighting, anyway, of the ivory-billed woodpecker he'd been in search of for years.

I stop my celebration dance to kneel and rub Mary's belly. "You're good luck, Little One."

Mary holds the rectangular laptop proudly on her very round belly and shakes her head, reveling in this last bit of good news. "Luca, come here," she yells. "Daddy's gonna have a book!"

In the corner of the living room, wearing a pair of ski goggles, he has Mary's humidifier cranked up high. He puts his finger over his lips, takes a deep breath as if going under water, and ducks into the dense mist. Emerging from the fog moments later, he wipes the perspiring lenses and, with a lengthy sigh of resignation, raises the goggles onto his head.

"Okay," he says. "Let me see this boring book."

⌣

We gather with friends to watch a Super Bowl in which the juggernaut falls to the underdog in the final minute of play. It's nearly midnight when I pull the car into the driveway, the pines above the house sifting wind, a waning wick moon smudged by a single cloud. I step out of the car into the falling snow, tiny flakes that in the porch light look charged with electricity. Carrying a sleeping Luca, I walk inside and, once down the hallway, place him gently in his bed.

Sitting up with a start, he says, "Story," then falls instantly back to sleep.

From the foot of his bed, I listen to a pair of mating great horned owls exchange calls. Five hoots from a tall backyard spruce tree—the male—followed by nine—the female. A brief screech from the female, announcing the union.

Out in the bright hallway, Mary meets me still wearing her peacoat and scarf. It takes me a moment to decode. The present is a wild season, someone said, not a ruse.

"Should I call Dillon?"

"It would appear so," she replies.

In the predawn hours before the peanut shells have been swept from the bar floors, before the streets have been plowed, before the cars parked by responsible nondriving drinkers have been ticketed, five days after her due date and three months after she nearly arrived small enough to cup in two hands, a healthy baby girl is born. As she grows, she will come to display what her middle-namesake, the surgeon-poet, called "fellowship with the essence."

"If you were a bird and didn't know what color your eyes were, what color would you want them to be?" is the kind of thing Molly Keats will often ask.

Or: "If I say the 'B' word, don't blame me because I don't know what it means."

Or: "I saw Luca's penis in a picture. He's had that thing *forever.*"

Or, as she will ask one dismal winter day with a blue colored pencil in hand: "How do you spell 'My heart leapt with joy?'"

NINE MONTHS, THREE YEARS LATER

November night sky strewn with stars, more than I've ever seen above Missoula, so many stars that within the distant wash I can scarcely distinguish the Big Dipper. We walk up the dark street wearing down coats, me tugging a wool cap over my ears, Mary huddled over a steaming mug of tea. She stops and drinks deeply, then strides further up the block, frozen deer droppings scattering in front of her boots. As she distances herself from me, I look up at the celestial ladle standing on its handle, the original ordering, the naming of which, was arbitrary. Do we strive to order, name what is ultimately chaos, or is there some ineffable order of which we gain mere glimpses, inklings?

"Can you see the Milky Way?" I ask.

"Chris," she says, ignoring my question. She rarely if ever calls me Chris, preferring Christopher, or many nicknames of endearment. "I have to tell you something."

In a speck of time my mind leaps between a dozen possible causes for her graveness, and I conclude that her beloved father has passed away.

"Is it your dad?"

"No. I—." She stops, stricken with that syllable, that single vowel, and begins to sob, her shoulders quaking below the suddenly distant and pitiless stars.

"You're pregnant?"

She exhales, her breath blooming before her face. "Yes."

"Do you know what Luca asked me at dinner tonight?"
Mary says.

We're back inside sitting on the worn couch, alternately dumbfounded with the news, silenced with fear, and
attempting deflated encouragements. Our cheeks ringing
red with night air and worry.

From the armrest I scrape dried applesauce. "What did
he ask you?"

She puts her index fingers and thumbs together, squeezes
them tight to make the space between them miniscule: "He
said, 'Was I ever this big?'"

I marvel at our four-year-old son's prescience, and watch
his mother's face quiver. "What did you tell him?"

"I said, 'Sure you were.'"

Gentle reader, if you are struggling to believe the timing of Luca's clairvoyance, you will find it even harder to
fathom that earlier in the day I had been writing a poem
addressed to a child in its mother's womb. I had started
the poem when Molly was still unborn and Mary was
bedridden with early onset labor contractions, and had
only this afternoon—nearly three years later!—returned
to an abandoned draft. I know this is hard to believe. But
place your thumbs and fingers together the way Mary just
did: Can you trust me this much? Steady those digits,
then, and regard the tiny diamond shape they make. If
you gaze through it, you can approximate the size of my
faith in our ability to raise a third.

"It's not that I'm morally opposed to the idea," I tell myself as I drive across town to teach after dropping Luca at his unaffordable-but-entirely-worth-it prekindergarten program and Molly at her quite-pricey-but-utterly-necessary-and-nurturing day care. "Given the money, I'd raise a dozen, mostly adopted, some ours. Buy a farm. Pull the pin. Get off the wheel. Add up enough crumb-crushers to forget their names more than occasionally. Hell, I'd fix Slinkies for a living."

This is hardly the first self-talk I've engaged in since Mary's revelation, and my conversation with myself continues for a few blocks. Not surprisingly, I get the last words— "Holy shit"—a phrase I've spouted so many times in the past week that I've begun to wonder precisely what holy shit, or *sanctus cacas*, might be. Is it a saint's defecation, or a movement sanctified by a holy person? Is it the chest vault tight with worry, or the four-in-the-morning desolation punctuated by the squeak of grinding teeth? The one-eyed glance at the flagging checking account, or the discovery of an old fragment by Jean Valentine: "Blessed are they who remember that what they now have they once longed for."

Against my better judgment, after dinner, after I've bathed Molly and Luca, clanked dishes into the dishwasher, and sung lullabies, I share the Valentine quote with Mary.

She leans against the broom with her back to me, then turns with a look of hieratic pain in her watery eyes: "But I can't do this. Not now."

A fiercely vital woman, Mary is grittier than anyone I know. But the knowledge that she spent the final third of her last pregnancy confined to bed rest—measuring contractions' duration and intensity, rolling around the house in an office chair for three months, reading scores of Internet articles on preemie survival—must fuel her trepidation. Not to mention Molly's actual birth, during which the arriving child kicked so hard she tore the placenta off the uterine wall. If thoughts tumble through Mary's brain like they do through mine, back and forth between the trivial (we're short on bedrooms) and the unforeseeable (which child will feel neglected and consequently be doomed?), she must be exhausted from the mental gymnastics.

Silent, I try to parse out when Mary could have gotten pregnant. Despite the fact that it took nearly two years of "trying" for her to conceive Luca and then Molly, Mary used oral contraception from soon after Molly stopped nursing up until a month ago. Inspired by new research on the long-term hormonal repercussions of oral contraception, as well as general discomfort, Mary planned to employ other means of birth control as soon as she began to menstruate, but she unknowingly ovulated and conceived before she even cycled, which made my vasectomy, scheduled a few months out, moot for the time being.

"Is this even possible?" I ask myself aloud.

"Is what possible?" Mary responds.

"Nothing," I say, and offer a tight-limbed hug.

She shirks my embrace. "No, say it."

"I'm just wondering if there's some book." I kneel down with the dustpan to scoop up the pile of crumbs, hair, bread ties, and a penny. "Some baby-planning literature that says getting pregnant under these circumstances can even be accomplished."

Now she is silent, mercifully—this living text in front of me elucidating all that needs elucidation. Bless her for not saying aloud what a fool I am.

⌒

We dicker over Thanksgiving plans. Mary wants a few close friends for dinner and I want our traditional over-the-mountain-top gathering of nearly thirty guests: mounds of fresh-cooked game and magnums of wine with which to wash down the feast, the children running up and down the stairs to sneak spoonfuls of homemade whipped cream before dessert, the sprawl of dishes at the end of the night some saintly friend agrees to wash, the impromptu music session around the fireplace to close the night, one tireless picker playing "Make Me Down a Pallet on Your Floor" while the singers sink into the couch with sleeping children on their laps.

The distraction of celebration wins out.

That Thursday snow falls heavy and wet but I'm too busy smoking duck and pheasant, sautéing three pots of green beans and basting the turkey, to shovel the walkway. The tracked-in slush melts and floods the entryway, spilling into the living room. Bobby lugs in a huge pot of elk shanks osso buco, John cradles a wide iron saucepan that holds an entire braised antelope shoulder simmered in juniper berries and carrots, and Spurgeon has brought slices of toasted baguette onto which he has slathered a red pepper and pine nut pesto topped with blade-thin cuts of grilled venison tenderloin. Esteban lugs several pies. Children are like pies, Chick was fond of saying: a parent's devotion to multiple children not divvied from a single pie, but rather, with each different child comes a separate pie of devotion, apple for one, meringue for another, coconut cream, and so on.

Thank you, pies, for reminding me of Chick. Thank you, dear friends, for coming. Thank you, Esteban, for filling my wine glass again. Thank you, children, for running around laughing and screaming and crying, for falling, knees first, onto the hardwood, for breaking two plates. Thank you, Joellen, for opening your guitar case and playing that Gillian Welch we love to sing. Thank you all for amply and exuberantly distracting me from my hidden cognitions and capacious fears. Thank you, Mary, sitting alone on the arm of the couch with the still-hushed-secret inside your body, sipping your "cocktail" of cranberry juice and soda water: I hope you can muster a seed's worth of gratitude for all of this noise.

Blissful shiver of memory: Mary leaning back to tell Luca, then eighteen months old, still in his car seat: "You're going to see so many things in this world. You've got a long journey ahead of you." For no reason that I knew of. Just to tell him. Just to say it.

Where did the winter, that quicksilver season of numb appendages and snowsuits, go?

It's April now and Mary's showing. Everyone is shocked to see her bump, her outie belly button pushing against a tightened camisole, and we're telling everyone that the pregnancy has warped past us because we spent the first six months of it in denial. To our closest friends we explain the long odds of it all: trying for two years before Luca, trying for nearly two more before Molly, then not even a single cycle before conception. To our closest friends we explain the long odds of it all; to others, acquaintances on the periphery whose unease with the news and supressed judgment we can't help but sense, we simply smile and nod.

I would be lying if I said I haven't registered occasional embarrassment at others' reactions that hint, however vaguely, at our social irresponsibility for our growing nuclear family. But the meadowlarks, returned from their wintering grounds and gushing song over fledging grasses, call me back into my physical body, which finds itself at work yet again on the river. Or maybe I'm easeful because Mary bristles with light, abloom with the life within her. She comes home early this morning from a walk in the greening hills punctuated by shooting stars and balsamroot, telling of a fox near the trail, a vixen with kits.

"They all disappeared into the grass for a minute or two, then the mom leapt up"—she makes an attacking gesture with her hands—"and pounced on something."

⌒

In many of the world's classrooms I have been a poor student, but I have studied light. I have seen it linger, kindling like a banked fire in a wrack of clouds at dusk. I have watched it strike the same fence post each month of the year, its blow in August that of a circus strongman, in December that of a child who can barely hoist a hammer. I have observed the way it forms with air and water, a kind of elemental trinity, an embodiment of all things essential and ungraspable. And longed for: rain on the tongue, wind in the hair, sun on the face, the barest of sanctions that slip ineffably through our fingers.

Edward Hopper once said that the only thing he "ever wanted to do was to paint sunlight on the side of a house." I would second that ideal occupation, but when Hopper said siding, I meant my son standing under our blossoming pear tree, holding a dandelion gone to seed, his lips moving in conversation with something, or with himself. I watch him stand there for several minutes, about as long as it took the sunlight to make its 92.4-million-mile way to his face, to say what it says to his skin this Mother's Day.

May: the month of morel-and-shallot cream sauces drizzled over charred sockeye, of never-enough mushrooms gathered by the children then shoveled post-saute, raccoon-like, with both hands into their mouths. The month of lilacs opening and daubing under our noses the earth's finest French perfume. To say nothing of the tacky cottonwood buds peeling apart and casting their scent, upon which heathens like me base my faith.

May: the way one of Mary's students, slurring the word, says her name.

I stand at the kitchen sink cleaning yesterday's harvest, tapping out the cavern of each morel, blowing soil from the caps' brain-like folds. At my feet, Molly sleeps in the jogger. An hour ago we ran along the creek and, standing on the cutbank together, felt fresh snowmelt rumbling cobbles under our feet. In the dining room Luca writes a makeshift Mother's Day card on the chalkboard easel. Mary's favorite, "To Live Is to Fly," plays quietly on the stereo, and leaf-steeped light pours through the west window.

"I'm hungry," Luca says.

"We'll eat after Mom wakes up. Morels, asparagus, and salmon. You want a snack?"

"I'm *really* hungry. Do we have to wait?"

"It's Mother's Day. Can't eat without Mom on Mother's Day."

"I don't want it to be Mother's Day. I don't ever want it to be Mother's Day again."

"Bud," I say, looking up from my preparations, "you're here because of your mom. You wouldn't be out picking morels with me or playing with your friends, you wouldn't be here on Earth at all without Mom."

From his hand the chalk falls to the floor, and without further warning he begins to bawl.

"I'm sorry," I say, trying to rescue the moment. "I was too hard on you."

"No, that's not why," he says through tears.

"What is it then?"

It takes him a while to settle. Finally he offers:

"I don't want to leave this Earth."

⁓

June's clearing waters burst with prolific hatches of aquatic insects: hypnotizing waves of caddis and giant bumbling sedges; several varieties of stoneflies, including the mythic *Pteronarcys californica*, whose mating flights ascend the afternoon canyons like miniature alien invasions; and mayflies such as the linebacker-stout green drake, often neglected by anglers in favor of larger bugs, but never by the river's biggest trout. At evening in the half-light, long after the last raft has been winched onto its trailer, a relatively dainty, just-emerged sulfur dun floats into a slick behind a boulder; a trout tilts toward it, and true summer, with its magnitude of angling riches, officially arrives.

For a few weeks, even the most grizzled, long-tenured guides can get along, so deep is our list of viable fishing options, so wide our field of play. You can get on early and pull streamers while shade still glazes the water, targeting an alpha trout that slid into the shallows after dark and hasn't returned to its midday station; you can join the masses during bankers' hours and, what with the ample pace and still imperfect water clarity, fare well despite jockeying with several boats; or you can sleep in late, cruise the farmer's market with, or for, your fishing partner, and later wet wade the witching hour just before dark when masses of ovipositing caddis fill the air with impossible density, land in your ears, your nose, your mouth, lay their eggs at waterline on your bare knees or thighs. Sit back on the bank and when it's too dark to see your fly, open another beer for your partner, a bottle of wine, maybe hum an old Ry Cooder tune because you doubtless are, "living in a poor man's Shangri-La."

Then get up and do it again.

Or broom the fishing for a morning and bathe yourself in tanager song, their plumage garishly bright in green willows. Follow a leap-able spring creek far into a meadow where the windblown grasses toss in sync with a lone chestnut mare's tail. Ignoring the mosquitos you stir, creep on all fours toward the shadow-fish you might or might not see finning in shallow, air-clear water, the largest brown trout—if it is indeed a trout and not a swaying bed of weeds—you've laid eyes on in years. Forget retrieving the rod you left at the boat and inch closer, watching the maw of the buck flash white as it opens to take a nymph, closer still. From your knees, ease your left arm under the cutbank, and when the fish sees your

upstream shadow and instinctively whirls toward its sanc-
tuary, feel all two and a half feet of it, kype to tail tip, slide
across your open palm.

It is Montana, after all, where these sorts of things can
happen.

⁓

Ten whole days before the mid-July due date. Safe to
have a few friends over for a bonfire, right? Some late-
night poem reading and mandolin picking, a few sips of
wine under the stars? As night falls, we gather the kids
into sleeping bags, their frames soften with the fetching
weight of slumber. Mary tucks Luca and Molly in bed and
sneaks off to sleep herself, but I stay up singing and hit
the sheets perfumed with wood smoke, my head aswirl
with Li Po's ancient lines:

> To wash and rinse our souls of their age-old sorrows
> We drained a hundred jugs of wine.
> A splendid night it was. . .
> In the clear moonlight we were loath to go to bed,
> But at last drunkenness overtook us;
> And we laid ourselves down on the empty mountain,
> The earth for a pillow, and the great heaven for a coverlet.

"Chris," Mary says.

Only it's morning now, it's dawn. I know the tone she's
using, but there's a dream to which I would prefer to return.
Sweet backyard crossbill high in the blue spruce, sing me
back to sleep.

"Chris," she says again. "I'm going to have this baby. Today. This morning!"

Excretia divina!

"Are you serious?"

Yes, she is.

Am I a full-fledged ass to move straight from the bed into the shower for a shave?

Yes, I am.

But I don't smell like bonfire and wine, when, a few hours later—after a relatively placid labor during which we hold hands and become instant best friends with the attending nurse—our daughter Lily Mae joins us on this "ground-of-many-gifts." Ten days before her due date. On Mary's birthday. At the exact hour and *precise minute* (10:32!) of Mary's birth, thirty-five years earlier.

Are you serious?

Yes, I am.

Numbers, said Hermes Trismegistus, are the secret words by which the world and heavens tell each other what will be.

THREE

Quiet, watchful, unquestionable as a pea, our month-old Lily is fair-haired and fair-skinned, lithe and hazel-eyed. As a good friend had it, while her dark-eyed, roughhousing, hairy-footed siblings may well be hobbits, Lily is decidedly an elf. I steer the boat down the tail end of the Alberton Gorge, a slow, quiet glide through a narrow canyon, while Mary shades the elfin one with the brim of her straw hat. Slurp of an oar blade, squeak of the oarlocks. Water lapping at the hull. Buoyant in their life vests, Luca and Molly dangle off the gunnel as I navigate the boat around a huge, two-story basalt outcropping atop of which balances a lodgepole pine. May's runoff put it there. At one time it was snow, rain, cloudburst in the headwater peaks, this water on which we float.

"Hard to imagine water that high," Mary says, looking up at the boulder. "With it being so low right now."

Sleeping now on her drowsy mother's breast, the nursing baby was once desire, coupling, atoms, zygote within egg— and yet it's hard to imagine her anywhere other than here.

We anchor at the mouth of Quartz Creek, whose deep emerald pulse frolics through the dry cobbles before joining the Clark Fork. While Mary nurses Lily, "the Bigs" and I hopscotch up the tributary on boulders that breathe a dry, mineral heat. There's no sign of any fellow creature whatsoever—no drying ouzel tracks or raccoon prints—until we reach the railroad trestle and come upon a transient's encampment: fire ring, coffee can, the cooked, clean ribs, spine, and gray-eyed skull of a cutthroat trout. Bluebottle flies blacken the carcass's stiff tail. Luca scours around for footprints. I test the coals for warmth, stir the ashes with a stick: the thinnest thread of smoke.

In a life properly lived, wrote a friend, you're a river. I take this to mean that headlong shots through roaring box canyons are inevitable; along with meanders, wanderings, in which the main channel finds itself far from its original course; tepid, drought-drained summers in which trout flag will be endured; as well as winters when water flows black and sinewy against the snow; eddies too, the hypnotic, elliptical movement of water running back on itself, around, and then around again.

Last fall, when Mary conceived, we were eddying.

For the first time in a long while life seemed, in October's holy glow, to have taken its foot off our necks. With two children finally both sleeping through the night, Mary had gone back to teaching full-time, and after guiding all season I had a full teaching schedule along with a couple of days a week to write and fill the freezer with wild food, to relish the season before the cold turned us all inside. Then, with the news of a third, we went cascading again, riding the cataract down a steeply pitched ravine.

In a life properly lived.

As a rower, I long ago realized that muscle and oar can only resist so much, that physical exertion is often inferior to ceding to the always-stronger water, then assessing a new current line and adjusting one's approach from there. Strangely, life has seemed simpler—albeit not financially, or logistically, or emotionally—since I resigned myself to the complexity of our current navigational equation. It's not that all my angst floated off downstream, just that I have far less time to tend it. Now and then I'll get to worrying about our ecological footprint and the gas our allegedly "fuel fit" minivan guzzles or doesn't, but I am reluctant to succumb to the opiate of collective guilt.

To raise a child mindfully is itself an act of radical activism. Che Guevara: "The true revolutionary is guided by a great feeling of love." The mindful parent knows that adding a child to the earth's ledger is consequential; that this act adds challenge, pressure, and acknowledged complicity to the everyday, sometimes driving the stakes straight through our faltering ozone. It's a daily self-subpoena of sorts to raise children with a mind on the earth's health as well, and some days the accompanying ennui is enough to fold me. But a conversation I had the other day with Molly led me to believe we might be okay, come what may. We'd been out picking watercress for a pesto recipe when she asked why we went to the outdoors to find food. I thought about it a while then finally ventured, "Because the earth is good to us."

"Yeah," Molly agreed. "She's our godmother."

⌒

For the better part of three decades, in every activity from schoolyard fights to athletic competitions, I have ardently guarded my groin against harm, but here I am currently exposing it willingly to scissors, needles, scalpels, and a surgical torch. Above me on the ceiling in the urology clinic operating room hangs a painting from the underappreciated psychedelic movement depicting a hunter with bow and arrow crouched on a promontory overlooking a deep sand-stone canyon peppered with game for the taking. Out of habit I begin to ponder the significance of this image as it applies to the loss of one's faculties to procreate; I am teasing out some vague meaning when a needle housing Novocain pierces the shriveled skin of my scrotum.

Women like Mary who have carried, labored, and birthed babies will rightly chortle at my cringing. But isn't this what our outpatient ribbon-clipping ceremony is all about, an attempt at faux martyrdom that might also result in our continued enjoyment of lovemaking without the worry of pregnancy, and without need of accompanying manufactured latex or the hormonal manipulation of oral contraception? *Indeed, martyrdom is mine!* I almost scream as the doctor tugs hard with hemostat on my numb vas deferens and brings a flame to his surgical torch.

"You might smell a little flesh burning here," he says. "Not the most pleasant thing. And then Veronica will be in to stitch you up. You'll want to get ahead of the pain with the Lortab I prescribed. I'd recommend picking it up on the way home before the local wears off. Veronica will give you some special briefs to wear, sort of like a jockstrap, to support things for a few days. Take it easy. No rowing for at least a week, no heavy lifting, and definitely no sex. Put a bag of frozen peas down there every hour or so to reduce the swelling. When you're feeling up to it, we'll get a semen sample and make sure the procedure worked entirely."

On the way home the local wears off and, dizzy with pain, I pick up the prescription along with a bag of Green Giant peas and a bottle of Smirnoff, the latter eventually stashed in the freezer. When the bag stuffed into my briefs thaws out, I hobble from the couch to the freezer for the second and decide to pour myself a few fingers worth of cold Russian water. No lemon, thanks. I have just reclined, albeit gingerly, in bed with the computer and cued up Netflix when I hear Mary and the kids come through the front door, with Luca, now nearly six, barreling down the short hallway to our bedroom with urgent queries.

"Mom says you got special underwear," he yells, hopping up onto the bed. "What part of you did they take out?"

⁓

Outside the window, August's hard pears hang unpicked from heavy limbs. Inside, on the floor, Mary's black dress: the dress I'd zipped her into and out of last night. We dined at a small bistro, splitting a salad of prawns and arugula, a cool green gazpacho, and sharing a rare rib steak. A steel-cold glass of white, followed by a couple Rhones. Then home to the bed where we were young. *Th-thunk* goes a pear landing on the parched, un-watered lawn.

I rise to boil water, and as day dawns cool we sip tea at the kitchen table, enjoying the rarity of a morning alone. Then come the boy's bare, scampering feet on the hardwood. Always the first to rise, he often looks stunned to see us in the morning, as if his nighttime dream journeys have been so extensive he can't believe we're actually still here in the house, right where he left us.

"I had two bad dreams and twenty-thirty good," he says, leaning his warm frame into my chest.

"What were the good dreams about?"

"Dragons."

"How about the bad ones?"

"Dragons."

"Did you have fun with Dillon?" Mary asks of his favored babysitter.

"We played in the sandbox and wrestled with the girls and had two bowls of ice cream for dessert but he said not to tell and then he sang me a special song before bed 'cause I'm the oldest."

"What was the special song?"

"I think it had dragons."

Mary looks quizzically at him for a moment, lets the matter lie. She's pouring her second cup of tea when she tips the spout upward and says, "Ah. Dillon sang you a song about *Puff.*"

"He was a *magic dragon.*"

Hoping to buy us time to drink another quiet cup of tea, I punch up the seventies cartoon version on YouTube and slide the computer screen in front of Luca. "This is the same song!" he exclaims and seems to be watching with interest, but before long his smile contorts into a wince, and then a grimace, and before I can ask what's the matter, he begins to sob suddenly like he'd been stung by a bee. Mary and I cock our heads like two dogs puzzled at their owner's action, then she gathers him into her arms and presses for an explanation.

"It said little boys don't live forever."

There's little use trying to explain that the line "dragons live forever, not so little boys" is a mere metaphor, a symbol for growing up—our young pupil will have none of it.

Finally, after he's found a hint of relief, he says, "I wanna go in my crib."

"Sweetheart," I respond, "you don't have a crib anymore. You got too big for it, remember? It's Lily's crib now." Which launches him into another torrent of sobs.

Even in the days before children, I knew their entrance into my world would render us exposed to life at its most raw, but I hadn't the faintest idea that we would be witness to the Fall itself.

Saw no grouse but feasted on the latest and sweetest of huckleberries I've ever picked. Straight from the bushes, cool and fermented, sugars concentrated as in a raisin. Also caught two brook trout in the tannin-rich creek flanked by ferns and thimbleberry fronds and hung them from a pine bough before gutting them in the stream. Later poached the small fish in butter, salt, cayenne, garlic slivers, and slices of pear from the backyard tree. The tiniest of forkfuls for Lily, who smiled initially, then grimaced, not quite sure what to make of the mouthful.

We're out in the snow dressing a snowman, eighteen-month-old Lily and I. Fir boughs for arms, pinecones for eyes, orange sandbox bucket for hat, carrot for—

"Hey, Lils, where's his nose?"

With tight, red cheeks the bundled girl turns and grins coyly, crunching her tiny first few teeth around the carrot.

Sunday evening, tucked in the corner of the living room decorating the Christmas tree as the snow falls almost weightlessly past the windows, the Bigs hanging ornaments with me, Mary and Lily cooking minestrone in the kitchen when, quite suddenly, I hear Lily cough: a single cough I expect to be followed by another, though when the second doesn't come, I worry that the cougher is choking.

Not altogether unfamiliar to a parent, the situation is nonetheless alarming.

"Sweetie," I yell from behind a limb. "You got that?"

"I got it," Mary calls back.

I position another ornament on a needly branch and wait to see if the hook will hold.

Then, a moment or two later: "Babe?" A dash of fright in her voice. "I need you."

By the time I float into the kitchen, past the bitten-into apple on the floor, Lily's cough has turned into a gag and Mary has her horizontal, positioned properly for toddler-food removal, and is performing hand thrusts with no positive results.

Their eyes—Mary's and Lily's—glisten with fear.

"Go back into the living room," I say, as sternly but tenderly as I can to the Bigs, who have huddled in the threshold.

"I don't like this," Luca says, retreating. "I don't like this."

When I take Lily in my arms she is stiff as a board. Still trying to gag, her body has gone tense with shock.

I try a couple of abdominal thrusts but can't get her drum-tight abdomen to cave.

How intrepidly the mind moves. I can't begin to gather all of what I am thinking as I hold Lily, listening to Mary whisper "Please No Please No Please No," but I know this moment lies far beyond my preparation.

Squeezing hard on her cheeks, I pry Lily's mouth open and try for a mouth sweep but am unable to free the piece of apple. I can touch the lodged piece though, and somehow, in a fit of desperation and against all instructional manuals and odds I manage to push it past the throat cavity and into the esophagus. Lily coughs once, gasps, and begins to cry: a loud and comforting cry, like the first one, just after a birth.

Good. Cry. Keep crying. Let us know you're alive.

Of course, once Lily begins to sob, Mary does as well, her entire body convulsing.

The Bigs are back in the room quickly—perhaps they never moved—holding their parents and their sister. For a spell, for the kids' sake, I try to diffuse the trauma. *Okay, everything's okay. Who wants a cookie? Let's go put a few more ornaments on the tree. Who wants to read a folk tale?* After we are settled, Mary says she needs a moment to herself, and heads upstairs to breathe.

On the carpet, I spot the offending apple—it had been in the center of the dining room table, and Lily, a most mobile toddler, had scaled a chair to reach it—and note the adult-sized bite she had taken out of it: a hunk as round as a silver dollar and thicker than a slice of bread. With Lily in my left arm, I zip it into the front pocket of my jacket. From her perch, Lily points to the corner of the living room with conviction. "Teet-teet, teet-teet," she exclaims. "Teet-teet." It's her word for bird, but I can't find a referent. I hold her tight against my hip and when dinner's ready I call the Bigs, call Mary. *Soup's on:* normalcy, please. Straight away, Molly arrives sucking on her index and middle fingers—she's worried—but Luca and Mary are missing. Maybe they've taken a walk. I check out front, in the garage, in the basement, and finally find them on the floor of her closet, her eyes still wet with tears. Luca sits next to her, his arm around her shoulders.

"He's been sitting here with me," she says. "This whole time. Not saying a thing, just holding his arm around me."

Some nights it takes hours to put the kids to bed. Someone wants a piece of bread with butter, someone forgot to brush his teeth, and someone else is thirsty for a cupful of milk. When we finally have the kids down, Mary and I sit on the old couch looking at the cold fireplace and talk, still breathless with fright, about how unmentionably stiff that body felt in our arms, how close we'd been to *it*. We aren't at all interested in blame but rather recognition of the dire straits we'd entered. When we're talked out, I stand on impulse, kiss Mary on the top of the head, and walk outside into the backyard. Flakes of snow melt on my upturned forehead. I unzip my jacket pocket and eat the entire apple on which Lily had choked. I eat the core, the seeds, I gnash my teeth around the stem, then fall to my knees and utter something in a tongue I cannot distinguish.

Back inside, the house is quiet, dark save for some warm orange light emanating from a candle on the kitchen table.

I can't hear her but I know where to find Mary: kneeling beside them, kissing their foreheads, their heads in her hands like warm bowls of broth. Stepping back from them, she can watch the calm water of sleep hold them buoyantly afloat. She's counting their breathing bodies. Three?

Yes, three.

In this way, with these bolts, I have stitched a quilt.
Cover me with it when I am most cold.

III.

THE NATURE OF WONDER

"We can seek truth without wonder's
assistance. But seek is all we'll do . . . "
—DAVID JAMES DUNCAN

HIGH WATER RISING

The boat felt shot from a sling. Despite my heaving oar strokes, the quaking alders blurred by. Kicked loose from the banks by rapidly rising water—the result of a thunderstorm in the headwaters, rain on sun-softened snowfields—in-stream particulate ticked against the drift boat's fiberglass hull. Holding lies passed by like apparitions. We overtook birds in flight. From the bow seat, aiming well downstream, my friend Jim Harrison made a sharp cast with a weighted streamer, which landed, due to our warping speed, even with the port oar. On a straightaway I looked sternward at our third, Dan—a Montana guide since the 1970s—and shook my head. Without my suggesting it, he had assembled the spare oar and pinned it, at the ready, under his thigh.

"Go another bend or two and I'll spell you," Dan said. He spit a stream of Skoal over the gunnel. "I'd smoke but the boat's going too fast to light a cigarette."

Twenty minutes passed before we reached a side channel two river miles downstream from our launch and eddied out. A bubble line trailed off the grassy island; finally some walking-pace water, a place to exhale. Harrison, a writer best known for a magnanimous output of prose and poetry that is rife with an eloquent and ravenous love of the earth, teased a parakeet-yellow streamer through the soft edge and managed to hook a brown trout, but I regarded the fish, half a yard long and nymph-fattened though it was, as a mere distraction. My focus was on the beast that is Rock Creek in runoff. Even in average flows, the water's steep pitch and boulder gardens make for arduous rowing; and during high-water events, when dead-falls suddenly loosed from logjams can form new strainers and render previously cleared channels impassable, the river inaptly named a creek can take a boat in its teeth and refuse to let go.

To complicate matters, I'd foregone the safer means of available transportation, a self-bailing raft that filters incoming water in and out of its floor, in favor of my very sinkable fiberglass drift boat. For all but the least sensible, Rock Creek in June is raft water; I had chosen the drifter, though, because Jim, at seventy-five years of age, had grown too unstable to fish from a slippery inflatable. Now, too ner-vous to peck at the lavish antipasto he had brought for lunch, I came to terms with my having underestimated the severity of the situation, with my having endangered my aging, not-so-nimble friend. If Jim pitched or the boat swamped, there would be no chance of rescue. Launching had been a bullish call, I concluded, one that was unimpeachably mine.

After lunch, Dan—Jim's friend and fishing partner of many years—spelled me on the oars. Our second heat fed us through a mini-gorge called the Microburst, where decades ago a sudden violent downdraft of wind felled hundreds of ponderosas. Locals call it "a heavy place," as it retains an ominous air. Without missing a stroke, though, Dan slipped us impeccably through two tight S-turns, ran us cork light through a tossy wave train, and, sculling masterfully, fought off a couple of grabby hydraulics. From the stern I watched him scan the hazards ahead of us. Impressively, he stayed several strokes in front of any pending threat. After he'd run the gauntlet, when it came time to swap roles again, I asked him how he'd become such a fine oarsman.

"Got good quick," he deadpanned. "Because I never learned to swim."

Two hours later, with the takeout in sight, we startled in unison to see the Granite County fire truck, sirens blaring, roaring up the ungraded washboard road.

"Luca, your father tells me that you like to ski," Harrison said in his characteristic nasally growl. He rested his ironwood cane on the dining room chair and, smoking an American Spirit to calm his nerves, positioned himself at the dinner table between father and son.

House rules: no smoking. We were making an exception, though, as we had just learned through the grapevine that a guided raft, floating roughly an hour behind ours on Rock Creek, had flipped on a standing wave and lost one of its passengers to a logjam. Just upstream of the Microburst, the experienced oarsman at the helm of that boat had taken the right channel. We'd taken the left. Rescue crews had failed to recover the missing body.

"When you're skiing down the mountain," Jim continued, boring his erratic, half-blind gaze into Luca's, "did you ever see a snow snake?"

"What's a snow snake?" the boy responded with an earnest rise.

I pushed a cheese plate across the table toward a trio of our mutual friends: a novelist, a sculptor, and the retired chair of the English Department. Mary nestled in beside me, Lily on one knee, Molls on the other. In the kitchen, Dan stood over the stove, tending to a roasting leg of lamb.

"A snow snake," Jim replied, smacking at his cigarette, "is a creature that lives under the snow and slithers beneath you while you're skiing."

Luca looked up, his eyes saucer wide.

Wiping cracker crumbs and bits of Spanish cheese from his goatee, Jim drew his face to Luca's. "When a snow snake finds you standing still, it pops its head up and wraps itself around your ankle. Pulling you under the ground forever."

"My goodness, Jim," said the retired English chair suddenly. She set down her glass of wine. "Why on earth would you say such a thing to a boy?"

"The world is a cruel place," he said. He puffed audibly from his cigarette and, rarely one to overdo the couth, hacked a grotesque cough. "The sooner he knows, the better."

⁓

I first met Jim after a reading he had given in Missoula to support the political campaign of Denise Juneau, a Blackfeet political upstart who would go on to become our state's first Native American superintendent of public instruction. Jim had waived his normally robust appearance fee, suggesting instead that donations be made to Juneau's campaign. Afterwards he treated several of the young writers in attendance to a pricey meal at an establishment known for its generous portions of pork belly. A friend of mine whose first book of poems Jim had championed was determined to introduce me to one of my literary heroes, despite my visible trepidation: my hands were shaking.

"Jim, I want you to meet my friend, Chris," Mandy Smoker said, flashing the ferocious, don't-trifle-with-me smile that's known to silence both conference room and tavern.

After growing up in far eastern Montana as a member of the Assiniboine nation, Mandy held the distinguished Richard Hugo Fellowship as a graduate student at the university, and later went on to become a powerhouse paradigm shifter as director of Indian Education for All. "He's the poet and fishing guide I was telling you about."

With no small measure of boredom, with a bear grunt, Jim glanced up from the bistro's wine menu.

"He's originally from Michigan," Mandy added.

"Who the fuck isn't?" Jim said. "Millions of people are. Where in Michigan?"

"East Lansing," I said.

"I went to school there, you know?"

"Yes, I'm aware of that."

"Exactly where in East Lansing?" he asked with suspicion.

"I grew up on Gainsborough. Half a block from Harrison Road."

"Well, why didn't you say so, son? Sit down, I'll buy you a drink!"

Later that summer we began fishing together.

The day after our treacherous float down Rock Creek, we didn't chance the river, which was still on a steep rise, standing straight up on the hydrograph. Instead we drove north to hunt for meadow mushrooms. Or so we said. Really we were "looking things over," Jim's phrase for taking a destination-less drive. After an intense day of rowing, my shoulder muscles felt gelatinous and my palms hived with new blisters. The mid-June morning was languid, and the green-as-they-get foothills were calling out *Verde*, *te que quiero, Verde,* in chorus with Federico García Lorca, the slain but poetically immortal Spanish writer. Given the surroundings and my physical exhaustion, I should have felt spent, if not relaxed, but reality had begun to sink in: we were one wrong river channel choice from having drowned.

At the wheel of Big Ron, Jim's white 4Runner, I twitched with anxiety.

"Let's pull over and have an early lunch," Jim said. Smoke purled thickly from his cigarette, making his gullied face in the window-parried shaft of light appear quite conjured, his bad eye wandering opposite his working eye, one of them, I'm not sure which, attracted to some bird or small god darting beyond my mortal perception. "There should be a word like 'supper' for lunching before noon. Plus, I can tell when a man needs a drink."

"I'm not sure I can handle it," I said, turning the rig off the highway and onto a gravel road just outside of Saint Ignatius. "Still a tad roughed up from last night."

"I'm a little bit hungover too, but that's to be expected of Marines of fly fishing. I'm famished from forging the smithy of my soul—I wrote a poem this morning! Come, we need sustenance."

Flanking the booming massif of the Mission Range, the dirt road skirted a modest family graveyard, its white stones decorated with lilacs and a few overwintered plastic bouquets. I gave it a glance but kept Big Ron aimed toward the wildlife refuge, where there'd be some birds to watch.

"The other day I told Linda what I wanted my gravestone to read. She wasn't happy."

One eye or not, Jim didn't miss much.

I once heard someone close to Jim's family say that the only person capable of writing the "true story" of Jim—including Jim—was Linda, his wife of more than fifty years, who was simply aloof to the task. Sharp, surpassingly gracious, unimpressed by displays of ego, Linda hovered above the fray. And for all the pomp around Jim's status as a legendary gourmand, Linda may have been the best cook in the house. You would feast with Jim at the picnic table for a few afternoon hours on dried pears and sardines and Iberian ham before it came time for him to retire to the desk for a late-afternoon work session, then you would wait at the yard's gate as he made his way slowly to the door, pausing every few steps to lean on his cane—and just as you would turn for the car, Linda would peek out the door. "Won't you stay for supper? Roast pork shoulder with garlic?" And though you were already gorged from the three-hour lunch, you would have to, albeit heroically, make space for some meat that had fallen off the bone.

"What did you propose as an epitaph?" I asked.

Jim snorted out a laugh. "'He Got His Work Done.' She said, 'But what about your family?'"

He had been bickering with one of his daughters, he continued, about what she had called his inattention to her youth. She said he hadn't taken her fishing when she was young. You fished sixty days a year, she leveled, and you never took us. I took you fishing, he replied.

"She held up two fingers: twice."

As I turned Big Ron past the old Woodcock place, narrowly avoiding a painted turtle crossing from pond to overflowing ditch, I felt Jim's admission hit me—harder, perhaps, than any line he ever published. (I've read most of them, revered many.) There was regret in his voice, the tremor of warning.

Above Ninepipe Reservoir, the air was filled with terns and nighthawks on the midday feed, dozens of sharp-winged insect eaters cutting through the air to intercept emergent damselflies and chironomids. In a small cove near the parking lot, four small birds spun dervish-like, stirring the otherwise glassy water, dislodging from the weeds below small particles of food that they dipped down occasionally to eat. Like oblong tops they turned and turned, doing something of which we humans are incapable.

"My God," Jim said. "Four phalaropes! We are blessed!"

Near the shore, I spread out our lunch: crackers, bread, cold cuts of lamb and whole cloves of garlic, fig spread, pickled brussels, several cheeses left over from a shipment a famous chef had sent Jim, some spicy Italian relish procured at Butte's Front Street Market. Like any antipasto meal, it became a test of combining in a single bite as many flavors as possible without maxing out the palate, of finding the proper ratio of spice, sweetness, and salt. I fancied a cracker topped with goat cheese, fig spread, a hot pepper, and some salty meat. Jim ripped off the end of the baguette and stuffed it with a garlic clove and a bloody cut of lamb, then shoved it in his mouth.

"I would watch this lamb from my studio window," he said, chewing unabashedly. "He was a sweetheart. Liked to put his forelegs on our fence so he could lean over and eat our lilacs. Our neighbor who raises them gives me pick each year."

Speeding on opposite vectors, two terns sliced above the cattails, narrowly avoiding collision.

"Where's your flask?" he asked.

Always a dragonfly, that darting mind of his.

"My vodka flask?"

"Last year I was flying to Paris with Dustin Hoffman, and we were lamenting the spate of interviews we had lined up upon arrival. 'Dustin,' I said, 'how do you put up with it all?' And he said, 'Jim, it's easy. I just fill up a water bottle with vodka and sip off it all through the day.' And I told him, 'I know a poet and a fishing guide in Montana who does the exact same thing!'"

I laughed. "I'm humbled to be mentioned in such elevated company."

"Don't get a big head. Mostly we were talking about how loathsome editors are, so the context was far from flattering."

Jim pulled a red from the cooler and gave us each an ample midday pour.

"Do you want to know how you can *believe*?" Jim asked.

"Absolutely," I said, not sure what he meant but going with it all the same. "Who wouldn't want to know?"

"Peacock"—author and grizzly bear expert Doug Peacock—"tells me that new, *indisputable*"—he fished a pack of smokes from the front pocket of his Carhartt T-shirt—"archaeological evidence points to the fact bears have been feeding on migrating cutworm moths in precisely the same drainage in the Front Range near Glacier Park for over thousands of years"—he lit a Spirit and took a drag—"and recently Peacock determined the bears now arrive *before* the moths. They *wait out* the moths' arrival, whereupon they eat themselves into a food coma! They say there are more nutrients per part in a cutworm moth than in a cutthroat trout. When they're done eating they're too gorged to walk so they just roll down the hill a little ways and nap in the shade."

Jim cleared his throat—a momentarily worrisome racket that recalled a yard dog snarling at a paperboy—and fixed my gaze: "And that, son, is how you can believe."

Later, gorged on our own protein-rich meal, we napped near one of my favorite confluences: a cottonwood dry wash that divvies a bear-laden creek bottom from the hard-rushing Flathead. It seemed appropriate to rest near the confluence of a tiny dewatered creek and a big blue river with Jim, whose work so eloquently marries the seemingly disparate—the sacred and the profane, the beautiful and the brutal—erasing delusions of separateness. Where the old cottonwoods dwindle, two conjoining bodies of water form a lazy back eddy, above which swallows are usually on the hunt. Nearby, at the lip of a deep-green swale, sits an old cabin, windowless, roof caved in by windfallen limbs. You could get mauled by a grizzly or bitten by a rattlesnake here, but it would be a finer place than most to breathe your last.

By the time I rose and took the quickest of revivifying dips in the cold river, it was early evening. Once Jim was up and his ample rump dusted off, we made for Missoula. The light—that enduring, loathe-to-extinguish, near-solstice June light—falling across the hills made the plains of greening sage look like brushed suede. Jim, the great monologist, was quiet and I left him to his thoughts. He jotted a thing or two in his notebook.

After a long silence he asked, "Did you see that dilapidated cabin back where we napped?"

"Sure I did."

"Do you know what it says to a young writer such as yourself?"

"No, what does it say?"

"It says: don't let your life become the sloppy leftovers of your work."

⤙

Not quite two months later, I thought of this dictum as the family and I barreled east down I-90 toward Michigan. It felt strange to aim the nuclear family carrier toward my birth state and register pangs of homesickness, but they were distinct, palpable as saliva. With Missoula well in the rearview, I watched my counterpart rivers slide past the truck window and pined for contact with their varied musculatures: the breaking haystacks of the Madison that can flip a boat without warning; the unrelenting Yellowstone with its wet-cement density against oar blade; the steep, gut-punching pitch of the Boulder. Ready to whip a gravel-spraying U-turn in an unauthorized median, I clenched the wheel and noted how the summer's oar callouses had already begun to soften on my palms.

After calling Montana home for fifteen years, we were moving the family to a peninsula in northern Michigan. Some scant reasoning: my finally having landed a steady teaching job; the notion of living closer to two ailing family members, Mary's father and my grandmother; and some well-deserved time off from teaching for Mary, who aimed to rear Lily through the toddler phase sans day care. In typical fashion, our finances were tenuous too—debt substantial, adjustable mortgage rate about to ratchet up to an unaffordable tier—and we hoped this venture might re-scaffold what seemed a teetering budgetary structure. We'll be back to visit in the summer, we had told our befuddled friends who helped stuff the garage with our belongings and promised to make sure the renters didn't trash our house. We're ready for an adventure, we had told one another, had assured the kids. But doubt abounded and there were tears from the driveway to the Great Divide.

Beside me in the passenger's seat, Mary tried to temper my wired state by transcribing into a notebook my frenetic observations. Magpies spraying from the wayside; antelope soldered to their shadows on the prairie; a single great spire of cumulus steepling eastward: quotidian Montana scenes to be sure, but images upon which I feared I might be glimpsing for the last. The dashboard was strewn with tail feathers of grouse and pheasant, a cottonwood bough, and a single river tooth, that surviving, pitch-heavy knot of a current-dissolved log. Rocks gathered from streambeds surrounded the gear-shift and filled the cup holders, comprising enough collective weight to anchor a boat. I picked up a piece of siltstone from the Blackfoot and admired the way its micro-laminated lay-ers of mud resembled a journal's beveled pages. Unabashed sentimentalist, I had packed in bloodshot manic mode.

"You can let go a little," Mary said, gently, as if reading my mind. She waited to see how I would take this comment. "A tight grip can't hold much."

THE DEADSTREAM

On Old Mission Peninsula, the lakeshore was pocked with raindrops. Barefoot, beneath the cries of swooping gulls, three-year-old Molly and I walked the wrack line: an endless braid of milfoil, dead alewife, the shells of invasive zebra mussels, and declawed crayfish. Inbound, quick-cresting breakers crashed on receding swashes, frothing the water around our ankles. After a morning of heat lightning and intermittent deluges, Lake Michigan churned on itself, more stirred than I'd seen it since our arrival.

"This weather will send the salmon up the creeks. We might even spot one from the house, cruising the drop-off," I told Molls, nodding up the bank toward the cottage we'd rented for the school year. When choosing between rentals we had ignored the ill-lit split-level's musty carpeting and ship-tight quarters, focusing instead on its proximity to the lake. Atop the bluff, a cool wind plundered the oak trees, and far above East Bay a vast current of air ripped through a sheet of cirrus.

Crouching, Molly lifted an alewife by its sickle-shaped tail. Victims of a viral hemorrhagic caused by the sudden cold snap, thousands of the goggle-eyed baitfish desiccated in the sun, coating the sand as far down-shore as the eye could see. She tiptoed into the water and dropped the minnow into an outgoing wave, where it tumbled for a moment in the meerschaum.

"I want to go back to my house."

"We're going back," I said. "Two minutes away, tops."

"Not that house," she said, pausing to flip another ale-wife with her toe. A hissing wave dematerialized our foot-prints. "The house with the mountain."

~

IMPASSE MUST PORTAGE: Montana Fish and Game often spray-paints this phrase on signs nailed to bankside trees, just after the rivers crest. Near the tail end of runoff, boating traffic builds on waterways that are by rights still too high and roily for the average boater to navigate. Channels that have been passable for years become blocked when large cottonwoods or ponderosas, having fallen away from slough-ing banks and ridden voluminous silt-stained currents, become lodged perpendicular to the river's flow: crown on one bank, root system on the other.

Despite blatant fluorescent paint, though, the wardens' signs aren't always heeded. It's not rare to come upon the swamped wreckage of a boat, a drifter, say, that someone tried to sneak through a chute, upended and filled with churning snowmelt, or an aluminum canoe bent by the riv-er's unyielding force. Each year in such encounters the lives of inexperienced and expert rowers alike are lost. Prior to such a tragedy, the rower might stand upstream of the snag assessing the scene: beneath the jumble of logs, pine-cones and mats of pollen swirl in recirculating flotsam. If the surrounding channel is relatively shallow, a boat can be portaged over a few downed trees, but this usually requires substantial effort, a quarter-mile slog across a submerged gravel bar, for example, through flooded grass and sharp, beaver-whittled willows. The alternative is to risk a first descent, a tight route through the pinch with little margin for error.

Years ago when I was still brazen, I tried to thread my raft through such a narrow passage, one that I should have portaged, and nearly joined the unfortunate aforementioned ranks. Ignoring the substantial lap line on shore—an indication that the river had dropped significantly overnight—I aimed my boat toward a shiny tongue that flowed over a downed ponderosa. Along with other fellow guides, I had safely passed through the funnel for several days, but the routine had bolstered my confidence and my confidence blinded my judgment: the log was a mere boat length away when I registered my miscalculation. Before I could reef on the oars and back the boat away from danger, the current shoved the raft sidelong, pinning the port tube and oarlock perilously against the trunk. Almost instantly the self-bailer filled with water; dry bags, gear, and tackle were instantly carried out of reach, swallowed and quickly regurgitated by a violent downstream hydraulic.

I looked toward my client Phil, my friend and doctor, who stood on shore at my insistence, and sized up the deteriorating situation. I was too angry with myself to be embarrassed, but also adrenalized enough not to panic. Inch the raft onto the log, I reasoned, lash a cam strap to the D-ring at the bow, and you might be able to yank the boat free before it becomes completely swamped, salvageable only with ropes and come-alongs. Fellow guides would doubtless arrive in short order, eager to lend aid, but not without giving me some ribbing first, and perhaps a hard-to-shake nickname.

Despite my apparent penchant for the ontological, I would trade existential for physical perils, as my body and ego often enjoy a repartee wherein the former takes over and the latter relinquishes control. After instructing Phil to position himself a hundred yards downstream on the bank so that he could nab the catch rope as the raft passed, I tiptoed high-side and around to the bow of the raft, my sandals' purchase precarious on the Hypalon rubber. I got to the log and perched there. Sloshing between my legs, fresh snowmelt greased the bark. A few inches at a time I managed to nudge the raft, free now of my weight and a hundred pounds of gear, closer to the tipping point. Now, mere current friction adhered boat to log, and if I hopped from trunk to bow, I wagered, I might lever the whole thing free. Full of pluck, if pluck can be associated with stupidity, I leapt high—a foot too far—but managed to half-pirouette midair and grasp the cam strap, which I gripped as I plunged into the water, sending the blue boat downstream swiftly over my head.

Little orbs of the oxygen I would moments later so desperately need spun like motes in front of my eyes. An amber stonefly nymph clambered for purchase like a small six-legged me. Parr marked, a young trout flitted back and forth at arm's length. However briefly, fleetingly, I marveled at the intensity of the quiet, the torrent of silence into which I'd been thrust. Then out of the churning underwater world a back current bucked me into the warm June afternoon and I found myself on the rock bar wringing out my shirt, picking detritus from the pockets of my shorts. Reluctantly, the way consciousness returns after a lucid dream, my breath returned to me in gags. I shot a thumbs-up shoreward and looked upstream at the moiling water, the strainer's tangled grip of logs and knobby, cobble-clutching roots: a blatant reminder of my errant choice.

‿

Back inside the house on Old Mission, Luca sat at the kitchen table with his half-eaten Cheerios, the once-saturated Os drying to the sides of the bowl. In his left hand he held a spoon, and in his right a green marker that hovered over a page of notebook paper already covered with figures.

Pouring a bowl for Molly, I asked her brother about his drawing.

"This is an elephant with a tiger on its back," he replied. "And that's a spider about to get stepped on by the elephant."

All of the characters were smiling except the spider, which seemed resigned to its fate.

"Too bad for the spider," I said. "I thought they were your favorite insect."

"Not anymore."

"No? Why not?"

"Just not. I like green leafhoppers better."

Unappeasable since our eastward migration, I would have given my forlorn kingdom for a healthy dose of "just not," anything to stop floundering in the hellish limbo of indecision. To my students at the fine arts boarding academy where I taught, I had read the Zen monk Ikkyū's seven-hundred-year-old advice: "Yesterday's clarity is today's stupidity. The universe has dark and light. Entrust oneself to change." But I lacked the existential mettle to heed these words myself.

Barb sharp and humble, my students were mostly as home-sick as I was. Playing on their longing, I would offer writing prompts like: *If you could repack your belongings in a bottomless backpack, what would you bring?*

"Write naked," I said, jotting the rest of the Denis Johnson quote on the dry-erase board: "That means to write what you would never say. Write in blood. As if ink is so precious you can't waste it. Write in exile, as if you are never going to get home again, and you have to call back every detail."

I urged them not to edit themselves, not to crank down on the imagination's faucet, rather to let the spigot run full blast. And while they engaged the prompts I played a few songs off the computer, something from Bon Iver's eponymous release, a soundtrack that far outgained my hipness but nonetheless elicited a few half-impressed shrugs. Then I asked for volunteers to share. With deft teenage aptitude they eluded eye contact with me until one—a tall visual artist with close-cropped bleached hair, freckles, and bright-red lipstick—popped up her hand and said in a genteel southern accent that she would bring her Hasselblad, two tripods, and her girlfriend's tongue. The class fell out laughing. I wanted to say something about the originality of these hypothetical items but dodged the bait. A compliment and I was a pervert, a suggestion and I was a prude. Instead, I shrugged, nodded my head with a wan smile.

"Anyone else?" While the cohort held its collective breath, I looked out the window at the school's expansive grounds, an eight-hundred-acre forest of white pine and hardwoods nestled between two inland lakes. "Fair enough. Moving on to questions about the reading."

"How about you," the visual artist said. "What would you bring?"

"Me?"

"And be honest. The voice majors say that lying raises your voice an octave and a minor B."

I pulled my gaze from my notes and glanced around the room. Every set of eyes, unreachable moments ago, now had me dead to rights.

"Okay," I began, and proceeded to describe the sloped line that Mount Jumbo's saddle scribes across the morning sky when the snow at horizon is tinted blue. I tried, anyway, but the words evaded me. I apologized. What a rube I was, nearly forty years old and homesick as a soldier. I expected this would sour me in their eyes, but they smiled and nodded to one another as if to say, *Vulnerability: A characteristic exhibited far too infrequently in adults. Perhaps we can trust this man.*

That I had replaced a veteran instructor, a beloved, iconoclastic misanthrope whose retirement after thirty-five years was mourned by former students and secretly cheered by the administration, added a certain pressure to my days. Ralph, as I'll call him, was one of the writers whose books my high school English teacher Colando had introduced me to nearly two decades prior. And while I was honored to succeed Ralph, I found his legacy, which included scores of former students turned published authors, daunting. A lone but humble wolf, Ralph dropped by the office upon my arrival and soon became an avuncular presence, offering advice, an open ear. After one particularly vacuous faculty meeting, I invited him out for a drink.

"How about a vodka at my place," he responded via
e-mail. "Straight from the freezer. In a chilled double-walled
glass. But only if that interests you. Afterward we should
head out to the bay to scout for steelhead. Come by after you
put the kids to bed?"

If, as is often the case, you've dug your own crooked channel into the mind's dark matter, and found that you can't,
despite multiple internal rants and graduate degrees, think
your way out of yourself, the quickest transport back to the
here and now is often a fish, or the pursuit thereof.

"You should know this spot if you expect to survive
around here," Ralph said, downshifting, leaning his white
Volvo station wagon into a sweeping turn at breakneck
speed. Headed north toward the coast, we passed a darkened
barbershop, a closed tavern on the outskirts of town, and a
credit union whose digital clock read: 36°, then 10:47, then
LET US CON, then *SOLIDATE*, then *YOUR LOANS!* "For
your sanity, I mean, not the fishing. You've gotta be crazy to
enjoy winter in northern Michigan. Hell, half of this county
is probably clinically insane."

Ralph's favorite word was "crazy." If he liked a person, he
called them crazy and made his eyes go all beady, smiled an
uninhibited smile. If he didn't like a person, he called them
crazy, then offered a blank look of utter disinterest.

"Isn't night fishing crazy?" he said. "You can't even see
the goddamned river bottom!"

Quills gossamer in the headlights, a porcupine emerged
from a cedar swamp and ambled across the road—Ralph
swerved onto the shoulder to avoid hitting the unfazed

creature. "Crazy porcupine," he said, as the gravel rattled against the undercarriage. Occasionally there were pairs of eyes waist-high and mammalian set like jewels at the verge of the trees, but mostly it was just the Volvo's high beams carving out the dark as we meandered toward the lakeshore. A road I'd never seen in daylight: abandoned drive-in movie theater, ice cream stand shuttered for the season, bait shop closed until morning. "The Deadstream," Ralph called it.

"Do you ever wonder," I asked, "why it is that so many writers like to fish?"

"Never. Except to say that every real writer and every real fisherman share one trait." He blasted the music and yelled: "They're bona fide batshit."

I rolled and I tumbled, I cried the whole night long, crooned the aged folk icon turned blues troubadour. *I rolled and I tumbled, I cried the whole night long. Woke up this mornin', I must have bet my money wrong.*

As thousands of passing jack pines outside the car blurred into a single band of green, I mulled Ralph's talismanic word. Perhaps it was crazy to have uprooted the family and moved to Michigan on what appeared to be the mere whim of a career move, but was it what one poet called "the right madness," or the wrong? Time would tell. With the hope of curing my recent insomnia, I had become fond of watching YouTube clips of Muhammad Ali's knockout of Joe Frazier, while imagining myself as Frazier, a habit that seemed far closer to the latter madness than the former.

"The students love you," Ralph said over the stereo. "And man, the poems they're writing since you got here. That first-quarter reading was a knockout. I know you're not looking for compliments. Just saying."

"They're amazing," I replied. "Super talented."

He turned down the Dylan. "But?"

"But nothing."

"Come on. You didn't invite me out to tell me what a ball you're having."

"I just thought the school was a stronghold of creativity not . . ." I listed a few of the administration's latest unconscionable edicts, which included requiring weekly self-evaluations, as well as the expunging of tenure. Ralph had previously warned me: the legendary Northwoods art school he had taught at now existed in name only. It had vanished, replaced by an institution run by moneyed honchos from the moneyed world, CEO-types without an artistic eyelash or a fingernail's worth of teaching experience who had overloaded a previously workable system with middle-management bean counters and uniformity police, placing the flex point per tradition on the working person, in this case the teaching artist. Since I had coveted the job for years, stalked it since graduate school, my expectations had been unduly primed, leading me to break the first rule of travel: no expectations. In this way I blamed much of my frustration on myself.

"I'm not trying to sound ungrateful," I said, "but I assumed they hired me to teach poetry, not process paperwork."

"Why do you think I retired? Those people are crazy. They'll latch onto you and suck you dry. I pushed against it every day. Fucking fascist lamprey."

An image of the loathed referent—a parasitic freshwater eel that attaches its circular jaws and fang-like teeth to the sides of game fish, leaving the host's flanks dotted with pale scars—flashed in my mind's eye.

"This is the first regular paycheck I've had since my paper route at age ten," I qualified. "I shouldn't be complaining. We have health insurance, for goodness' sake. Enough about me. Have you been writing at all?"

Though he'd authored several acclaimed books, Ralph, per the rumors, claimed to despise writing. "I like *to have written*," he responded. "I'm leery of ambition, Junior. You ought to ask that same question of a rock on the shoreline tonight. Ask it if it's been writing. A rock has the proper amount of ambition."

He cracked the car window and continued. "Half of being a writer is surviving the world. The other half is surviving yourself, or selves, as the case too often is. That's what I've been working on. Speaking of, you realize our mutual pal Harrison used to live just north of here? Wouldn't you love to stretch out the lines he wrote, all thirty-some book's worth, in twelve-point Courier, just to see how many miles they covered?"

The wind was no longer an inland wind: I could smell the coast.

"What line would you start with?" I asked.

"Easy: 'We are more than dying flies in a shithouse though we are that too.'"

"Our minds buzz like bees," I countered, "but not like the bees' minds."

"My year-old daughter's red robe hangs from the doorknob shouting 'Stop.'"

"*Letters to Yesenin*. My favorite from that era."

"I knew I liked you, Junior. You're no factotum newt," he said, rolling down the window to the rubber. "So how's the family adjusting to the move?"

I noted his abrupt subject change, his unerring emotional antenna. A series of letter-poems written by Harrison
to the Russian poet Sergei Yesenin, who hung himself at age
thirty, *Letters* is no Hallmarkian epistolary collection, but
rather a sequence of soliloquies that stares down depression,
mental illness, and confronts the sometimes comes-to-worse
consequences of fighting such psychological battles. To
broach this book, and potentially my own afflictions, was to
go deeper than Ralph wished on this given night.

"They seem to be doing great," I said of the family, letting
the heavy stuff slide. "Making friends. Enjoying the lake."

"But you miss it, don't you? The mountains."

Something about the nocturnal drive ablated my
inhibitions—if we were having a conversation in the daylight, I would never have ceded to this pace of reveal.

"When you were a kid, did you ever have a pillow you
slept with," I said, "that you couldn't fall asleep without?"

━━⌇━━

Not even ichthyologists can explain precisely what initiates
the migratory journey of anadromous fish. But somewhere in its lacustrine home a steelhead senses something
beyond our human ken—the angle of light, for example,
or the alkalinity of a river mouth altered due to decaying
maple leaves—and aims toward its birth water to answer
a reproductive call. To reach meter-specific locations
imprinted in its DNA from the time it was a smolt, the
single-minded salmonid will ascend waterfalls and fish
ladders, negotiate municipal culverts, even venture across
flooded highways in the push toward the river of its birth.

Studies have documented that a steelhead spawning in river A, live shocked and tagged and helicoptered overland to river B, will about-face and swim downstream to its birth water in order to reenter river A, traveling up to one hundred fifty miles if needed. Upon entering streams in late fall, the Great Lakes steelhead Ralph and I were searching for often stage in-stream for several months before eventually spawning toward spring. Once they mate, they drop back to the lake (or ocean for wild Pacific steelhead) and live several more seasons, capable of multiple spawning journeys in a lifetime.

"Holler if you spot anything," Ralph said as we parted ways near the river. "But don't get all hot and bothered over a salmon. There'll still be a few coho around." Like steelhead, Great Lakes salmon also migrate out of Lake Michigan to spawn, but since they largely forgo feeding for procreation, they're considered less than sporting targets. They decay in-stream too, and, unlike steelhead, die shortly after mating. And while we were targeting steelhead as game fish, I admitted to myself that I felt, for the time being, more melancholy kinship with the on-its-last-swim salmon. "I'll scout a couple of holding pools upstream. You head down to the mouth. Remember not to shine your headlamp on the water. Illegal."

"Didn't bring one."

"Good. Your eyes will adjust that much quicker."

At the mouth, the reflection of a waning gibbous cast a milky sheen across the water, providing ample light to see by. The river slurred toward its finish. Before long, I heard a stationary rustling upstream and, moving toward the commotion, discerned a salmon on the pearl-colored gravel: a buck, sentry on a well-aged spawning bed. Lanky from territorial battles with smaller jacks, tail shredded, misaligned kype jaw bulbous and scarred, the fish was not long for this bardo. In a few days, with its fat reserves sapped, it would keel over and begin to fall, bend by bend, back toward the lake, where raccoons, coyotes, and crayfish, to name just a few, will scavenge the protein-rich carcass. Even the eye sockets: picked clean by gulls.

Its flesh peppered with decay, the fish was easy to track through the flickering shallows. Watching it sway in the current, I sensed my nocturnal faculties taking rein, the reptilian edge wearing off, and in this defogged state began to acknowledge my persistent mental struggles. Accretive guilt at moving the family twelve hundred miles from home. Fear that this exploit would eventually bankrupt us and hinder us from returning to Montana. Embarrassment that the job I idealized for a decade had turned sour. And worse, the crippling worry that these changes would tease out my most depressive tendencies. In daylight these encumbrances scurried from me, remained vague and thus more agitating, but under the cover of darkness there was nothing to do but sit with them and accept the bedrock truth. Founded as they were, these inhibitions were wearing me away, preventing me from any kind of progression.

The night cooled swiftly and the river, suddenly warmer than the air, exhaled a fog pungent with cedar. A cloud passed over the moon, aglow and faceted like a cracked-open geode. I shook my head. Foolishly I had once courted madness, and now, with its weight pressed fully upon me, could barely draw a full breath.

As a young writer I had idealized this writer's depiction of mania and that one's delusions; imitated her fugal downward spirals and romanticized his book of nightmares. True, these troubled literary predecessors made laudatory works of art that served as balms to readers in times of anguish. But to think that I once sought out mental disequilibrium, in hopes of making my own work more potent, shames me. A force as capable of fueling personal destruction as it was stoking creativity, madness wasn't some noble pursuit; it was simply madness, an unwelcome, discernable presence that I found myself fighting hard to evict.

I crouched to touch the river's flesh, a momentary consolation. From the edge of my shadow appeared something black and calligraphic: a spooked lamprey tacking upriver. I bent down and fished a stone from the shore, then hucked it in the lamprey's direction, hoping to harry the eel past the spawned-out buck.

OLD MISSION

"I haven't seen a horse in so long," Luca said to Molly. He scratched himself behind his right ear. "I haven't seen a horse in so long—"stopped to scratch behind his left ear too—"I'm beginning to think they're extinct."

"My teacher has a horse," Molly said. "She says that's why she got a divorce from her husband. She said she liked her horse more than him."

"I'm not getting married," Luca said.

"You know you want a wife," Molls responded, scratching her brown hair vigorously. "Life stinks without one."

"How do you know?"

"I don't. But Dad's got one."

"He's a poet. He's got a hard life."

Sketching out a grocery list, I resisted the temptation to interrupt the kids, to spin their conversation in my favor. Near my feet on the linoleum, Molly was at work on an extensive series of self-portraits composed on the backs of recycled cereal boxes and energy bills: drawings made almost daily with immense concentration and an enviable disregard for results. In most of the drawings there were two stick figures: the "artist," depicted with drawing utensil in hand; and another smiling female figure wearing a crown. Listening to the sound of her scissor blades opening and slicing through paper, I recalled the tender image of my mother clipping coupons at the breakfast table underneath her colossally large pink hair dryer. When I looked down to praise Molly's progress, though, I discovered that she had taken her scissors to the twenty-dollar bill I had set aside for groceries, cut it into strips, and glued the strips into the hands of her subjects.

All too aware of what the cash would have added to the tightrope of our weekly bottom line, I crouched down and fingered the shreddings.

"Sweetie, why'd you do that?"

"'Cause they needed more monies."

A true child is the opposite of time.

⌒

Thousands of hours: that's how many I've spent poring over the anatomical details of tiny aquatic insects—noting, for example, the way a mayfly dun's tails double in length and its opaque wings become translucent as it molts to enter the imago stage—a course of study that has left me well qualified to pick nits. To be clear, this is not a reference to miniscule edits of students' poems or line items in the family budget, where we could have spent seven dollars on bulk almonds instead of ten, but rather literal nits, the impossibly clingy eggs of lice, which we discovered in the Bigs' scalps shortly after their school sent home a yellow half-sheet, warning families in the district of the threat.

With little choice in the matter, soon I became a student of the louse, of its oblong abdomen red with a child's blood, its six legs and long-evolved claws capable of gripping the thinnest brown strands of hair. I numbered these hairs, splitting them with fine-toothed comb and harsh bathroom light. I researched piperonyl butoxide, the pyrethrum with which I shampooed their scalps after homeopathic treatments of olive oil and shower caps failed. I observed the scratched-red necklines and the otherwise tender provinces behind the ears. I measured the uncanny speed of the louse itself, as it scurried behind a lobe or down the sideburn, as compared to their stationary, specter-white eggs left behind after the nymphs have hatched and only a week away from adulthood where they'll start the whole cycle over again. I apologized to the kids for what I cursed at these malefactor eggs, unrepeatable phrases that fell upon their un-stopped ears, prosecutable utterances that I should have forgone for the equally true but less impeachable: *hideous necromancers*.

And, after several weeks of scouring the footholds of hairs, I had nearly eradicated these Beelzebubs of domestic torture when the phone began to ring with a similar level of incessance.

Our renters—phone call number 1—rang sheepishly from Missoula to inform us that an L-joint in the copper piping failed in our washroom, flooding the basement. I didn't panic until—call number 2—the insurance assessor reported that our tenants had set up an elaborate marijuana growing operation in the adjoining room and, following the flood, a potent strain of mold has begun to grow on the drywall, which would need to be torn down. While demo, remediation, and remodeling took place, we put the renters' deposit toward our mortgage to offset the lost rental income, a mendable situation. But because of the complicated and extensive nature of the claim, our homeowners' insurance dropped us—call number 3—whereupon our mortgage company—call number 4—unbeknownst to us, locked us into a backdoor fallback policy (see fine print) that cost three times that of our preexisting one.

Call 5: Can't our original policy be reactivated? I begged to an automated voice mailbox.

Call 6: No.

In one magnetic swipe, the money we'd salted away to pay off our sizeable debt vanished. Worse yet, the interest rate on our adjustable-rate mortgage was due to adjust upward by two percentage points if our debt-to-income ratio didn't improve, a feat that seemed reachable prior to the news.

Interviewer: How do you know when a poem of yours is finished?

Frank O'Hara: The telephone rings.

⌒

Some winter days in Michigan you wonder if you've gone color-blind, so resolute are the grays—of brittle skeleton beech trees, of cement and sidewalk slush, of your own skin without pigment. The species of snow are myriad, and all taste the same: like copper, brass, blood at the back of your throat. The state emblem is a boy with his tongue frozen to the flagpole. Neck craned, he watches his schoolmates laugh at him from the warm classroom, the windows steaming, their mittens drying atop the radiator. The flag luffs in the wind, its chain clanking against the pole. As he waits for the custodian's rescue, the cold deepens, draws him into himself, where he's not at all fond of the company.

As the days shortened and the aperture tightened, I tried to convince myself that my sanity teetered due to drastic circumstantial changes rather than inherent mental and chemical imbalances, but self-diagnosis is inherently flawed. With adequate insurance, I should have sought out therapy. Likely my mistrust of "mind doctors" arrived in my adolescence ("kill the father," mine a successful psychologist) and, due to a persistent immaturity, never departed. To shirk expert help was irresponsible, if excusable, as perhaps I feared becoming again "the patient" that I so often was, by proxy, as a child. But because I refused to talk with anyone about my discordancy, I ended up talking mostly to myself, only compounding inner turmoil and consternation.

What is this, I often asked myself, the same old dire straits story again? Isn't it the guide's job after all to steer the boat and his guests away from danger, rather than toward it?

I thought a lot about a short poem by Pablo Neruda that I quoted frequently to the students: "Pardon me, if when I want / to tell the story of my life / it's the land I talk about. / This is the land. / It grows in your blood / and you grow. If it dies in your blood / you die out." Body and land are inseparable. I had spent nearly two decades growing into a place, a little valley where some rivers meet, from which I had suddenly eradicated myself. How did I expect to feel settled?

That was my empathetic side talking. On my worst days I became certain that the children would inherit my depressive tendencies, a conviction that gutted me to the spine. Full-vent survival mode meant amplifying my (manic?) energy for games and projects and irreverent humor. I cut cardboard "binoculars" from cereal boxes through which we stared at the lake. I built igloos and bonfires down at the beach. I scheduled nightly wrestling matches with Lily, which ended with her delivering a fatal blow, after which I would writhe, give out a couple of death throes, then go stiff. One night, my eyes were closed momentarily when I felt something sharp pierce my cheek.

I pulled my face away from Lily's open mouth. .

She blushed. "When I see something so cute, I just want to bite it."

At peace for the moment, I kissed her goodnight and tucked her in, and once downstairs began shuffling through a stack of papers, catching glimpse of the mail—on top of the pile, a red-stamped, time-sensitive envelope from the mortgage company—and felt myself slide into a melancholic ditch. It only took a moment, so deeply were my mental patterns scored, before I was spinning in an eddy of anxiety. In the living room as the Bigs stared through their cardboard cutouts, I wondered: With such surround, how could I be so inconsolable? But I was. Irrefutably, I was.

Brave daughter of a bipolar father, Mary could sense what I was hiding. While her father's condition was long ago mediated by the prescribed use of lithium, her traumatic childhood memories of his episodes remained vivid. No doubt my behavior revivified them, and she feared a repeat performance.

"You're reminding me of my dad and his episodes," she said one morning as we lay awake before dawn. "One minute you're totally happy with the kids," she continues. "The next—"

"I can't just make myself *feel* better," I said, hijacking her inquiry into my well-being with self-martyrdom.

Out the window the predawn sky was muted: no stars.

"Anyway, you're positing."

Gently she reached toward my face. "Babe, you don't seem okay."

I curled back from her hands and racked my memory: *You don't seem okay.* She had never said those words to me. An honest response would have required more psychological fortitude than I could muster, so I slipped out of bed and found my way to the closet, where I slumped down and began to study the little white rope above that hung from the barest of bulbs. Unfinished pressed gypsum, the drywall faced me down like a blank page of printer paper.

He who thinks he can do more for a blank page than a blank page can do for him, a teacher of mine used to say, is probably in the wrong profession. *If you could begin to fill the page of this wall with words,* a voice asked me, *what would you write?*

"Dad, dad!" came a voice from the other room. Then the Bigs were there, standing over me, their pajama-covered bodies emanating warmth. "You have to see the sunrise! It's like a cut from God."

I put on a coat and hat and walked down to the shore. Above the brightening rosette bay a strand of snow geese parted an almost liquid wind, the birds' undersides turning opalescent with lake-refracted light. Through the ozone their calls fell invisibly toward my feet. And there, in the wet sand above wrack line, lay two well-defined coyote prints. Frail lines sprayed out from the footpads where the creature's fur had swept the ground. Six feet farther down the beach, two more. Gauging by the distance between them, the tracks were left by a running animal, a loping one. What lengthened its gait, I wondered, inspired its strides?

As morning wore on, while shaving my whiskers with one hand and feeding Lily with the other, I employed my anti-Zen Zen, a phrase I had coined to describe the sort of meditation practiced not in silent temples but amid the chaos of raising children. Note: the sound of one hand shaving and one hand feeding a hungry daughter is the sound of said daughter not crying. I was doing "just one thing," as the wise teachers instruct, but that one thing was simultaneously filling lunch boxes with cream-cheese-and-jelly sandwiches, heating water for tea, praising Molly's crayon drawing, and prepping another bowl of rice cereal and pureed prunes for Lily.

Behind a rush of humid fall wind, Mary entered the living room through the front door, her face flushed from a run along the lake. We kissed briefly, the fecund scent of coastline lingering on my cheek, took in the quotidian chaos of the morning, and shook our heads in unison. Raising three children was like fording a swift, waist-high stream whose stones are covered with moss; it's possible, but move heron-slow, measure each step, or you'll topple and end up who knows how far downstream.

In reality our daily existence as parents had morphed into a combination of the chaotic and the monastic, some hybrid of the unwritten novels *Love in the Time of Diapers* and *The Electric Kool-Aid Patience Test*. We woke in the dark to feed Lily, waiting for the thump of the Bigs' feet on the stairs, then made oats and slugged down tea. We dressed the children and read them stories before school, then swept the floors and rinsed the dishes. We laundered small sets of pajamas, wondering how apple juice soaked into cotton managed to smell precisely like urine. We wiped noses, clearing the orifices of yellow ooze and crusted green pebbles. Some hours later we made dinner, swept the floors again. Bathed the children, brushed their small teeth, read more stories. Then it was time for lullabies: Luca wanted "Fishing a Stream I Once Fished as a Kid," and for Molly "Wagon Wheel." Mary sang "Edelweiss" to Lils.

Ah, so this was vespers.

And as my head hit the pillow fourteen hours removed from the morning's Cheerios, I contemplated that endless supply: O after O after O. *Hold fast to their wonder,* a voice inside of me uttered, a poised voice that seemed to arise of its own volition. *If nothing else, trust that.*

GOOD HARBOR

One day at school in Hybrid Genres our discussion centered on the first stanza of a famous poem, an account of a development company's bulldozing of a pristine alpine meadow, then splintered into the subject of landscape, the landscape of home, how it feels to be wedded to a place, to know a place not as a tourist but as an intimate, and the trauma caused when such ties are severed. "Eden under asphalt," said one. "I can't write about home when I'm there," said another. "Hemingway wrote about Michigan when he lived in France." "Hemingway was a buffoon," said a third, one of the brightest students in the class. "But he did say, 'Finish what you start.'"

After class I drove the long way home through the hills above the Boardman River, where, against stout banks of snow, oak trees stood in high relief, barren save for a few brick-colored clutches of leaves. With ample time to spare before dinner, I wound up a two-track and crested a knuckle of land, a vantage from which I could overlook both the river's meander and the distant bay specked in whitecaps. What stubborn fool couldn't be happy here? I asked myself, admiring the view. This fool, it would appear. Happiness, of course, is no one's right, the mere mention of it a privilege.

From this aspect, I could see the simple riches that surrounded me: a sense of privacy, few social distractions, and an intimacy with family. And as much as I complained, what job in this declining empire wasn't without its bureaucratic failings? But I couldn't shake the notion that I had broken a kind of covenant I'd long ago struck with the rivers of the West, that I had abandoned the life the mountains and moving waters had bestowed on me, and in so doing had lost touch with my most feral and truest self. After that has been relinquished, what's left to give the ones around you? Society, with its mirage of accomplishment and responsibility, would say a lot. But what could I possibly hand down to my children that is more durable than my passion for and stewardship of a beloved landscape and its inhabitants, both human and inhuman?

Mulling this notion on the way back to the highway, I popped in a CD, the demos of a musician friend's new album. I was enjoying the nakedness of the composition—untidy melody, little warble of a bottleneck slide, boot sole tapping against the floor—relishing the sparseness of the thing before it has been accompanied by other instruments played by other talented musicians, when something gray spilled from a stand of beech and flew across the road. I jerked the wheel to avoid the flushing grouse, but it flared too late, thwacking against the windshield, and fell instantly dead in the two-track.

Breastbone snapped. Slaver of blood and one sprig of wintergreen protruding from its beak. With the bird's limp warmth filling my palm, I fanned out its banded tail feathers, its flight rudder, and apologized for my inattention. To claim the roadkill bird legally, I would have had to call a warden whose office was probably twenty miles away, and who would have needed to meet me at the scene to ensure that I didn't illegally poach the game, before issuing a valid permit. If I bury the grouse in the bracken and dormant ferns, I thought, a coyote will find it soon, no later than nightfall; it wouldn't be wasted to the greater ecosystem, this much was certain. But nearly a year had passed since we had shared a family dinner of wildfowl.

I set the warm grouse on the passenger seat beside my books and put the car in gear.

Down at the dock, each wave arrived with a mother-hush. With Molly by my side, I picked the grouse's cape, rump, and breast feathers. In the glow of the streetlight I showed her which leg and wing joints to cut, which slice of membrane opened the chest cavity and freed the organs. Together we drew the intestines, which she tossed into the lake, food for the crayfish whose pincers she collected. Then we removed the sweetbreads and organs, and the ticker the size of a raspberry.

"Do you want to try some grouse meat for dinner tonight?" I asked.

"Not tonight," she said. After a silence: "What about the wings? What do you make with those?"

"We'll save them. I bet Ralph knows a couple of bird hunters who could use them for training dogs."

"I wish we could get a dog."

"Oh yeah? What would you name it?"

"Loveheart," she said without hesitation, like she'd been waiting all day for someone to ask her.

After seasoning the bird with lemon juice, salt, olive oil, cayenne, and fresh thyme, I browned it on the stovetop, then roasted it in the oven for an hour. I poured a pan reduction—made from trimmings, red wine vinegar, agave syrup, and red pepper flakes—over the cooked bird's crisp skin. Alongside slices of radish and pear, cuts of the bird's light flesh were served. A rare dinnertime hush fell over our table as everyone, even high-chaired Lily, tucked into the meal. Save for the sounds of cutlery clanking against plates or someone chewing with audible satisfaction, the room was uncharacteristically quiet for the duration of the meal. Later, I was doing the dishes with the window open when I heard the Bigs' living room chatter suddenly hush.

Assuming that a lamp had been broken or bowl of cereal had spilled, I hurried to investigate. But Luca and Molls were staring out the window, drop-jawed, as a huge moon, two days from full, rose out of the land beyond the bay. Someone flicked out the lights and we huddled on the couch, watching. After their bath, Mary and Lily joined us in the living room, the little one's sleepy eyes thrown open by the spectacle in our window. For a while I closed my own and listened to their voices marvel at the far-off rock, the coppery afterimage glowing behind my eyelids like that of a stared-at flame. Something rose in me too: the understanding that their inherent, undiluted wonder had the power to rescue me from myself.

It seemed like as good a night as any to watch the moon rise and, several hours later, on the west side of a peninsula, set. So when the house was quiet with sleepers, I rustled together my fishing gear and a thermos of tea, threw on my cold weather gear, and left a note for Mary: 3 a.m. Headed to the lake for a few hours. Straight to school from there.

The snow fell soft and dense, lighting the shoreline like a strobe. Though high humidity coupled with increased river volume promised to tease a few fresh steelhead upstream from the lake, fish were low on my list of cares. Waist-deep in the dark water, I peeled fly line from the reel and let it unspool until it hung downstream like viscera. There were portions of mind that I wanted to send downstream, too, but not my body—the mass of cells, electrons, and neurons that could go sledding with the kids, eat fresh grouse, make love with a beautiful partner. As for the stubborn mental sediment, I trusted the current would carve it away.

With the river lapping at the rim of my waders, I took a few steps upstream and rolled out another cast. The fly landed with a light splash, the reverberation traveling up leader, line and graphite rod before registering in my hand. Once taut, the line swung, sweeping a soft hackle fly through the water column. When the line had come parallel to the bank, I took three more steps upstream, lifted the rod, and snapped out another cast. Tighten, swing, sweep. Three more steps, cast. Repeat. For a few hours like that I combed the river—every riffle and trench, every boil created by recumbent rock, every chute and sag—but failed to move a single fish. I reeled up, pinned my fly, and started toward the hillside parking lot. From there I would have a view of the river as it made its final swooping turn before entering, through a spit of sand, the bay.

Winding through the mossy trunks, the path was well lit for the moonlight and fresh snow, the latter of which clumped to the felt bottoms of my boots. I took my time, no class to teach for hours. Rabbit track. Deer droppings melted into the snow. Insular forest warmth. Somewhere in the still trees an owl called with an unsteady rhythm, like a child trying to make an empty bottle hoot. Great gray, I thought, and sent out my human rendition. No response. More rabbit track. Several tiny spiders crawling from a swatch of wind-blown lichen. And just before the trail emerged, the rabbit track stopped dead. A few steps later I crouched to parse an ornate print the preying owl had left—outstretched wings, a round face, flat, save for the eye sockets and beak, and a fili-gree of markings made by the tips of sharp feathers. Walking on, I gave the imprint a wide berth as I might a fine vase or a glass sculpture in a museum.

Looking out across Lake Michigan, I sat against the car's bumper. Steam from the long-steeped tea unfolded over my face. Faintly, to the south of the big setting moon, the western horizon emitted a mirage of light. Chicago's sub-urban North Shore and Milwaukee were both hundreds of miles distant, but on calm nights light particles bent by cold air can travel vast distances across the water. Chicago, an otherwise anonymous metropolis at this hour, Mary's city, on the outskirts of which her father, early riser, was likely shuffling down the stairs in his slippers toward the morning *Tribune*.

Nearly eighty years old, he still clocked full workdays at his insurance office, still scheduled regular calls to his clients though his long-term accounts were staked, business rela-tionships steadfast. There were always children to inquire about, or grandchildren, always the Bears' long-suffering receiving corps to discuss. He didn't fish, didn't golf, or play cards, and so his pastime was conviviality, gracious conversation in which he could engage nearly anyone at any time. Tollboth workers, supermarket checkers, passersby on the street. Though he rarely spoke of the grave psychological trials he had endured—the interventions, the breakdowns, the failed prescriptions, the hospitalizations—they left in their wake a specific courage, the kind that is requisite for a human being who hopes to regularly extend small kindnesses to fellow human beings.

Thinking of him, I felt a wave of everyday compassion ripple toward me and tried to gather a bit of what he might offer to a threadbare friend. *The world takes enough from us; pass on what mercies you can to whomever you can, yourself included.*

I watched the moon set, then walked back down to the lakeshore to ply the mouth.

There, the sound of sheering water startled me: a fish was working its way through the rip. Kneeling to bring the shallow river mouth to eye level, I spotted a single mint-silver steelhead surfing the current tongue, readying itself at the threshold. It had probably milled along the break all night, chasing off smaller competitors, foraging on baitfish, piling on pre-spawn calories, and would likely be a sucker for a short cast and a tightly swung fly. Scooting in, it stationed itself in the tail-out, a prime lie. It wouldn't take more than a few casts in this low light to hook him, I wagered.

Fingering the damp, soft-hackled fly on the rod's hook keeper, I watched the water pour like quicksilver over the fish's snout, imagining the way the rod would buckle under that depth-honed muscle—then put my hand back in my pocket. Better to let the fish preserve its well-earned calories, to start up the river unmolested, where it will face enough obstacles to its survival. After a moment the fish scooted on. In that soft place, I stood awhile longer until I sensed at my back the eastern sky bluing subtly with dawn, then turned to walk toward it.

PARR MARKS

High on the wall in the alcove of the building where I taught hung a striking six-by-eight-foot oil-on-wood painting by Tatyana Leykin. Through the textured, deep blues of the painting's background float three asexual human nudes, along with several triangular shapes and five mauve fish resembling carp or koi, one of which has risen to the water's surface, belly up.

Walking up the stairs with me one frigid Sunday, Molly stopped in her tracks and laid eyes on the underwater scene.

"Oh yeah," she said, pointing to the human figure in a semi-fetal position. "I remember that."

Since she had never set foot in this portion of the building, she couldn't have recalled the painting itself, so it must have triggered a memory of—what, skinny-dipping somewhere unbeknownst to her parents with large fish and geometrical shapes? Perhaps a scene from a movie? Or a brief moment spent immersed in a lake or pool, a bright disk of light cleaving the glassy surface?

"Molly, come on!" Ralph yelled up the stairs. "Let's copy our faces on the copy machine." And, giggling, down the stairs she hopped before I could quiz her on the painting.

At the base of the stairwell rested Ralph's tricked-out snow sled, loaned to us for the afternoon so that father and daughter could try their hand at high-speed downhill hammerheading, a new mode of winter chicanery Ralph had devised to help pass the epoch-long month of February. He had cleared a switchback trail through the woods just off campus and smoothed a track fit for a luge. At night, he would soak a Hula-Hoop in white gas and set it ablaze at the end of the track, then video his sled crossing a fiery finish line. The right madness. I hollered downstairs, urged the two pranksters to the door, and together we three walked toward the sledding course, snow pants swishing. A Sunday kind of feeling on campus, most of the students holed up in their dorms or rehearsal rooms. A scentless wind stirred wraiths of dry snow, danced a brittle oak leaf across the quad. From an open studio window, oboe notes floated off like parasols. Once at the trailhead, we stared uphill into a bric-a-brac of snow glare and pine-cast shadow.

"You're on your own from here, Junior. I got my laps in this morning. Smoothed down the track for you real nice. Just follow the flagging tape," Ralph said, pointing uphill. He rifled through his pocket then and bent to show Molly the Xerox of their faces under the hood of the copy machine. She stared at the paper, then into Ralph's mirrored sunglasses, and began to fiddle with the chinstraps of her bright-pink helmet before removing it altogether.

"You need the helmet to protect your noggin," I told her.

"I like my smile better with no helmet."

"You can't sled without a helmet on, Sweets."

"I don't like it," she said, pointing up to Ralph, whose white hair stood wildly around his wind-chapped face. "He doesn't have one."

"I got nothing left to protect," Ralph said, rapping his fist on his skull. "Besides, that pink helmet is awesome. I'm wearing the same color underwear."

With a screaming slapstick laugh that tickled my heart chakra, Molly rolled onto the sled and refastened her chinstrap.

I thanked Ralph once again for his generosity. "For everything. I feel like I keep needing to thank you."

"Anything to keep you around." He folded the Xerox portrait and zipped it back into his pocket, dug at a samara with his boot. "But you know. Maybe the best thing that happens from this whole deal is that you learn where you're supposed to be."

"Come again?"

"I had a good run here, at school."

"A grave understatement," I laughed. I took stock of the scores of published authors Ralph taught over the years, the vaunted reading series he established that had hosted luminaries like Oliver, Snyder, and Kinnell, in addition to the countless young artists he mentored and nurtured onto meaningful paths as makers and mindful fashioners of language.

"Real good run," he continued. "But I should have gone back to Pittsburgh. That was it for me. The only place I ever felt right. You probably only get one."

I stood silenced, leveled by Ralph's revelation.

"You know, my dad was the basketball coach there."

"I did know that."

I had once read a *Sports Illustrated* interview where the reporter asked Ralph's dad, who coached at the university, what it was like to have a poet for a son, if that wasn't a little strange. Coach replied, "Nothing's stranger than dressing twelve kids up in tank-tops and short shorts, rolling a ball out onto the court, and watching thousands of fans scream and yell for them."

"For a while he thought I could be a ballplayer, or a coach," Ralph went on. "There were opportunities, favors people owed him. I was good enough, but it wasn't for me. I wanted to write."

"Did it hurt things between you?"

"Not in the least. It might have dug at him some, but he didn't show it. One day he sat down next to me at the breakfast table with the *Gazette* in his lap and said, 'I've thought about it for a while and it's better to fail on your own path than to succeed on another's.'"

With gloved fingers, I rubbed my temples. From the otherwise quiet distance came the sound of a snowmobile: a revved engine, a goosed throttle.

"Daddy," Molly said, "you have to hold my hand so I don't get hit by a car."

"No cars out here," Ralph said, hoisting Molly to my shoulders. "*Oof-da.* Just idiots chasing coyotes on their snowmobiles. You guys don't need to worry about them, though. You're hammerheaders. Course record is sixty-seven seconds flat."

On my chest facing downhill, nose a few inches from the ground, gloves gripping the sled's steering wheel, I dug in my boot toes to steady the sled, then Molls jumped on, the sled's waxed skis shifting beneath us. She wriggled and wrapped her arms under my shoulders like straps on a backpack.

"You ready?"

"Yep," she said, scooping a mitten-full of snow into her mouth.

The first turn was smooth, just a simple jackleg we took without much momentum, but soon we were at gravity's mercy, gaining speed, leaning into banked turns, floating down a long straightaway, me steering with the handles, Molly gripping me tighter under my shoulders as our legs flared out on a sharp turn, snow spraying at our faces, me hollering, "Hold on, kiddo, hold on tight!," Molls laughing one long "Yee-eee-eee-eee-ess!" If the sled had rolled, I would have had a broken arm to explain, a snapped collarbone, but I found myself easing off the hand brakes as we gained speed and the bare trees blurred past.

When the hammerhead had coasted to a rest at the bottom of the hill, we sprinted up for another run, racing each other, huffing the trail. By late afternoon with six runs under our belt, too exhausted to climb the hill again, we headed toward the car and the promise of hot chocolate. For a while I carried a dozing Molly on my back, but eventually my lower right lumbar began to grind against a disk and I had to set her down. She seemed unfazed, wandering off-trail and into the drifts, postholing and falling face-first into a snowbank, coming up smiling, almost amused by her efforts to keep up, her two steps to my one. The leaden rivulet we followed downhill curled through a cedar bog, through the belly of which wound a small spring lined by dormant ferns, swamp buttercup, and forget-me-nots. Beside the clear pool, Molly plopped down heavy and peered into the water.

The shallow pool harbored a school of salmon fry so tiny they could have been classified as alevin, transparent pre-fry no more than six months old, that had only recently hatched and slipped their egg sack. Camouflaged by watercress then revealed in shifting columns of light, the fry were only distinguishable against vegetation and pebble by their parr marks.

In the woods' terraced silence, we rested.

During Molly's final months in her mother's womb, those tenuous ninety days of bed rest when her lungs were the size of seedpods and we worried she would arrive too early, too small to survive without great intervention, she must have developed a spectacular fortitude. She twisted through the fecund darkness of Mary's uterus, absorbing the reverberations of our fears and frenetic energy, or so molecular physicists tell us. Much occurs in those porous nine months, in that single long starless night, that imprints a person's psyche and is irrevocably retained.

"You're a pretty tough girl to make this hike," I finally said.

"Yep," she said, her cheeks bright red, ice beading a lock of brown hair that had escaped from her helmet. "When I got tired, Bumfer carried me."

Evening sifted down through the black branches.

"Who's Bumfer?" I asked.

"My friend."

I was inclined to inquire further, but something stopped me.

"And where is Bumfer right now?" I asked.

She smiled and nodded, looked down at her chest, then back up at me, as if I well knew the answer.

Watching the salmon fry shift through the waters of their birth, I let the matter lie in the mystery from which it had sprung: a child's empathic imagination, which promised to lead me to far richer, wilder locations than my prim rationale.

Gusting hard from the south, the wind off East Bay was redolent of earthworms and flowing culverts. Softening earth. Face upturned, I sat in the car outside the Traverse City airport terminal watching Debra Magpie Earling's flight approach. My friend and former colleague was due in momentarily from Montana to give a craft talk and reading at school, where I had been teaching her acclaimed first novel, *Perma Red*, for several weeks, reveling in how thoroughly the students took to the book's gritty narrative and its indomitable young female protagonist. An enrolled member of the Confederated Salish and Kootenai Tribes of the Flathead Nation, Debra is the great-granddaughter of Paul Charlo, the last federally recognized Chief of the Bitterroot Salish. After spending childhood summers on her mother's allotment property on the Flathead Reservation, she came to stay at age eighteen, taking a job as the first public defender in the tribal court system. During a prep lecture I showed the students images of the Reservation and surrounding country but stressed how difficult it is for a snapshot to capture the physical and historical scope of the Western landscape. Think of it this way, I continued, while scrolling to a photo of the National Bison Range, there were sixty million bison roaming the plains when Lewis and Clark arrived; half a century later, there were fewer than a thousand. For millennia, tribes lived sustainably with the animal, and in fifty years they were nearly gone.

Though we hadn't seen each other in months, I had, as ever, a ream of stories to tell Debra, with one in particular rising to mind, the account of a late-summer Montana magpie encounter in which I had had to dispatch a wounded bird. The tall black tail of the bird had canted in the wind, casting a shadow on wet Clark Fork sand flecked with pyrite and centuries-old mine tailings. Since it hadn't spooked from my oncoming raft, I assumed the bird, cousin to crows and jays, was dead, assumed the late-July wind, not breath, made its white breast feathers move. Stepping out of the boat for a closer look, though, I saw its fly-rimmed eyes blink twice. I shooed the bluebottles and flipped the bird over with a stick. Though free of wounds or blood, the bird's abdomen heaved and fell with labored breaths. It didn't flush as I stomped, just opened its beak and gave a mawkish gasp. Perhaps it had been poisoned (as some ranchers planted traps to keep *Corvidae* away from harvested hay) or had scavenged off the illegally poisoned carcass of a coyote or fox. To dispatch a songbird such as a magpie, even a dying one, would have been against the law, but to leave one suffering broke another code. From a nearby logjam, I dug out a piece of driftwood and, walking back, weighed it in my hands, brought the smooth, flat piece over the bird's head, and let it fall.

Back in the parking lot, I watched Debra's plane circle the field, reclining the seat and setting my face in full sun. Elated for the students to meet Debra, to be in her ever-generous presence, I was also hoping that a visit from one of my mentors would put me in contact with the landscape for which I was so pathetically homesick. I listened to the wind and, awash in white noise, fell fast asleep. I slept no longer than a minute or two it seemed, but it was long enough to dream of traversing a favorite bird-hunting covert, late in a plentiful season. I reached the prized thicket of hawthorn and snowberries when out of the sky a vast covey of birds began to swarm my head and attack my bare face and neck. I soon recognized the small tornado of partridge, grouse, and pheasant as the game birds I had killed and eaten that season. Under the spiked branches I cowered until out of the mauve sky a magpie descended and, squawking wildly, ushered the flock of vengeful birds away.

Waking with a start at the roar of the approaching plane's engine, I turned to watch as, from the fuselage and wings, the Bombardier's landing gears unfolded and Debra's plane appeared ready to coast onto the strip. But just as it drew level with the tower, the nose tipped up, the engines roared, and the aircraft banked north over East Bay. Watching the plane disappear into a raft of cumuli, I walked inside to investigate. Decked in blue vest and red tie, the airline attendant didn't look up from his computer screen to answer me. "Sorry, sir, no word."

"They were a few hundred feet from touching down," I implored. "What went wrong?"

"No word from the airline yet," he repeated, a response that only piqued my curiosity.

After texting Debra, I began to ponder my magpie daymare. By rights I deserved to be accosted, even attacked by the birds I had harvested. But what of the magpie's intercession? Of course, the whole thing could have been a subconscious conjuring by my overinflated ego, an elaborate attempt to pat myself on the back for putting the magpie out of its misery. We don't decide our own penance for the carnage we've caused in the world, though, even in our dreams. So it struck me that the dream was about consequences, and about how on occasion, by way of undeserved aid from the natural world—"grace" is the old word—we are spared from what we actually deserve.

There are subjects, his dreams included, into which a middle-aged white man such as myself should avoid delving in public; another that comes to mind is the cosmology of Indigenous people, even if his approach to the subject is reverential—perhaps especially if his approach to the subject is reverential, as the dramatic irony at play only deepens within such a dynamic. Over nearly two centuries, through countless methods of destruction both intentional and unintentional, colonialist culture has done a thorough job of poleaxing Indigenous people from their belief systems, from their deep foothold in the earth, and our brutal crimes against humanity have left both practical and existential scars. True, there are good and nuanced intentions that I'm ignoring, but now is not the hour to irradiate nuance, but rather to morph from directive givers into listeners.

One semester in Missoula, while teaching Debra's Traditional Storytelling class during her sabbatical, I learned, despite my verbose tendencies, to settle into such a role. When I say "Debra's" class, I mean that she is synonymous with the course, not only because she designed it and has taught it every fall for going on two decades, but because she is a nonpareil oral storyteller. Her writing speaks for itself (*Perma Red* won several national awards and earned her a Guggenheim Fellowship), but to listen to Debra tell a story is to come face-to-face with elemental presence—pitched water running over rock, fire breathing inside a burning log, leaf shadow levitating near the forest floor. Emanation. And so the teaching appointment, while a distinct honor, mortified me. To squelch my nerves each week I focused my full imagination on the students' stories, those long-shut-in traumas unearthed in horrifying but courageous renderings, whose unifying substance was that of suffering.

One night midway through the semester, a young Salish student stood up before the class in the center of our circle beside the wonky store-bought electrical "fire" with its waving plastic flames and said that he intended to tell his tribal origin story.

"But the story I'm about to tell belongs to my culture," he added. "I ask you not to repeat it, any of it, without permission."

A silence fell over the gathering of forty-some students as he waited for us to affirm his request. Then, with a poise and eloquence that had evaded him in earlier presentations, he honored us with a tale that seemed to come from beyond the senses. Listening, I wondered why he had withheld the story from us until now; perhaps we had yet to prove ourselves trustworthy. The narrative was gripping, but what transported me was envisioning the process by which the story had endured one hundred fifty years of cultural siege, from teller to listener to teller, ad infinitum. And not as a mere relic: rather, it had been preserved like an untouched numen, a grove of aspens at the lip of a steep canyon threaded by a clear spring. And I sat there in the blood thrum of it, this young man's rendering of a very old story, comprehending that the more we evolve as listeners—to our collective stories, everyone's, including the land's—the more will be revealed to us.

An hour later my cell phone rang: Debra was calling to tell me that her plane had landed safely at a nearby rural airport. She mispronounced the name of the town nearest the makeshift airstrip. "Anyway, it's just a runway in the middle of a field," she said. I apologized for the scare and told her I was on my way. The plan had been for us to share a nice lunch with Mary, maybe enjoy a midday glass of wine, I told her, but with the extra drive time we'd have to head straight to school, where she would be whisked off to present a craft lecture and then, following an early dinner, give her reading.

"Oh, we're already on a bus headed your way," she said. "They gave us wine coolers and everything. Wait till you see this journal I bought at the bookstore in Minneapolis. I can't resist them. I have so many. Maybe I'll leave this one with a student."

Outside the bus station we shared a hug, a three-armed embrace since Debra dragged a roller suitcase and cradled under her elbow a cardboard box on top of which was stacked a six-pack of wine coolers, one top-popped and empty. The box was for me, she explained, from a mutual poet friend of ours. Well, go on, open it. I took my car key to the tape and removed the wadded-up newspaper pages to find a bundle of sage, along with a fragrant braid of sweet-grass and a jar filled with chokecherry jelly. Taped to the lid of the jar was a postcard, along with a note: "All the syrup turned to jelly unlike other years where all the jelly turned to syrup. Oh well, I hope you like it on your toast. Love, M."

On the front of the card was a photograph of Square Butte rising over a foreground of greening high-grass prairie. When I could fight off the pangs of regret for long enough to think of Montana, I envisioned a gallery of cottonwoods that looked out on this very butte, and in particular one old tree within the stand of trees that I hold dear. I had last seen that tree on a late-December morning, just before sunrise when the sky to the south boiled with reds and pinks. No wind, but a few brittle aphid-bulbed leaves, hangers on from fall, rattled against each other in the breath of dawn. Coarse bark, deep grooves between the wales. She is the kind of tree one is inclined to listen to, and I did, as I'd done before. After a spell I picked a fallen branch from the ground and snapped off the smallest memento twig, the gnarled pinky finger of an old woman.

Certain rules, set down long before my people struck our banal but rampant camp of cul-de-sacs, prevent me from talking about the butte itself. This code is more than culturally prudent; to stare at this landform long enough in any light is to let the fist of it knock the air from your lungs, to feel it grip your throat and shake the would-be words in your mouth to dust. I put the postcard inside the left pocket of my sportscoat and tapped my chest.

After Debra's craft lecture, we stood by the thawing lake at dusk, just off campus so she could smoke a cigarette without violating school rules. A few hundred yards from shore, backgrounded by cobalt sky, a light-blue ice fishing shanty had begun to sink through the slowly melting ice into the periwinkle water. There was open water at our feet too, and a squadron of *Hexagenia* nymphs undulating through the warming shallows. The first smoke was for small talk, but by the second we were riffing the way we always had about work habits and obsessions, about tone-deaf administrations, and scraping by financially in pursuit of the durable made thing. After a self-conscious laugh, I detailed my pervading homesickness, how it coats experience like a pathetic but nonetheless potent adolescent love. Debra nodded and lit a final smoke—"just a half," she said—and soon we were exchanging tales of the uncanny, in other words, ghost stories, a favorite pastime of ours.

Then it was time for the reading.

Before introducing Debra, I examined the students' eyes, those luminous undefiled landscapes. Though the entire assembly appeared primed, one female student sat tallest, clutching a cup of tea apart from her normal cohort and exuding a focalized expectation. Like the character Louise White Elk, this young student had been subjected to the pains of abuse both domestic and cultural at a young age. During our conferences she had revealed that Louise's brutal survival story had given her "permission" to exhume her own past, and that during the dig the possibility of her own authorial voice had been discovered. What greater gift could a book and its maker bestow on an aspiring writer? As the students applauded my introduction, I made a mental note to introduce the two after the reading.

Shuffling her papers at the podium, Debra thanked the robust audience for its welcome, the students for their palpable attention, and the school for its hospitality. "I apologize if I seem a bit jittery," she said, "but I just had a change of heart. While I had planned to read from my novel, a ghost-story session with your instructor here"— she sent an owlish smile my way—"has compelled me to share instead from a work in progress written in the voice of Sacagawea."

"You must be glad to have Chris here," Debra continued. "We sure miss him back in Montana. But not only that, the land misses him. The land itself misses him."

My ears hummed for minutes, even as I saw Debra turning the pages of her manuscript as she read. Dizzied, I heard nothing but the echo of her proclamation, the suddenly plausible abundance of it. The land itself. Could she begin to fathom what she offered me by way of these words? They were a blessing, yes, but also a kind of passage, a shaft of fall light shining down on a trace path that leads out of a previously impenetrable wood.

One Sunday in early March on a sentimental whim, I headed up the Leelanau Peninsula to pay a visit to the Harrison's old French Road farm, where Jim and Linda raised their daughters, and where, for several decades, Jim worked in a barn turned office, producing a prodigious body of work. I had directions from Jim and permission from the current owner, who was standing at the end of a long, muddy driveway in a pair of coveralls and a red Stormy Kromer when I arrived, checkerboarded in elm shadows.

Before getting out of the car, I rang Jim to tell him that I had found the place.

"You would have made a good stalker," he said. "I heard you're not going to renew your contract for next year."

"You can christen a wolf, right?" I responded, riffing on Kooser. "But he'll eventually ask, 'Which way is the woods?'"

I wanted to say something more romantic about shirking societal duty for a more sacramental one, but in reality I was going back to Montana to row a boat and write because it seemed a more tolerable existence, threadbare or not, than one that required allegiance to daily staff meetings and interdepartmental audits over artistry and creative spirit, to name just a pair. Financially, we were down to the dregs, but we were headed back to a place where living off the dregs made the most sense, where we might still get to see the seeds we planted years ago taking root, the eventual branches bearing fruit.

"Call me back when you're done with *the grand tour*," he said.

Set against a hill caped in hardwoods, the farm was modest—just a barn, an outbuilding, and a two-story Tudor—the spread barely earning the moniker. Via the novels and poems, the place had amassed a sort of mythical status in my imagination, but I reminded myself that these physical surroundings were merely what inspired a created setting, not the setting itself. That distinction, between an author's work and their actual life, is a line similar to the one Jim drew between the author and the always fictionalized, regardless of genre, first-person "I."

Like a warm docent, the current owner led me through the house, his narration fading into the corners of the rooms as lines and scenes from Jim's work flared in my mind. The living room where Jim listened to Bach's suites and absorbed that musical form as a poetic one, the window beside which he drank too much and passed out only to be woken by his daughter: *There are flies in your mouth, Daddy.* The kitchen where the famed painters and bird-dog runners cooked the epic, post-hunt, gout-inducing meals. And out the north window, the barn where the asshole rooster he compared to himself kept on with its incessant banging, and the beam where he did pull-ups between chapters. From which he must have imagined, while writing *Yesenin*, hanging the rope.

The rafters bent shafts of light and the slats mitered shadows across the lingering patches of snow.

A hand on my shoulder. "Let me show you across the road."

Over the high pasture where trillium and scotch broom would soon grow, a raven and crow jousted. Against the trunk of a white pine, a pileated woodpecker probed for grubs, stopped to listen, then extended its neck into the bole of the tree past half a century's worth of rings.

"I'll leave you to it," the owner said, turning back toward the house.

I leaned back against a lichen-covered boulder and looked up at a sumac. Like spoors, the bush's fuzzed red seedpods burst against the blue sky. A male cardinal chased a female through the branches, before finally relenting. Rising off the suddenly textured bay, a wind flowed uphill and over me, rustling a patch of dormant grass, parting the tawny blades, and loosing a single gray moth that fluttered momentarily above the meadow before falling back to the earth again.

Jim once wrote a poem called "Not Writing My Name" that could have been conceived not far from here, about *thinking about* then deciding against writing one's name in the snow. "What star-crossed jock ego would churn through those / drifts to write a name invisible except to crows?" The answer of course is Jim's, a personality trait he worked hard to conquer, along with many other banes. Following his beloved Rilke's advice, he had aimed early on in his career to turn his demons into angels. But there was carnage along the way, of course, relationships severed, addictions and depressions barely endured. A perfect human he wasn't, far from it, but he embraced his fallibility with perfection. "Vulnerability is a writer's best defense. Why do I fundamentally reject this?"

On impulse I stood up and thanked the place, the surround of it, for sustaining an artist who went further than most wish to go, who took the deepest trails in, and let himself remain lost there awhile before returning to us with news of the way out—deliverance . . . is never far away, but often quite invisible—who kept insisting, despite all, "We are here / to be curious, not consoled." It might seem odd to thank a place, but it's a gesture I often find myself making, we human creatures existing at the mercy of the landscape the way a character exists, for better or worse, at the mercy of language.

"You didn't find my old coke grinder out there by the boulder, did you? Another story for the river. We must fish this summer, Dommer." After leaving the farm and thanking the gracious owner, I had called Jim to gush about my visit, but he cut me off before I could moon.

"Anyway, what's for dinner?" he asked.

"I'm in the parking lot of Burritt's right now trying to decide between salmon and whitefish."

"I would think a poet of your considerable talent would know the answer to that question. Did I tell you I'm taking the month off from writing? But then again, I am thirty-two books ahead of you, so get trucking!"

Inside the market, the aproned butcher shook his head at me. Behind him and the fish display case, a window-shaped square of sunlight blared against the back wall. One by one the shadows of gutter-loosed droplets fell through it. Clock, chrome paper towel dispenser, bucket and mop leaning against the door. In the cooler behind their price tags, various cuts of salmon, lake trout, walleye, and whitefish were tidily arranged. "A thaw like this? Wave goodbye to your shanty. Once that ice goes punk, I don't risk it. Just let it sink. It'll be perch habitat next year."

Waiting, I thumbed through the discount rack of wine.

"Sorry, what'd you want again?" he asked. "Two of the whitefish, was it?"

"Yes, sir."

He shuffled the crushed ice around with his blue plastic glove, pointed out two filets nearest me.

"How about these?"

"Perfect."

Paused before grabbing them.

"You're not gonna fry them, are you?"

"No, sir. Blackened in the broiler. Maybe a little caper sauce on top."

He slid them into a plastic bag. "They're all yours, then," he said, slapping the fish on the scale.

While the tag was printing, I grabbed a lemon and a jar of capers and set eyes on the premium wine rack, soon honing in on a Baryshnikov-nimble Gamay I couldn't afford, a bottle Jim was fond of. Primates all, we can't avoid our predisposition toward imitation. And while there is much from his example to disregard, Jim's taste in wine was nearly infallible. I grabbed the bottle and set it on the counter. Ring it up, I said with machismo. Back inside the car, though, I was pulling the credit card receipt from the brown paper bag and making banking calculations in my head. Finally I ceded to the blunt numbers and was considering how to return the bottle of wine when something hit the hood of the car.

Hand on my rearview, the butcher stood next to my window, his white coat blinding.

I rolled down the window.

"Forgot your capers and lemon," he said, handing them to me, then pointed to my tailgate. "I was gonna put 'em back on the shelf but I saw your license plate. Lived there eighteen years. In Cut Bank, then in Helena. Sometimes I get so homesick for it. So I just wanted to say: *Montana*."

For dinner I served the filets—one blackened with caper sauce, one broiled with butter and salt for the kids—alongside the jaunty Château Thivin, a fragrant, earthy red whose initial tautness conjured Mary's body on a spring day shortly after we met, her shucked overalls tossed into the calico shade of an orchard's budding limbs, a luminous memory of the senses that we attempted, when the house was quiet, to resurrect.

~

Lily sucked her right thumb. Sometimes while sucking this thumb, she rested the four unused fingers of her hand on her left cheek. Sunday afternoon on the living room couch. We had just woken from our respective naps. Why the fingers sometimes, I asked her, and other times not?

"When my cheek is cold I put my fingers here." She stuck her thumb back in her mouth, running her fingers across her sleep-flushed skin to show me. "Until my cheek is warm."

This is precisely the brand of unfettered individual genius, I thought, to which Walt Whitman urged each of us to be faithful.

At that, a triangle of sunlight found her cheek, a triangle with rounded edges that morphed into something resembling a wing, the wind from which Whitman himself would give his ceiling fan of a thousand hummingbirds in heaven to feel flutter across his skin.

GREAT-GRANDMOTHER

The perpetually sudden arrival of a Michigan spring. Survivors, we emerge from winter in a stupor, puzzled by the effulgence of warmth, by the skull-penetrating songs of birds returned from parts south. But soon we are bolstered, dime-light, and fit to sing ourselves. Radiating from the long-bare branches and long-frozen lawns, the color green returns: we run toward it in T-shirts, genuflect in rays of sunshine. Like church chimes, baseballs ring off aluminum bats. The cardboard "Closed" signs in the windows of ice cream shops are traded for spunky soft-servers. Humid dusk. Peepers calling from the swamps.

On the cusp of spring in 1925, my maternal grandmother was born, and shortly thereafter was crowned baby of the year at the Michigan State Fair. Save for a black-and-white portrait taken in the fair's photo booth and a trophy engraved with the words "Prettiest Baby," few mementos of Shirley Burns's childhood remain. Nearly nine decades later, standing beside her bed at Friendship Manor Assisted Living Center, I ran a finger down the tarnished silver trophy, which was stationed on her windowsill. We were leaving the next morning to move back to Montana; she had visited us there a few times, and she was insistent I take the trophy with me in her stead.

"You can bring it on the boat," she said with a laugh that quickly turned into a cough.

"Do you remember floating the Blackfoot with me?" I asked.

"When you tried to kill me?"

She hadn't forgotten a thing. Smiling, I recalled floating with her upstream of where the Blackfoot meets the Clark Fork, the sheer joy in her eyes as we crested a small wave morphing into genuine fear as we shot our first rapid, her good hand's white-knuckle grip on the boat seat.

When I was a child the windowsills of her small home near 9 Mile Road in Detroit were adorned with knickknacks. I would play with them—a miniature British double-decker bus, a letter opener disguised as a tiny bamboo-sheathed samurai sword, and others now fuzzy in my memory—and ask her where they'd come from. Perhaps she held mixed feelings about being in the wind—those rambling years during which the items had been collected, and was hesitant to recollect around my mom who had been left in a relative's care then—because Shirley offered little in response.

Now, standing at her bedside, I felt the need to prod her again. I was loath to doubt her resiliency, but persistent infections and multiple strokes had weakened her bladder and liver beyond repair. After calculating the slim odds of her visiting Montana again, of me returning to Michigan while she was still with us, I was feeling unreasonably desperate for some last kernel of her enigmatic personality, a keepsake of sorts.

"The best place you've ever been? Tell me," I asked, as with Luca's help, I eased her out of bed and into her wheelchair. "You went all over the world, right?"

She was quiet as we steered her out of her room toward the Friendship Manor cafeteria.

"I don't think about those places very much," she said once we were in the lunch line. She pointed at what she wanted for lunch, a square of red Jell-O constellated with bits of mandarin orange. "Here with you today. That's enough to think about."

She strained to reach the leather fanny pack that hung from the handle of the wheelchair, and eventually gave up with a huff.

"Honey," she said, turning to Luca. "Go in there and take out a five-dollar bill. Will you get us each a Milky Way bar from the vending machine? Push the letter *B*, then the number 4. And keep the change."

With a dutiful nod Luca took the bill and banked for the hallway.

"I would go for the Snickers," she confided, "but the peanuts are hard to chew."

Following a favorable Social Security snafu a few years prior, Shirley moved to Friendship Manor, an otherwise unaffordable physical rehab center, where the doting staff weaned her from the booze and nicotine. Almost in the face of well-balanced meals cooked by a staff chef, she consumed mostly candy bars, Jell-O, and pudding. Despite this staunch, nutrition-free diet, and the toll multiple brain and bladder surgeries had taken on her body, she appeared grounded, sturdy, well lit.

I pointed at a bowl of cooked green beans—she looked up at me and frowned—then slid a chilled dish of tapioca onto the green plastic tray. We found a table and ate.

After Friendship Manor's dining hall was cleared of lunch and readied for bingo, we settled in for a few rounds. On our frequent downstate visits, we had become regulars at bingo hour, to the extent that the normally strict officiator warmed to the girls and even allowed them to pull, after the brass wheel had shuffled them, the settled bingo balls. A bingo savant, Shirley monitored four cards at once, her acumen alienating her from her fellow residents. Bingo was a wickedly competitive pastime at Friendship Manor, and while she counted many residents as friends, she was relentless. She was even short with her grandson, scowling or rolling her eyes when I tried to make conversation with residents. With an arthritic finger, she tapped my card when I missed a call, N-37, and shortly thereafter won on a four corners. "That's a good bingo," the caller affirmed.

After several rounds we gathered outside in the court-yard underneath a budding crab apple and a few talkative robins. While Molly and Lily took turns pushing Shirley around the patio, she waved from her wheelchair at passing staff members, clearly proud to be surrounded by family. Back and forth through the soil-scented air, Luca and I tossed a Nerf football. After a while my mom arrived with cheese-burgers for an early supper; Shirley nibbled at one, barely unwrapping it from its wax paper, while the girls rubbed lotion on her liver-spotted forearms. Then it was time for Shirley's nap, my mom said, time for us to say goodbye.

I looked across the courtyard at Luca, who stood with both hands in the air, waiting to catch another imaginary touchdown. I was barely older than that, I thought, when I learned that an apparently healthy person could go golf-ing on a summer afternoon and end the day in a wheelchair, unable to walk or speak, a small portion of hemorrhaged brain removed from their cranium. When Shirley returned home from the hospital, I refused, stubborn eight-year-old that I was, to leave her side. Football in hand three decades later, spring sun heating my dark thatch of hair, I felt the same youthful ache of reluctance.

"Give Gram-Gram a kiss," my mom told the kids. "Tell her you love her and you'll call from Montana."

"We can hang out a little longer," I said. "Everybody's feeling fine."

"It's a long drive, son. You don't want to be driving in the dark."

Shirley read my resistance.

"Don't worry, honey," she said, sparing me from having to say any more. She smiled and reached out for my hand with her stroke-bent one. "I'm the first grandma and the last grandma."

She raised her good hand and waved goodbye.

HOME PSALM

It's well after midnight when we reach Montana, crossing
the state line just west of Sentinel Butte, North Dakota.
Wired on green tea and adrenaline, I drive on with my four
passengers sleeping, the U-Haul trailer snaking through the
darkness behind us. The CD player skips so I fiddle with
the radio, searching for an acceptable accompaniment to the
all but empty road. As a boy, I would watch Shirley tune
the AM while she sipped coffee, twisting her thumb and
forefinger around the silver dial, searching for the frequency
she wanted, past a station to some static, back to the station,
Paul Harvey's voice, then past it again in search of a song. The
Seek button renders nothing but static, so I tune manually,
eventually sticking to a grainy station that pours out cantina
music, a ballad some seasonal cowpoke come north to work
the Big Sky summer might be listening to right now, feet up
on his bunk, hat over his eyes as he holds lightly to a thin
thread of home.

The rising sun fills the back window. Luca stirs, asks
where we are. I wink, raise my eyebrows in the rearview.
"Montana?" he asks. I nod. "Montana!" he screams, over and
over, until he nearly goes hoarse. As the others roust, I roll
down the windows. A damp wind teems with the scent of
rain-wet sage. Gushing in, meadowlark song fills the cab. I
pull over and step out and walk toward a vast ranch's fence
line, at which grows a wild rose bush, its early yellow blooms

gaudy against the gray-blue sky. I snap a thin, thorny branch from the bush and bury my nose in the flower.

Then, I do. Why wouldn't I? I kiss the ground.

～

There's a hawk moth in our bathtub, still alive, wings fluttering, leaving a frail coat of iridescent scales against the porcelain when we finally arrive in Missoula. A feast of elk prepared by friends, accompanied by countless bottles and toasts, with wild roses floating on wine. On our first Blackfoot float, a bald eagle soaring over the river drops a recently captured brown trout into the water, the freshly dead fish arriving, moments later, downstream at my feet, and hours later, stuffed with onions, potatoes, lemon, and dill, atop our hot grill. I want to tell you of these happenings, this week of welcomings.

But first, to look for morels with Lils.

She kneels next to a fallen cottonwood, setting keen, earth-round, earth-reflecting eyes on a drove of morels, a stash viewable only to the prostrate.

"Psst, Dadda," she says. "I'm finding everything I see."

Walking on, inspired by her attentiveness, I turn Lily's words over in my mind as I would a koan. Though I've picked this cottonwood bottom for longer than Luca's been alive and know the aimless drainage well, every encounter hereafter seems an initial one, my senses not so much noticing as capturing, or being captured by, the earth's inhabitants. I ruminate for a while on my friend Debra's words about the land having missed me. How could we ever know if the land is communicating with us? Either it's a far-fetched and fanciful idea, or it is rote, in that the land is always communicating with us, and we're simply ill-attuned to its frequency. Plum blossom with slight hints of chokecherry lofting on the June air, I hear you. Scent of leaks loosed by our footfalls, wafting up from wet earth, speak my wild name. Tiny white bloom of false Solomon's seal flaring out from the undergrowth, toward your voice I incline.

Charged with her rapt attention, I begin to catalog our surroundings. I show Lily a wild strawberry that will soon fruit; the violet splash of a clematis flower, its viny tendrils; on the drying hills, early bear grass and camas, balsamroot already beginning to parch; I show her the bed of a cow elk in a fen; a grouse, a vireo, a common yellow throat, a yellow warbler, a tanager, swallows, geese, a nest full of peeping owlets. I list it all, what one could eat were one lost in the woods, what one should avoid.

But the longer my litany gets, the more the gesture feels false. After all, what else have she and her siblings provided me if not survival instructions, their spirit of wonder and rapturous curiosity sustaining me through the deepest of discordances?

You can't pick morels again for the first time. But you can watch a child picking them for the first time, the mushrooms' blond reflections blooming in the window-wide eyes of the free ones, who free the rest of us.

By the time the dew has burned off the grass, Lily stands in the trough of a shallow swale holding a paper sack heavy with her harvest: wild asparagus thick as a garden hose; several varieties of mushroom, scaly hedgehogs, waxy caps, and of course morels, those thumbprints of the gods. Bag in tow, she lags a few steps behind me. I stop at the rise to wait, hear a red-shafted flicker call from the canopy. Cheeks flushed, she stares into the budding branches, their wide grasp of sky. So that it won't spill when we wade the shallow channel, I zip Lily's cache inside my backpack and lift her to my shoulders. As my sandals shift on the rocks, my trunk wobbles a little, and I feel her knees, thorn scraped and sweaty, tighten pleasantly around my neck. Together we begin to ford.

⁓

Late July. The week when the grasshoppers in western Montana finally sprout wings large enough to propel them through the air. Though I've been forewarned that she can no longer speak, I call Shirley on the phone. A morphine-Ativan cocktail has rendered her sentience questionable, but there won't be many more chances. A hospice nurse answers, speaks with me momentarily, and places the phone near Shirley's ear. I say a few words that feel insufficient. Returning, the nurse thanks me gently for calling, and says that Shirley has been a wonderful patient, very peaceful. My mom has been steady by her side but is down the hall talking with staff at the moment. Quality control, I laugh. Daughter cub turned mother bear. Then the nurse says if there is anything else I want to tell Shirley, anything, now is the time.

I clear my throat and look around the cool garage, where I've come for privacy. From a nail on the wall, Lily's life jacket hangs, still damp from last night's dunk in the creek. Lacking words, I hum to Shirley the first verse to "Doxology," four four-beat lines of a hymn I know she loves, and that I heard her sing last winter in the Friendship Manor Choir Club. When I would stay with her as a boy, she used to tuck me into bed each night, ritually, her voice sandy from cigarettes, breath sweet from three martinis, with a saying she'd invented. "Do you remember what you used to tell me when you'd tuck me into bed?" I ask her, knowing she can't answer. I pause, then conjure her old phrase: "If you wake up before I wake up, get me up. And if I wake up before you wake up, I'll get you up."

~

The snappy horseradish made my nose run and my eyes water all through the late-summer dinner at Jim's. The evening was a big affair, with most of the Harrisons' Livingston-based family tableside enjoying baked ham, beans, slaw, all prepped exquisitely by Linda and their novelist daughter Jamie. Celebrating nothing but fine company and the long September light, we were nearly a dozen, eating and talking and drinking red wine, opening bottles that ascended gradually in nuance and conversed intently with the horseradish. I had brought along my friend Jeff, a musician who happened to be touring Montana, and whose songwriting acumen is trumped only by his taste in wine. To wit, I thought I was holding a high face card in a fairly well-aged Barolo, which was met with much appreciation. But when Jeff pulled a dusty '63 Coltibuono from his kit bag, the table, full of well-versed drinkers, went quiet. We relished the gift in small glasses, tickled that it was possible to step from the high-elevation Barolo to the stratospheric Chianti, which, as Jim reminded us, "could easily have sucked" had it been corked or turned. Later, Jeff played two sets at Livingston's Murray Bar to a modest but raucous crowd all snap-shirted and sun-dressed and dancing to songs I wouldn't previously have thought of as dance tunes. Post-show, we had a round, and then another, this one bought for the singer and his poet-roadie by a plucky sixty-something brunette wearing horn-rimmed glasses and looking vaguely familiar. After a while she vanished, and the bartender, sweeping up his tips with a coaster, said, "Well boys, you just missed your chance to buy Lois Lane a drink." We stared back. "Margot Kidder? Superman?" Sonofabitch, one of us said. Dammit, said the other. Another Livingston Sunday night.

We don't pop out of our respective sleeping bags the follow-ing morning so much as eke, but a face full of the cold water tumbling past our camp revives us from the previous night's debauch. Along a north-flowing creek the maps call a river, flanked by stark granitic peaks, we hike to where a fan of Jeff's told us to start fishing, family land, a private stretch. You want upstream or down? Jeff asks. Both, I say. And I do.

"Good to be back?"

"Best kind of good."

"Life's too short not to do what you want."

The water upstream flows clear and deep against a verdant bank; down, it turns heavy right, forming a riffle corner above which mayfly spinners have begun to congre-gate. We agree to work in opposite directions for an hour, then double back to the starting point. After a few fish, I find myself less interested in trout than in the square of apple cake leftover from dinner, so I sit down on a log and unwrap it from a square of tinfoil. Baked by Jim's daughter Anna Hjortsberg—a bookseller who could clearly swap her formidable skills for a baker's apron should she tire of the "tournament of hunchbacks" that is literature—the cake is perfect, even when polished off with fingers tacky with trout slime. I fold the tinfoil into my pocket and wade back to meet Jeff, the current at my back putting a lift in my sandaled step. Several bends later with the trailhead in sight, I startle to see a dog crossing the water, a big black dog that I decide, after a moment, is in fact a bear.

But it isn't a bear. It's a black wolf, followed soon after by its smaller black mate. When, momentarily, Jeff appears downstream at the bend, I catch his eyes to make sure that he is seeing what I am seeing, that it isn't a delusion. He nods wide-eyed, mouths *wolves*. In the living river we stand with two black wolves between us, their musculatures resisting the current, their hackles high, dark coats bristling with sunlight. When they finish crossing, they shake dry—a half-glance toward me—then flow up the tawny side hill and lope downcountry, calling through a warm fall wind to the rest of their pack, which begins to answer from the other side of the river, first with a succession of yips, and then in a feral, unrepeatable melody that melds into utterly sacrosanct song.

A THIMBLEFUL

Suddenly—or what feels like it—the yellow leaves fall to the ground, wet with rain and soon enough, snow. Cottonwoods, aspens too, the unruly backyard pear; the lawn sprinkled with their bright coins. The grasses redden on the mountain, fade, and drape to the ground revealing antlers shed in summer, the bones of a stillborn fawn, the skull of a coyote.

After Shirley's cremation, my mom insisted that we not travel back for the memorial, assuring me that we would have our own ceremony later in Montana. In the weeks before she died, Shirley's skin took on an oddly luminous sheen that belied her failing body and religious diet of chocolate bars, my mom said. The Desert Fathers exhibited a similar phenomenon too, I mused to her over the phone, those emaciated old monks who starved themselves but meditated with such ferocity that their humming neocortexes were said to emit a glow, a subtle penumbra that shone on the sandstone walls of their caves. That's a nice story, honey, she said, or something to that effect. We'll see you in the fall.

I would be suspicious of such tales too, had I not watched Montana's larches hum with bright yellow each October before they drop their needles, the same larches that are at peak color when my parents arrive to scatter Shirley's ashes in the Blackfoot. On the stretch I once floated with her, I steer the boat alongside fireweed bushes and their blazing reflections. In a plastic bag from the

Myrtle Park Crematory, my mom holds her mother's "cremated remains," as the label on the ziplock reads. While
she spent most of the past several years caring for Shirley,
overseeing meals, bathing, doctors' visits, even pedicures,
my mom seems against erecting even a figurative memorial.
She doesn't say a word, and despite the masses who clamor
for some illusion of closure, sides with the river, eschewing
the notion altogether.

The anchored boat tacks across the pool. Once it settles
against the tightened rope, I take a handful of the ashes and
let the granules fall into the river. The sound is childhood:
a fistful of sand dropped into a lake's still shallows. My dad
does the same, and then my mom empties the bag over the
gunnel. Spreading downstream through the blue current on
their way to the Pacific, the ashes look a little like a galaxy,
streaming across a boundless firmament.

It's June again. Nine months since we scattered Shirley's
ashes on the beat I'm rowing today, my first Blackfoot run
this year. A week ago, peak snowmelt pushed rocks the size
of bowling balls out of their centuries-old holds; if you sat
still long enough and listened, you could hear the riverbed
shifting, deep bellows of tumbling boulders punctuated by
hackle-raising scrapes. I had planned to float a different river,
a smaller, clearer, more settled one, but while driving up
the valley I spotted veritable congregations of just-hatched
salmonflies huddled together for warmth in the bankside
alders, fist-sized clusters of protein that I knew would soon
precipitate a frenzied piscine feeding period.

A cool rain drips from the hood of my coat to my hat brim. I pull on the oars, navigating the boat through a wave train and around a violent hydraulic, keeping my clients' casts in range of the fertile banks. After peppering the undercuts with tight shots, the anglers grunt as their offerings speed past good lies unmolested. They pick up, fire again. Eventually a fish strikes but the hook set is missed. I eddy out to rest my shoulders—my early season deltoids not quite prepared for the heavy current—and kick the stern into the flow. More well-placed casts and grunting. A sigh, a shrug. Then, off a riprap bank, a heavy trout is hooked. Sculling for a moment, I look for an inside bend, some slower water in which to eddy and temper the fish's scorching runs, but we round several bends before finding a suitable run to net the fish. Released, the trout—a large, densely spotted hen cutthroat so gorged on stone flies that her belly is distended with still-wriggling, undigested insects—rights itself against the sandy bottom.

I'm admiring the fish's translucent caudal fins when I spot something white, what appears to be a bone, half buried in the still-murky shallows. Curious, I tug up my sleeve, reach down, and draw it out. A small, worn stone Buddha, the size of a chess piece, drips between my thumb and forefinger. Dumbfounded, superstitious anglers to a man, we marvel at the find, wondering aloud how far the rotund, smiling figurine traveled to get to this precise spot where we had anchored the boat. It is concluded that our arrival in this location, and the statue's, could have quite easily been otherwise.

After dinner that evening, I e-mail a picture of the statue, along with a brief account of its unearthing, to a poet friend, an old teacher. "That's Hotei," he writes back, "the happy Buddha. He found you because you were paying attention."

My scattershot, late-night cyber searching informs me that Hotei loved to drink beer and was happiest as a rambler. Known as the magnanimous, laughing, ample-bellied Buddha, Hotei is often rendered with one palm pressed against his ample waistline. The caretaker of children and somewhat kitsch patron of bartenders, he's said to be an incarnation of a hermit whose name meant "cloth sack," one of which he carried on his back, mostly empty save for a wish-granting fan and candy he gave to youth.

I close the computer and let my head fall onto the pillow.

On summer days I launch the boat, row for several hours, my arms moving like a swimmer's until I reach the take-out, winch the boat onto the trailer, and drive home spent, hands calloused, hoping there's a glass of wine left in last night's bottle. In a fugue of images, the weeks pass, with memory's net grasping little. Cascades of orange and yellow tanagers. Riots of birdsong after rain. A young bull moose lifting a mouthful of watercress, velvet antlers dripping. What the mind forgets, though, the body retains, as the land expresses itself in us and through us. I've come to understand that the body is an extension of the earth, and vice versa. Some mornings I wake after rowing to feel the reverberations, the sloshing churns and glides, of the torsional river in my joints.

Thus, a few weeks pass before I think to e-mail my mom a picture of the figurine, to tell her that I'd found the Hotei, which I've taken to carrying as a talisman in my boat, while fishing the same stretch of river on which we'd scattered Shirley's ashes last fall, down which I'd taken her floating a decade earlier.

"Quite a coincidence," my mom writes back. "You probably don't remember because you were so young, but Shirley had a wooden Buddha just like that. The fat one. She kept it on her windowsill on Evelyn Street. It wasn't like she was a Buddhist or anything. I think she got it on a trip to Hawaii."

⁓

I back-row, holding the boat under a rock wall to watch a stone descend, tier by switchbacking tier, a worn game trail. Where the stone falls into the water, I anchor, solo on the Blackfoot this still October afternoon, the canyon quiet save for a cow elk calling from the wind-thinned ridge spine, and the upstream riffle throwing its voice against the cliff. Standing on the rower's bench, I survey the air-clear shallows: void of trout but covered with promise in the form of autumn sedge cases, inside which meaty larvae, favored trout forage, prepare to pupate, slip their case, and ascend, wings fully formed, in an air bubble of their own making. When in flight, the mature sedge is erratic, a bumbler, but the larva itself possesses an extremely nimble set of jaws and forelegs, appendages capable of constructing rock cases from thousands of the streambed's tiniest of pebbles, twigs, and sand grains. I tug up my sleeve and reach through the water to pluck one from its hold on a boulder. Closed at the aft, the case is as thick around as a cigarette, and from its fore the tip of the larva's orangish head protrudes, like a smoldering ember. I place it back underwater and wait for it to seat itself before retiring to my fly box to find a decent approximation.

For all the hours I've spent on moving water, a thimbleful: that's all I've managed to ascertain. My failure to glean more, my stone-headedness, does not deter me, though, and I keep planting myself bankside or on the current to listen.

A river is a thread sewn into time that is not subject to time, or at least not subject in the way we humans are. Because it appears to flow horizontally, we liken it to clocks and calendars, but it moves vertically as well, descending from peak to seawater, lapping at layers of strata, reading and rereading the deckled edges of the earth, softening rocks the glaciers teased forth, conversing with the eons, the *kalpas*. Because of this, the angler standing in the river casting is not so much absolved of time as disburdened of it, able to shirk its weight—for some moments anyway—before, with a dull thud, a trout strikes his swinging fly and he returns to pretending that he set himself in this cliff-shadowed stretch in search of a fish.

After a brief run, the middling rainbow cedes and flails at the surface, lethargic in the cool flows. It appears ready to come to hand but suddenly balks, shooting across the thermocline with renewed vigor—an inexplicable burst, until I make out the lengthening gray-green shape that pursues it, a three-foot native bull trout, as large a specimen as I've ever seen, tooth-studded white mouth agape, kype jaw cocked. I let my line go loose, hoping the suddenly frantic rainbow will make use of the slack and de-hook itself. But the piscivorous bull wastes no motion, and soon the water is afroth, the rainbow engulfed. Protruding from the predator's closed jaw: the mere tip of the rainbow's tail.

Pewter fish into pewter pool, the bull trout sinks. Against that descent I bend the rod—tug forehand low, backhand high, corking the graphite, exhausting all angles—but the fish that swallowed my fish merely sulks, immovable on my light tackle. Last ditch, I pull slack from the reel and toss my rod into the bankside fireweed in order to eliminate tension altogether; if I can fool the bull into believing that it is no longer connected to my line, that its prey is no longer attached to a danger, I might just coax it shoreward. Following the fly line, using its modicum of tension to steady myself, I walk toward the center of the pool across the exposed tops of boulders caked in dry moss and flaky pupa exoskeletons. When I reach the clear monofilament leader, twelve feet between the fish and me, I pull steady, like someone drawing a full pail from a well. Gradually, the bull begins to rise off the bottom and, a few inches at a time, its fins just out of reach, I manage to bring it near enough to note a single roe-colored spot on its flank among countless white ones, a single planet, Mars, standing out from a spill of stars.

At an arm's length, though, it anchors in and sulks.

No moves left, I plunge my arm into the water: momentum and desire and a dose of the right madness carrying my whole side under, and then my head and neck and torso. Bony, threadbare with age, the bull's tail is easy to discern from the depths. I make two breaststrokes toward it, grazing it with my fingertips before water's gravity catches me and pulls me to the surface, a bubble-clung ascent. Then in one swift headshake, the bull flares its gills and regurgitates the entire tooth-scarred-but-still-kicking rainbow, before departing the pool through the shallows.

Treading, I watch a puff of trout-stirred sediment disperse in the current, the chalky, bottom-hung particulate that contains bits of decomposing leaves, decaying crayfish, milt from spawning whitefish, diluted merganser droppings. Maybe even the tiniest follicle of a two-legged creature's cremated remains. It's a far-fetched but nonetheless tangible possibility, that a sedge larva living in this run could have used the ashes, miniscule bits of those cremated remains, to form its case, the likes of which I was imitating this afternoon with my fly.

Elementally speaking, after all, nothing has a permanent home. Some part of everything eventually abides everywhere. "Rock of Ages, cleave for me," Shirley sang as a youth in the Baptist choir. "Let me hide myself in Thee." We are matter and long to be received by an earth that conceived us, which accepts and reconstitutes us, its children, each of us, without exception, every one. The journey is long, and then we start homeward, fathomless as to what home might make of us.

NOTES

Like its author, this book is a hybrid of sorts. As a work of creative nonfiction, it employs elements of memoir and reportage in search of story and emotional truth. Narrative, fictional, and chronological liberties have been taken throughout its composition. In the interest of fluidity and continuity, I've occasionally omitted citations from the body text, electing instead to provide these attributions in a chapter-by-chapter list below. Much of this book was drafted using fifteen years' worth of handwritten journal entries, a fallible source to say the least; any factual errors herein are the fault of the author (or at the very least his penmanship) not the fact checker. Sometimes, owing to my fondness for folktales and campfire talk, I have chosen to render things the way they were told to me in those days and moments, not the way they were later journalistically reported or verified; see for instance, in "Begin, O Small Boy, To Be Born," the case of the missing boy (Kenny Gherkin) or, in "Seeds," the mention of trillium, which was actually used, contrary to the character Dixie's proposed employment thereof, as medicine, especially for women, during childbirth.

"The river," Gary Snyder reminds us, "is all of it everywhere"— so too the story.

PREFACE

1   *Myriad enduring relationships of the landscape* Lopez, *Crossing Open Ground*, 67.

3   *A sensorial empathy with the living land* Abram, *The Spell of the Sensuous*, 69.

HEADWATERS

13   *Eternity compressed into a moment* Maclean, *A River Runs Through It*, 44.

THUNDERBIRD MOTEL

23   *Form is never more than an extension of content* Creeley, quoted in Olson, "Projective Verse."

DOSTOYEVSKY'S KOAN

33   *The floods left few remnants beyond fossilized seaweed* Andrews, *Down from the Mountain*, 33. Andrews' narrative on the geologic history of the region helped shape this chapter.

34   *The hallucination of innocence* Cates, *High Desert Journal* "What Is the West?" interview with David Allen Cates.

43   *How can this throat* Neruda (trans. Tarn), *Selected Poems*, 291.

VISITORS

46   *The name came from the French trappers* Fuller, *The Confederated Salish and Kuteni Tribes of the Flathead Reservation*. E. O. Fuller's 1974 book was integral to the composition of this chapter.

55   *Delusions of reality of nonfiction* Harrison, *The Ancient Minstrel*, 4.

55   *It is difficult to undo our own damage* Dillard, *Teaching a Stone to Talk*.

SEEDS

65   *Extensive knowledge just eases the burden of the* mystery Keats, from a letter to John Hamilton Reynolds dated May 3, 1818.

EMISSARIES

74   *Poets talk about 'spots of time'* Maclean, *A River Runs Through It*, 44.

BEGIN, O SMALL BOY, TO BE BORN

83   *Begin, O small boy, to be born* Oppen, *New Collected Poems*, 104.

NEIGHBORS

111   *There would seem to be nothing more obvious* Kundera, *The Art of the Novel*, 14.

119   *Ford's Kink and Double Twist* Clifton, *Barbs, Prongs, Points, Prickers, and Stickers: A Complete and Illustrated Catalog of Antique Barbed Wire*, 160.

FIRST FALL

126 *Every gun is loaded and cocked* Harrison, *After Ikkyu and Other Poems*, 57.

134 *A week before the summer solstice* Scott, *Missoulian*, June 27, 2010. The elegiac passage on Spurgeon is very much indebted to Tristan Scott's fine, memory-stirring memorial tribute.

THE RIVER OF REAL TIME

139 *One needs to work to achieve enlightenment* Basho, *The Essential Haiku* (ed. Hass), 238.

BED REST

147 *Rilke wrote that our youthful conversations* Rilke, "The Unfortunate Fate of Childhood Dolls," republished in *The Paris Review* online.

THE CREATUREHOOD

161 *And we're in trouble when we don't know which story is ours* Kittredge, *Taking Care: Thoughts on Storytelling and Belief*, 52.

164 *Or as the cyberneticist Gregory Bateson says* Kuipers, *The Deer Camp*, 41. Many of the ideas on the ethics of hunting, such as the quoted passage on Lake Erie and the notion of our sharing a "collective imagination" with the land, are gleaned from Dean Kuipers' marvelous book, in particular his examinations of Paul Shepard's classics, *The Tender Carnivore and the Sacred Game* and *Nature and Madness*, both of which were also influential to the composition of this passage.

165 *The gritty work of the soul is accomplished in the feminine vale* Hillman, *A Blue Fire*, 115. Additionally, the "mate with the cosmos" line comes from a letter from the 14th Dali Lama that Hillman quotes in this passage.

167 *Expounding on Bateson, eco-philosopher Paul Shepard contends* Shepard, *Nature and Madness*, 4.

167 *The hunter knows that he does not know* Ortega y Gasset, *Meditations on Hunting*, 150; quoted in Shepard, *Nature and Madness*, 22.

ROAD TO THE BUFFALO

171 *Season of mists and mellow fruitfulness* Keats, *Complete Poems and Selected Letters of John Keats*.

182 *Inherent in story is the power to reorder* Lopez, *Crossing Open Ground*, 68.

HEATHEN

185 *They even bribed grand jurors who were assigned to look into bribery* Egan, *Lasso the Wind*, 148. Egan's chapter "The Colony" on Butte was integral to the composition of this chapter, and tireless upper

Clark Fork conservationist Casey Hackathorn helped greatly with
mining statistics and illustrative language.

186 *Physical changes made to a river conflict with natural processes*
Leopold, *A View of the River.*

189 *Mountains belong to the people living there* Dogen, Mountains and
Waters Sutra.

BRIGHT RIVER, BLACK STARS

194 *Coyote was walking through the forest* Matthews, *Rocky Mountain
Natural History Guide*, 368-369. Matthews' text from Raven
Editions (2003) contains a version of the traditional Clatsop tale,
"Coyote and the Cedar," retold at bedtime. See page 282 in *The River
You Touch* for discussion on the ethics of sharing traditional myths.

199 *We live in a cage of light* Ikkyu (trans. Berg), *Crow with No Mouth*, 55.

201 *The present is a wild season, not a ruse* Vizenor, *The Trickster of
Liberty: Native Heirs to a Wild Baronage.*

NINE MONTHS, THREE YEARS LATER

214 *Numbers, said Hermes Trismegistus* Howell, *Love's Last Number.*

THREE

205 *Blessed are they who remember* Valentine, *The River at Wolf.*

216 *In a life properly lived, wrote a friend, you're a river* Harrison,
The Art of Fiction interview with Jim Fergus, *The Paris Review*,
Summer 1988.

THE DEADSTREAM

245 *Yesterday's clarity is today's stupidity* Ikkyu (ed. Arntzen), *Ikkyu
and the Crazy Cloud Anthology*, 291.

246 *Write naked* Johnson, quoted in *The New Yorker.*

249 *I rolled and I tumbled, I cried the whole night long* Dylan, "Rollin'
and Tumblin.'"

249 *The right madness* Hugo, *Making Certain It Goes On*, 416.

251 *We are more than dying flies* Harrison, *After Ikkyu and Other
Poems*, vii.

251 *Our minds buzz like bees* Harrison, *After Ikkyu and Other Poems*, 3.

251 *My year-old daughter's red robe* Harrison, *Collected Poems*, 199.

OLD MISSION

260 *Pardon me* Neruda (trans. O'Daly), *Still Another Day.*

PARR MARKS

289 *What star-crossed jock ego* Harrison, *Collected Poems*, 277.

290 *Deliverance is never far away* Harrison, *Virginia Quarterly Review*,
interview by Jon Schneider.

290 *We are here to be curious* Harrison, *In Search of Small Gods*, 24.

ACKNOWLEDGMENTS

I'm deeply grateful to my undergraduate mentor, the brilliant poet Jack Ridl. Jack was a legendary professor (scores of his former students are now published authors) and anyone who knows him will recognize the Pittsburgh reference in "Parr Marks" as having come from his life. At a pivotal point, Jack shared this liberating story with me; for this and so much else, my debts to him remain deep. Otherwise, the character of Ralph—bless creative nonfiction—is based on Mike Delp, another Michigan legend who helped deliver me more than once from the proverbial weeds.

I am indebted to the late and nonpareil Brian Doyle for his early editorial guidance; portions of "The Nature of Wonder" first appeared in his Portland Magazine. The phrase "the nature of wonder" came from Hannah Fries, former editor at Orion, in which passages of this book first appeared: I'm grateful to both parties. In a different form, portions of Book II and Book III originally appeared in the Sun, as "Three" and "My Anti-Zen Zen"—my thanks to the wonderful editorial staff there. Thanks to Jonah Ogles, formerly of Outside, which published portions of "High Water Rising" in altered form. My abiding gratitude as well to Bill Sisson, Founding Editor at Anglers Journal, for a long editorial leash and continual support.

Thank you to Jeffrey Foucault for being my first reader and most demanding reader; to Nickolas Butler for talking important parts of the book out of me; to Melissa Stephenson,

Lowry Bass, and John Larison for close readings of early drafts; to Robin Troy and Paul Mosely and Peter Picard for believing in Beargrass; to retired ELHS English faculty Beth Lawrence for reading, always rigorously, my work for the past thirty years; to Esteban and Amelia, who know their real names, for carving out the first channel; to Phil Gardner for looking after our family; to Joe McMahon for the stand-up desk and Caleb Kasper for the shed; to Casey Hackathorn and Tina Barrett for repairing, respectively, Montana's rivers and grieving hearts; to Kirby Kim and Julie Stevenson for indispensable advice and guidance; to Bob DeMott, who gave me faith in my initial fluvial writings; to the Modern Huntsman crew for going far afield and dragging me along; to Dan Mahoney for showing me the ridgeline; to Kerry and Missy Sprouse for taking us in; to Tim O'Leary and Kelly Webster for shared vision; to Missoula, a rare real one, and the incredible creatures that make it such.

Abiding gratitude to my wonderful colleagues in the Creative Writing Program at the University of Montana: Brian Blanchfield, Judy Blunt, Boris Fishman, Sean Hill, Keetje Kuipers, Sam McPhee, Emily Ruskovich, Robert Stubblefield, and Erin Saldin; and to my fabulous students (teachers all).

Thank you to Billy Conway (in memoriam), David Duncan, Jeff Foucault, Jason McGerr, Brett (and Gretchen) Simmons, and Jimmy Watts for kinship, music, and fresh Dungeness; to AD, Law, Poppy, and Rocker for going all the way back; to the Drake, Hellman, Hurd, Miller, Alexander, Bates, Murphree, and Warnock crews for plying the river with me; to the rivers.

A huge whoop of gratitude to the entire world-class publishing team at Milkweed Editions, especially: Shannon Blackmer, Katie Hill, Claire Laine, Joey McGarvey, Marketing Director extraordinaire Yanna Demkiewicz, Creative Director and transcendent book designer Mary Austin Speaker, Managing Editor of meticulous brilliance Broc Rossell, and lastly, my trusted friend and editor, Publisher and CEO Daniel Slager.

Thank you to my parents, Dianne and Richard Dombrowski, for nothing shy of everything.

Thank you to Mary, Luca, Molly, Lily, and Zeke—not a word of this without you.

Erick Petersen

CHRIS DOMBROWSKI is the author of *The River You Touch*. He is also the author of *Body of Water: A Sage, A Seeker, and the World's Most Elusive Fish*, and of three acclaimed collections of poems. Currently the Assistant Director of the Creative Writing Program at the University of Montana, he lives with his family in Missoula.

milkweed
EDITIONS

Founded as a nonprofit organization in 1980, Milkweed Editions is an independent publisher. Our mission is to identify, nurture, and publish transformative literature, and to build an engaged community around it.

Milkweed Editions is based in Bdé Óta Othúŋwe (Minneapolis) within Mní Sota Makhóčhe, the traditional homeland of the Dakhóta people. Residing here since time immemorial, Dakhóta people still call Mní Sota Makhóčhe home, with four federally recognized Dakhóta nations and many more Dakhóta people residing in what is now the state of Minnesota. Due to continued legacies of colonization, genocide, and forced removal, generations of Dakhóta people remain disenfranchised from their traditional homeland. Presently, Mní Sota Makhóčhe has become a refuge and home for many Indigenous nations and peoples, including seven federally recognized Ojibwe nations. We humbly encourage our readers to reflect upon the historical legacies held in the lands they occupy.

milkweed.org

Milkweed Editions, an independent nonprofit publisher, gratefully acknowledges sustaining support from our Board of Directors; the Alan B. Slifka Foundation and its president, Riva Ariella Ritvo-Slifka; the Amazon Literary Partnership; the Ballard Spahr Foundation; *Copper Nickel*; the McKnight Foundation; the National Endowment for the Arts; the National Poetry Series; and other generous contributions from foundations, corporations, and individuals. Also, this activity is made possible by the voters of Minnesota through a Minnesota State Arts Board Operating Support grant, thanks to a legislative appropriation from the arts and cultural heritage fund. For a full listing of Milkweed Editions supporters, please visit milkweed.org.

Interior design by Tijqua Daiker and Mary Austin Speaker
Typeset in Adobe Jenson

Adobe Jenson was designed by Robert Slimbach for
Adobe and released in 1996. Slimbach based Jenson's
roman styles on a text face cut by fifteenth-century type
designer Nicolas Jenson, and its italics are based on
type created by Ludovico Vicentino degli Arrighi, a late
fifteenth-century papal scribe and type designer.